Zack Wheat

ALSO BY JOE NIESE

Burleigh Grimes: Baseball's Last Legal Spitballer (McFarland, 2013)

WITH BOB DORAIS

Gus Dorais: Gridiron Innovator, All-American and Hall of Fame Coach (McFarland, 2018)

Zack Wheat
The Life of the Brooklyn Dodgers Hall of Famer

Joe Niese

McFarland & Company, Inc., Publishers
Jefferson, North Carolina

LIBRARY OF CONGRESS CATALOGUING-IN-PUBLICATION DATA

Names: Niese, Joe, author.
Title: Zack Wheat : the life of the Brooklyn Dodgers Hall of Famer / Joe Niese.
Description: Jefferson, North Carolina : McFarland & Company, Inc., Publishers, 2021 | Includes bibliographical references and index.
Identifiers: LCCN 2020047152 | ISBN 9781476680149 (paperback) ∞
ISBN 9781476641829 (ebook)
Subjects: LCSH: Wheat, Zachariah David, 1888–1972. | Baseball players—United States—Biography. | Outfielders—United States—Biography. | Brooklyn Dodgers (Baseball team)—History. | Baseball Hall of Famers.
Classification: LCC GV865.W447 N54 2021 | DDC 796.357092 [B]—dc23
LC record available at https://lccn.loc.gov/2020047152

BRITISH LIBRARY CATALOGUING DATA ARE AVAILABLE

ISBN (print) 978-1-4766-8014-9
ISBN (ebook) 978-1-4766-4182-9

© 2020 Joe Niese. All rights reserved

No part of this book may be reproduced or transmitted in any form or by any means, electronic or mechanical, including photocopying or recording, or by any information storage and retrieval system, without permission in writing from the publisher.

On the cover: Brooklyn Dodgers left fielder Zack Wheat in 1912 (photograph by Charles M. Conlon)

Printed in the United States of America

*McFarland & Company, Inc., Publishers
Box 611, Jefferson, North Carolina 28640
www.mcfarlandpub.com*

For my parents,
Marvin and Mary Niese

Table of Contents

Acknowledgments ix
Preface 1
Prologue 3

1. Off the Prairie, Birth to 1909   5
2. A Star in the Making, 1910–1912   14
3. Uncle Robbie, 1913–1915   34
4. A Pennant for Brooklyn, 1916   56
5. Uncertain Times, 1917–1919   72
6. A Whole New Ball Game, 1920   88
7. Captain Wheat, 1921–1923   104
8. A Season to Remember, 1924   126
9. Calm Amidst the Storm, 1925–1927   136
10. A Baseball Man Through Thick and Thin   158

Appendix: Major League Statistics 177
Chapter Notes 181
Bibliography 189
Index 191

Acknowledgments

I have the pleasure of sending a round of gratitude for helping this book see the light of day. Many were involved in one capacity or another in the research and writing process. A majority are the same people who have supported and assisted me through my other projects. I am grateful to all the names listed below as well as those that went unmentioned.

I must start by acknowledging my wonderful wife, Sara, and our three great kids: Oliver, Evelyn, and Henry. Your support means so much and continues to inspire me.

A special thanks to:

My parents, Marvin and Mary; brothers, Andy and Marty; sister-in-law, Brandie; and nieces, Allison and Lilly.

My great in-laws and extended family—the Slatterys and Hahns.

Kenny Dixon, owner of a collection of Zack Wheat memorabilia that is second to none. Kenny was just as enthusiastic about this project as I was. His generosity in sharing information and photographs was so helpful. Kenny, his wife, children, and grandchildren were so hospitable when I traveled to Hamilton, Missouri. The visit was just the inspiration I needed at the time.

McFarland & Company, Inc., who has continued to show faith in my work over the years, especially Gary Mitchem, Senior Acquisitions Editor.

Others who I conversed with about the project, especially Chuck Clark, Bob Dorais, Greg King, and Alan Wheat (Zack's great-grandson).

Libraries (both physical and digital) are the backbone of my research. I want to once again acknowledge the talented IFLS Library System interlibrary loan department—Maureen Welch and Gayle Spindler—and the great staff at the Chippewa Falls Public Library.

Other persons and their corresponding institutions include Judy Vilmer at the Caldwell County (Missouri) Historical Society, John Horne and Katherine Adriaanse at the National Baseball Hall of Fame Library (Cooperstown, New York), Cleveland Public Library, Library of Congress, and Kansas City Public Library.

Acknowledgments

All the authors and researchers who have written about the storied history of the Dodgers over the years. A special thanks to two of them, Lyle Spatz and John Zinn, who provided blurbs for the book.

The Society for American Baseball Research community (SABR). I'm particularly thankful for the work done by the SABR Baseball Biography Project as well as the resources made available to SABR members.

A shout out to my coaches and teammates on the diamond over the years—from Little League up through the Chippewa River Baseball League. Also, to the neighborhood crew who I played endless hours of ball with—those summer days are some of my fondest memories.

Preface

For decades, it was a foregone conclusion that Zack Wheat was the greatest player in Dodgers franchise history. Then, time took its toll. The number of fans who remembered him in his prime during the Deadball Era, and then his magnificent batting numbers of the first half of the 1920s, dwindled. Players from Brooklyn's World Series teams of the 1940s and '50s endeared themselves to a new generation, and then the team moved to Los Angeles after the 1957 season and made new memories over the next six decades.

Legendary sportswriter Frank Graham gave a perfect summation of Wheat's career—and why, despite his on-field accomplishments, his name is now known to so few:

> There was nothing dynamic about him, however, on the field or off. He showed up at the ball park every day. He played an almost faultless game in left field, he got his base hits, drove in runs and won a lot of tough ones. Then he went home to a rented apartment in Brooklyn or to the hotel when the club was on the road … and showed up at the ball park the next day. He never got into rows with the umpires, he never had a fist fight or even a quarrel with a teammates or an opposing player. Even the enemy pitchers had to like him, though he knocked their brains out.[1]

In their book, *The 100 Greatest Baseball Players of All Time*, Lawrence Ritter and Donald Honig wrote of Wheat, "He became during his tenure probably the most popular man ever to play in Brooklyn. Zack earned this admiration by his quiet, gentlemanly comportment, and also for the way he bashed line drives in all directions."[2]

Wheat spent a good part of his major league career with the Brooklyn Dodgers being overshadowed, first by John McGraw and his perennial contenders, the New York Giants; then by the larger than life persona of Babe Ruth, the New York Yankees, and the Liveball Era. So, it's no surprise that even in Wheat's hometown, Hamilton, Missouri, population of less than 2,000, he is overshadowed by another person of fame—James Cash Penny—founder of the JCPenney department store retail chain. Not that Wheat is altogether forgotten in Caldwell County. His image is on a mural

Preface

in downtown Hamilton, and a local brewery produces "Zach's Wheat" beer. Nearby, there is a Zack Wheat Memorial at Zach Wheat Memorial Sports Complex (yes, the spellings are different) in close proximity to his longtime home in Polo. A stretch of Highway 13 in the county is named "Zack Wheat Memorial Highway." In Sunrise Beach, Missouri—where Wheat resided for decades—there is the Zack Wheat American Legion Post 624, a Zack Wheat Drive, and, at one time, a Zack Wheat Little League team.

Baseball is one of the most researched American sports, if not the most researched; so there is no shortage of resources. I looked at dozens of books relating to both Dodgers history and specific player biographies. I relied heavily on a number of digitized newspaper databases, including newspapers.com, and used the following websites for statistical information: baseball-almanac.com, baseball-reference.com, and retrosheet.org. As a member of SABR, I was also privy to a number of other resources that helped fill in gaps.

There are a few items to address regarding wording within the book. First is the spelling of Wheat's first name—"Zack" or "Zach." I have decided to spell it "Zack"; it will be spelled "Zach" only when quoted from a source. The other wording is how to address the Brooklyn Dodgers. Wheat played during an era when the club was known by a few different monikers, including Superbas, Robins, and Dodgers. For continuity and familiarity, I will use "Dodgers" but address the other names when necessary.

I thought I knew a lot about baseball history, and then I started writing about it. As I worked on my first book, *Burleigh Grimes: Baseball's Last Legal Spitballer*, I was schooled in ball players of the day. The name that kept standing out to me was Grimes's longtime Brooklyn teammate, Wheat. I was surprised to see that he hadn't been the subject of a full-length biography, especially in light of the number of books written about the Dodgers franchise and particularly the Brooklyn years. There are few stones from the franchise that have been left unturned, and Wheat's story is one of them.

Prologue

On the afternoon of February 1, 1959, the phone rang at Zack Wheat's Sunrise Beach resort cabin on Lake of the Ozarks. Located in the central Missouri range of the Ozark Mountains, it had been the Wheats' home for over two decades. On the other end was John George (J.G.) Taylor Spink, publisher of the *Sporting News* and chairman of the Veterans Committee for the Baseball Hall of Fame. He was calling to inform Wheat that he had been unanimously voted into the Hall of Fame.

Wheat likely anticipated the moment. After all, Spink's son, C.C. Johnson Spink, was present at the resort. Despite his prior knowledge, the long-time Brooklyn Dodgers outfielder had problems controlling his emotions. "That makes me feel mighty proud and feel real good," a choked up Wheat told Spinks. "It's the greatest thing that can happen to you in baseball. I feel a little younger, too, on being honored. I'm 70 years old, you know."[1]

It was not an easy journey to the Hall of Fame for Wheat over the past quarter century. Unable to find work in major league baseball and still feeling the effects of a near fatal car crash in the mid–1930s, Wheat became the second Dodger player to be named to the Hall of Fame (Dazzy Vance, 1955) and the third native Missourian (Clark Griffith, 1946 and Carl Hubbell, 1947). Two years earlier, in 1957, Wheat was elected by the Veterans Committee, before it was pointed out that he was ineligible. He had been retired less than 30 years, the minimum for election by the committee. The year before, 1958, no new members entered the Hall of Fame for the first time since 1950. For many, the induction was long overdue, as the 5'10", 170-pound, tobacco-chewing Wheat had long been regarded as one of the greatest Brooklyn ball players of all time.

J.G. Taylor Spink complimented Wheat's all-around game, calling him the "perfect ball player, who was always thinking."[2]

A tear-filled call went out to Wheat's daughter, Mary Gottschall. By the end of the conversation, she was making plans to travel to Cooperstown in July.

Prologue

Wheat and his wife, Daisy, who had to compose herself throughout the visit, regaled Spink with stories of Wheat's career for the next few hours. They were often interrupted by congratulatory calls from reporters and baseball luminaries, such as the former president and GM of the Cincinnati Reds and current National League president, Warren Giles, and the great Branch Rickey, currently an executive with the Pittsburgh Pirates and a member of the Veterans Committee that voted Wheat in. The former Dodger General Manager said, "Old Zack was the best outfielder Brooklyn had, and he was one of the game's truly great batsmen."[3]

When sportswriter Murray Robinson, a Brooklyn native who grew up a fan of Wheat, called on his idol, he asked about the New York City borough. "My heart is still in Brooklyn," Wheat responded with a quiver. "Brooklyn had the most loyal fans in the country."[4]

Wheat receiving the call about his induction into the National Baseball Hall of Fame in 1959 (courtesy *Sporting News*. All rights reserved. Reprinted with permission).

1

Off the Prairie, Birth to 1909

Caldwell County lies in northeast Missouri, roughly 60 miles from Kansas City, Missouri. Originally the northern part of Ray County, Caldwell County was established on December 29, 1836, a designated safe haven for Mormon settlers who were experiencing religious persecution. They were expelled from Jackson County in 1833, living as refugees in Clay County until Caldwell County was incorporated. Originally consisting of one-third timber and two-thirds prairie, the new district enabled these pioneers to find success living on its expansive offerings. The tranquil setting was short-lived as the county became a main battleground during the Missouri Mormon War, leading to all Latter Day Saints being exiled from the state.

Following the Mormon exodus, Caldwell County's population dropped from over 5,000 to a few hundred. The next few decades were ones of transition, as the railroad came to the area and the population—and establishment of towns—grew. The agrarian culture flourished as newcomers arrived. On one of these farms, Zachariah David Wheat was born on May 23, 1888. The Wheat farm was located between Hamilton, the county's largest city—and place most often listed as his birthplace—and Kingston, a railway town and the county seat. He was the first son of Basil Curtis Wheat and the former Julia Davis Scott. It was not the first child for Basil; he had six children with his first wife, Mary, who died in 1884. Basil and Julia married March 2, 1886, and Zack came along a few years later. Brothers McKinley Davis (1893) and Basil Curtis, Jr. (1896) followed. It has been theorized that Zack was named after Zachary Taylor, the 12th president of the United States, and Jefferson Davis, the only president of the Confederate States, but those names, as well as those of his brothers, had been in the Wheat family for generations.[1]

During Wheat's major league career, there were mentions of his Native American heritage, since his mother, Julia, identified as a "full-blooded" Cherokee. It was a narrative that was repeated for years and never confirmed or denied by Wheat, who was tan with dark features. As early as his first professional season in 1908 with the Shreveport Pirates of the Texas League, he was referred to as "Cherokee" Wheat, when a local paper was giving players nicknames. A few years into his major league career with Brooklyn, a member of the organization made reference to his Cherokee heritage to the press as a positive marketing ploy. It was rarely mentioned in Brooklyn newspapers, but *Baseball Magazine* made frequent references to it for several years. The most sensational of these was a January 1917, full-length article titled "Zach Wheat, Most Graceful Outfielder: What a Heritage of Indian Blood Has Done for Zach Wheat." The piece was wrought with stereotypes of the day to describe him, including: "The lithe muscles, the panther-like motions of the Indian are his by divine right."[2]

By the next decade, Wheat's native heritage—which his wife Daisy said wasn't accurate—had disappeared as a reference point for sportswriters. There are a few mentions (no box scores to confirm) of him barnstorming with the All Nations baseball team, comprised of players of different ethnicities. If he did in fact have a Cherokee lineage, it would have made him one of baseball's early Native American stars, and, historically, one of the greatest indigenous players to ever play professionally. At the time he would have been amongst a group of players that included future Hall of Fame pitcher, Charles Albert "Chief" Bender (Chippewa); catcher, John Tortes "Chief" Meyers (Cahuilla band of Mission Indians); and outfielder, the great Jim Thorpe (Sac and Fox). To this day, Wheat continues to be mentioned as a Native American.

In 1916, when Wheat and Meyers were teammates on the pennant-winning Dodgers club, Meyers was asked if they "talk Indian." "As near as I can make out, Zack's tribal speech and mine differ about as widely as French and Russian," said the catcher. "I have it on Zack in one way, though: I speak three languages—English, Spanish and the Cahuilla tongue, while Zack speaks only two—English and Cherokee."[3]

Wheat was coy and at times playful regarding his lineage. When asked if his brother, Mack, was also Cherokee, Wheat replied: "Like myself, he is an Indian, only he is wild."[4]

According to Zack's daughter, Mary, the family genealogist, the Wheats had French ancestry, first coming to England as refugees, changing their name from Duplis to Wheat. They were descendants of Moses Wheat, a Puritan who fled England aboard the Mayflower, helping found Concord, Massachusetts, in 1635. Eventually, the Wheat family migrated to Virginia, settling in Bedford County near the Peaks of Otter, nestled in a part of the Blue Ridge Mountains that would take their name—Wheats Valley. From there, children of an earlier Zachariah Wheat ventured over the mountains

1. Off the Prairie, Birth to 1909

into Kentucky. Among those offspring was Zack's father, Basil, who settled in western Missouri.

When Zack Wheat was six, his family moved to Kansas City, Missouri. A year later they settled in the adjacent, Kansas City, Kansas. In 1886, the city reincorporated, consolidating five municipalities including "old" Kansas City. In the years that followed, "KCK," as it was known, experienced a population boom. The Wheats lived at a few different locations throughout the years, and members of the Wheat family would reside in the city for decades. Zack also maintained a house there for much of his life. His father, Basil, took on work as a hog salesman at the stock yards for the firm of Larrimore, Stagner & Pieronet commission merchants. By nine, Wheat was helping his father around the stock yard.[5]

From an early age, Zack wanted two things: to own a farm and be a baseball player. He would eventually accomplish both, but baseball quickly became the main goal. The game was growing in Kansas during the first decade of the 1900s. Universities all over the state fielded teams, the Missouri Valley League flourished, and the Western Association expanded to several cities within the state in 1905. By the end of the decade, Kansas' golden age of professional baseball began with the creation of Class A minor league baseball, as 25 cities and towns had teams in organized ball in all different classes.

Wheat was enthralled by all aspects of the game. As a youngster, he used to travel to his uncle's farm, gather green apples, and throw them at the lambs. When he broke the leg of one of the animals, he was reprimanded and this practice stopped. Wheat's interest in baseball grew, and by age 11, he and boys from the neighborhood had their mothers sew uniforms to wear to play sandlot ball. Zack regularly attended games at the "Hungry Hill" ball field at Walnut Street and Stewart Avenue. He pleaded with managers of various teams for a chance to play, but was always refused. He would then scour the crowd for someone to play catch with throughout the game. If there were no takers, he would incessantly throw handfuls of rocks.

Wheat attended Longfellow Elementary, before dropping out of school after eighth grade, in the spring of 1902. That summer, at 14, Wheat finally cracked a lineup at Hungry Hill, joining the Jones Boulevards. Over the next few years, he played for several semipro teams, including another local sandlot nine, the C.A. Mays, then the Prairie Roses at Chelsea Park, followed by the Schmelzers of the Intercity League. A right-handed throwing first baseman and left-handed batter, Wheat was gaining a reputation as a power hitter, but his fielding left much to be desired. Alfred H. Spink wrote that in his early days, Wheat was "like a wooden man" when fielding ground

Zack Wheat

As a teenager, Wheat (back row, second from left) played for a few different semi-pro teams in Kansas City, Kansas, including the Prairie Roses (Kenny Dixon photo collection).

balls, and "efforts to catch a fly ball were awful and frequently resulted in failure." Even catching a thrown ball was "not always a sure thing."[6]

At 17, Wheat played for Enterprise, a semi-pro team in Enterprise, Kansas, for $60 a month. His defense was suspect, but he could hit, evident by the long home run he supposedly hit in his first at bat. The Central Kansas League team was managed by Ralph W. Hoffman, later longtime president of the Kansas Flour Mills Corporation. Off the field, Wheat worked as a clerk at the Hoffman Mills in Enterprise. He learned his on-field tolerance from Hoffman, who told him that a player getting kicked out of a game for fighting or arguing "hurt nobody but himself, and his manger and his team, if he was put out a game, and that it was worse if he was suspended."[7]

The following spring, in 1907, Wheat signed on to play with the Union Club Nine, a Kansas City, Kansas outfit sponsored by the Union Club, a fraternal organization focused on fitness. Zack became the main source of income for his mother and two younger brothers. He sent a majority of his money home to them from his job at the Morris (Nelson) & Company, a meatpacking facility, first as a yardman, then a driver. When Wheat was a member of the Union team, it was said, "if he failed to get a home run every game the fans would think him sick."[8]

During his summer with Union, Wheat was called home because of the death of his father, Basil. He had been sick for a few years, but the latest illness had been ongoing for several months, before he finally passed away on July 21, 1907, at his home in Quindaro, Kansas. Since Basil had been unable to work, family funds were greatly depleted.

In the fall of 1907, Budge Cable, a pitcher and teammate of Wheat's on Union, received a letter from Dale Gear. A former major league pitcher and outfielder, he was the new manager of the Shreveport (Louisiana) Pirates, who were moving from the Southern Association, to the eight-team, Class-C Texas League, replacing the Temple Boll Weevils. The Pirates would be the league's only non–Texas team. Gear was looking for prospects, specifically an outfielder and first baseman for the 1908 season, and asked Cable to send a few players down for tryouts in February. Wheat pleaded with Cable, "Let me go. Send me. I can play first base."

"Pshaw, you can't catch a balloon," was Cable's reply.

"Well, if I can't I can hit them where the fielders can't get then," responded Wheat confidently.[9]

Cable relented, suggesting himself, Wheat, and Joe Dear, the team's catcher, as candidates. According to Alport F. Hager of the *Kansas City Kansan*: "At that time Dear and Cable were considered the one best bet along the baseball line in this city and the 'bugs' called Wheat 'excessive baggage,' and laughed at his even going away."[10]

Wheat's professional baseball journey began with the Pirates and player-manager, Gear. In early workouts, it was evident to him that Wheat wasn't a first baseman. Besides, that position was occupied by the larger, heavier-hitting, Chick Gandil. He would spend nearly a decade in the major leagues, but is remembered best as being a member of the Chicago White Sox and the 1919 World Series Black Sox scandal, which ended his career.

Gear was certain about Wheat's abilities as a hitter, batting him leadoff from early on. "He's the one who taught me to hit line drives," Wheat said of Gear.[11] A brief trial at shortstop followed, but Wheat's ground ball fielding was so bad that Gear moved Wheat to left field, a position the youngster was unfamiliar with. It was said that Wheat had ordinary speed from home to first, but there were few that ran the way he did from first to third. Gear hoped this would translate to play in the outfield. Each morning the two worked out together at the Shreveport grounds, with Gear drilling Wheat on all aspects of outfielding.

Wheat made a decent transition to the outfield, but he benefited heavily from the speed and fielding abilities of centerfielder Tony Thebo—who stole 80 bases—until he was acclimated. "I'll take all the fly balls, and then you do the hitting for me," Wheat recalled Thebo saying.[12] Wheat's .268 average was among the leaders on the eventual sixth-place club, but he struggled mightily on defense (12 errors in 92 games), with ground balls the cause of several of those. "Gear showed a lot of patience with me," said Wheat three decades later.[13] A blessing came early in the summer when a bone in his left arm was broken when he was hit by a pitch. For a month he watched from the bench, observing proper outfield play.

Despite the setbacks, Wheat played well enough to be mentioned as being considered by a few major league clubs. In late August, his option was picked up by the Mobile Sea Gulls of the Class A, Southern Association, for a pitcher and cash. "We gave a worn-out pitcher, a broken bat and a coon dog for you," replied manager, Tom Fisher, when Wheat inquired what it took to acquire him. "I didn't care then, I just wanted to play baseball," Wheat later said.[14]

In 24 games, Wheat batted .226 (19-for-84) for Fisher's fifth-place club. The manager pitched one season for the Boston Beaneaters in 1904, throwing for Shreveport from 1901–'03, and '05–'07, coaching the Pirates. Wheat's play was hampered by a hip injury suffered when an opponent stuck a bat in front of him as he slid into home. Several years later he described it as the "most painful experience" he ever had, thinking he had broken several ribs. He figured that if he had struck it on the corner of his hip, he would have been permanently injured.[15]

Shortly after the season, Wheat headed home with teammate, Lee Garvin. On September 20, they stopped at Sportsman's Park in St. Louis to watch the St. Louis Browns and Washington Senators. It was the first major league game that Wheat had ever attended. He saw Rube Waddell in his first year for the Browns—and last dominant season of his career—strike out 17, besting the Senators' promising 20-year-old right hander, Walter Johnson, 2–1, in ten innings. "After I saw Waddell that day," recalled Wheat years later, "I wasn't sure I wanted to be a big leaguer."[16]

Wheat returned to Mobile in 1909, this time to play for new manager, George Reed. According to American League umpire, Billy Evans, one team gave Wheat a tryout for several days during spring training, only to turn him away. "I'll play my head off in the Southern League and make them give me a chance," said Wheat of the rejection. "I'll make those fellows who said I didn't have big league class take back such statements."[17]

Wheat showed a little more pop in his bat from the leadoff spot in 1909—.246 with 20 doubles. More importantly he improved his defense—21

1. Off the Prairie, Birth to 1909

assists with just ten errors. The Sea Gulls were in first place in mid–June (they finished in fifth), and his play was being recognized. "Wheat is playing a dandy article of ball for the Sea Gulls and may have a chance to show in a higher class next year," wrote the *Montgomery Advertiser*.[18]

George L. Solomon, a traveling salesman from New York, saw Wheat play while working in the South. He mentioned the young outfielder to his friend, Charles Ebbets, owner of the Brooklyn Dodgers of the National League.[19] Ebbets dispatched Larry Sutton, whom the owner had befriended at the 1908–'09 offseason winter meetings in New York. The 1909 season was Sutton's first summer as a scout—considered to be the earliest person to hold the position in a full-time manner. He was the first of a handful of scouts hired by Ebbets over the next few years, later joined by former Brooklyn player, Tom Daly.

A proofreader and printer for several newspapers, Sutton had been involved in professional baseball for over three decades as an umpire, manager, owner, and, now, scout. Said to be large and humorless, Sutton's scouting territory was "limited only by his imagination and his budget for traveling expenses."[20] He was superstitious, always carrying an umbrella and favoring fair-haired ball players because he thought they were better suited for the hot summer on the ball diamond.

Wheat was struggling and about to be released when Sutton headed south in mid–July. Wheat was particularly bad at the Sea Gulls home park that had a sandy diamond, making it difficult to utilize his speed. Of late, Wheat had been suffering from symptoms that equated to malaria. "I don't know how much this

Wheat had mixed results in the minor leagues before his surprise signing by Brooklyn Dodgers scout Larry Sutton and subsequent call-up to the major leagues in September 1909 (Kenny Dixon photo collection).

affected my work, but it affected it a good deal," recalled Wheat. "I never felt in first-class shape until I came north, and then the malaria seemed to leave."[21]

In 1925, Al Demaree, who spent eight seasons as a big league pitcher, recounted the story of Wheat's signing to the Associated Press:

> Zack Wheat, the great Brooklyn outfielder was playing with Mobile, Ala., in 1909, and was hitting only about .240; in fact, he was going so badly that Jackson, president of the club that year, despairing of his ever amounting to anything, mailed him his unconditional release to the hotel where he was stopping. That same night Jackson awakened by the ringing of his phone. A voice at the other end of the wire was reading him this telegram "Brooklyn club will give $4,500 for Zach Wheat, Wire answer. Larry Sutton." Jackson thought somebody was kidding him, and wouldn't believe it until the telegraph company verified the wire. Wheat never received his notice of release, as the Mobile president was over bright and early to Wheat's hotel waiting for the first delivery of mail.[22]

Sutton signed Wheat on July 15. A few days earlier, Sutton had attended a doubleheader between Mobile and the Memphis Turtles, taking notice of both Wheat and the Memphis first baseman. He recommended that Ebbets obtain him in the fall. The player was Jack Daubert—the Southern Association's leading hitter in '09—who was drafted by Brooklyn on September 1. That same summer, Sutton also scouted outfielder, Hy Myers (purchased July 15), and catcher, Otto Miller, drafted the same day as Daubert. They were just a few of a litany of players signed by Sutton during his three decades with the club. Other players included: Dazzy Vance, Casey Stengel, Leon Cadore, George Cutshaw, Hank DeBerry, Ed "Jeff" Pfeffer, and Sherry Smith—the last two who he signed on the same day. Sutton helped build the foundation for Brooklyn's 1916 pennant-winning club, signing 11 of the players on the World Series roster for under $15,000.

According to sportswriter and baseball historian, Lee Allen, Ebbets was still at a loss after the signing. "What do you expect me to do with a player who hit for such a low average in a minor league?" he implored.

"Put him in the outfield," Sutton assured. "That's where he plays. This fellow's a ballplayer; I don't care what he hit."[23]

On August 29, Ebbets purchased Wheat's contract from Mobile for $1,200. The signing puzzled many, but the injury-riddled, second-division Dodgers, managed by first-year player-manager, Harry Lumley, had little to lose. It was a difficult season for Lumley, once one of Brooklyn's most popular players. His on-field performance had slipped, thanks to bad knees and the subsequent weight gain, drawing the ire of the home crowd. He broke a finger in the second game of the 1909 season, missed a month of play, and ended up appearing in only 55 games. All of this was compounded by his easygoing managerial style, which didn't work well.

1. Off the Prairie, Birth to 1909

Reed figured it would be a brief stay, expecting he'd see Wheat back in Mobile the following spring. He was given first class transportation and $7.50 to cover meals and tips to New York City. "My journey to Brooklyn was like the Lewis and Clark expedition," he said years later. "It took about four days of sitting up and riding in day coaches. I still remember how hard those seats were."[24]

When Wheat arrived at Jersey City, he took all of his belongs—a suitcase and a baseball bat—and stepped onto a ferry. "I was the most surprised guy in the world when it started to move," he recounted with a laugh decades later.[25] He became lost his first day in the big city, wandering into a bar for a beer, sandwich, and directions to the Polo Grounds. From the bench he watched Brooklyn drop two of three to New York. Exhibiting the bravado that got him into minor league ball, Wheat supposedly showed up at Charles Ebbets' office on a Friday off day. "Say, Mr. Ebbets, I came here to get in your outfield and I want a chance to land there," said Wheat. "If I can't do better than any of that gang playing out here for Lumley, I'll pay my own way back to Mobile."[26]

Wheat was equally as confident when he spoke with Lumley, who questioned his tepid minor league numbers. "I had malaria all summer," he told his new manager. "But it didn't seem to bother me when I left Mobile. I think I'll hit all right up here."[27]

2

A Star in the Making, 1910–1912

Charles Hercules Ebbets was a lifetime resident of New York City, born in Greenwich Village on October 29, 1859. By the age of 23, he had already amassed a resume that included architect, book publisher, and door-to-door salesman. He married Minnie in 1878 and had four children: Charles, Jr., Florence, Lydia, and Anna Marie. According to John Saccoman, "[A]n unsuccessful campaign for the New York Senate convinced him to devote his considerable talents to baseball rather than politics."[1] In 1883, Ebbets began working as a clerk, bookkeeper, and scorecard salesman for the Brooklyn Grays of the minor league Inter-State Association of Professional Baseball. It was the franchise's first year of existence. The next season, the Grays joined the American Association. In 1889, the now Bridegrooms were league champions. They moved over to the National League, winning the 1890 pennant.

In January 1898, Brooklyn became one of the five boroughs of New York City. It was a move not accepted by many Brooklynites, who continued to act as a separate entity. That same year, Ebbets became president of the Bridegrooms—or "Grooms" for short, following the January 4 death of longtime team president, Charles Byrne, one of the franchise's founding members, and for a few seasons, team manager. Ebbets would spend the next 27 years as team president. Within five years of taking over, he owned all but a few stocks, which he bought out over the next decade. During the 1898 campaign, Ebbets became the third manager of the season for Brooklyn. On June 10, he took over for Mike Griffins, after his four-game tenure, succeeding Billy Barnie. Ebbets lasted the duration of the season, ending with a personal mark of 38–68, a majority of the club's 54–91, eighth-place finish.

The fate of the franchise changed the following season, in 1899, when Ned Hanlon and Harry Von der Horst, owners of fellow National League club, the Baltimore Orioles, acquired a half-interest in the Dodgers. Despite being president of the Orioles, Hanlon, who guided Baltimore to three consecutive pennants from 1894 to 1896, took over managerial duties for

2. A Star in the Making, 1910–1912

Brooklyn. The team would soon be referred to as the "Superbas," in a nod to a popular vaudevillian acrobatic troupe, Hanlon's Superbas. Brooklyn's roster was littered with the most talented players from Baltimore: outfielders, Willie Keeler and Joe Kelley; shortstop Hughie Jennings; and pitchers, Jim Hughes and Doc McJames. Though his time with Brooklyn was brief, Keeler, a native of the borough, who "hit 'em where they ain't," would predate Wheat as the franchise's batting standout and fan favorite in the outfield. The '99 club took over first place on May 22, and ended up winning the franchise's second National League pennant and first 100-win season, 101–47. They repeated as champions in 1900, but the American League began raiding National League rosters. The Dodgers spent the remainder of the decade spiraling towards the bottom of the standings, leading to Wheat's debut.

Ebbets had seen much change to the Brooklyn franchise and baseball as a whole in his quarter century with the club, having much to do with that change. In the previous decade, Ebbets instituted innovations that were adopted all over the major leagues. In 1904, he devised the 154-game

Charles Ebbets began working for the Brooklyn Dodgers franchise in 1883, selling scorecards. By 1898, he owned the team, a position he held until his death in April 1925 (Library of Congress, Prints & Photographs Division [LC-DIG-ggbain-05526]).

schedule, mapped out by the distance between clubs. Two years later, in 1906, he pushed for separate batting and fielding practices for each team. He also provided dressing rooms for both home and visiting clubs. It was a particular blessing for the out-of-town teams, who had previously dressed at the team hotel. This new luxury came with lockers and running water—both hot and cold. He was laughed at by other owners when he said that baseball was still in its infancy during the first decade of the 1900s, but he was certain that much change lay ahead. In 1905, he conceived the rain check portion of a ticket that could be used in case of a rainout, and in 1913 helped implement the player's draft, where teams with the worst records got the first picks. Finally, in 1924, he helped formulate the 2-3-2 World Series format.[2]

Much of the good that Ebbets did for the game was sometimes overshadowed by his combative approach to money matters. Longtime New York sportswriter and baseball historian, Frank Graham, described Ebbets as such:

> Of necessity, he fought with almost everybody over money matters. He cut the ballplayers' salaries where he could, and when he had to give a player an increase, did so grudgingly. He bickered with the sporting goods manufacturers over the price of bats, balls, and uniforms. He watched carefully over every penny taken in at the gate, constantly lecturing his employees on the subject of economy, and refused to approve many small bills presented to him or delayed payment of them as long as possible.[3]

On September 11, 1909, Wheat's name was in the Brooklyn lineup, batting second and playing left field against the Giants. It was a fitting introduction for Wheat, as he would be an integral part of one of baseball's biggest rivalry. In fact, the first recorded game between a team from Brooklyn and New York dated back to October 1845. On the mound for Wheat's first start was one of the game's best—Christy Mathewson. In the clubhouse, regular left-fielder Wally Clement quipped, "We always like to see young guys come up at the end of the season to give us regulars a little vacation."[4]

Wheat loved retelling the story: "Well, I gave him a vacation all right—for 18 years."

In the nightcap—a 10-1 Brooklyn victory, Wheat played center—one of just a handful of games he played there in his career. He again batted second, collecting the first two hits of his career—a pair of singles off the Giants' hard-drinking right-hander, Bugs Raymond.

A week later, Wheat had Brooklyn's only hit in a 6-0 loss to the eventual World Series champion Pirates in Pittsburgh, coming off future Hall of Famer Vic Willis. Willis and his catcher, George Gibson, got crossed up on Wheat's tapper in front of the plate in the third inning. When Gibson finally retrieved the ball and threw it to first, Wheat was already across the bag. Willis' effort

2. A Star in the Making, 1910–1912

was the closest any pitcher would come to a no-hitter at Forbes Field. Wheat's play in the field also gained him an ovation from the Pittsburgh crowd when he went out to his position to start the bottom of the eighth inning.

Brooklyn fans could only follow their new outfielder's exploits from afar. It took three weeks from Wheat's debut for the Dodgers to finally return to Washington Park for an October 2 doubleheader against the Boston Doves. Wheat played both games, going hitless, but his presence pleased the fans, who sat through the chilly games. The *Brooklyn Daily Eagle* wrote, "his work in the field, especially in the second game, earned him applause from the shivering fans."[5]

Washington Park sat between 3rd and 4th Avenues and 1st and 3rd Streets in Brooklyn's Park Slope neighborhood. Built in just 45 days, it was the fourth home for Brooklyn's professional ball club, having previously played at: Capitoline Skating Lake and Base-ball Ground, 1862–78; Washington Park, 1879–90, and Eastern Park, 1891–97. Ebbets moved the franchise to the current location in 1898 after taking over control of the franchise. With an original capacity of roughly 10,000, the current ballpark had a wooden facade, a covered grandstand that stretched from first base to third base, and uncovered bleachers down the left and right field lines. Beyond the right field wall were the Ginney Flats apartments, where tenants watched games. As time went on, Ebbets used as much space as he could, adding seats 15 feet from home plate. For highly attended games, standing room was installed on-field around the perimeter of the outfield. The outfield dimensions when Wheat arrived were left field, 376 feet; left-center, 444; center field, 425; and right field, 302 feet. The outfield fences were 12 feet high in left and centerfield and 42 feet in right field, made up of 13 feet of brick and topped by 29 feet of canvas.

In one of the games from Wheat's home debut series against Boston, he was left questioning whether he had the grit to play in the major leagues. He foul-tipped a ball that knocked loose the middle fingernail on Doves catcher Frank Bowerman's left hand. Time was called to give Bowerman a quick respite. Wheat watched incredulously as the catcher took off his mask and mitt, rolled the injured digit in the dirt, and, without a word, bit the nail of his finger and spit it aside. He put the helmet on, squatted behind the plate, and called to the pitcher, "Let's get this busher."

"Zack, old boy, I don't think you'll make the grade in the big leagues," Wheat recalled thinking to himself.[6]

Wheat had slipped into a week-long slump before his debut in Brooklyn, but over his last six games of the season—all at Washington Park—he went 12-for-25. During his month-long stint (26 games) Wheat batted .304, with seven doubles and three triples. He signed his 1910 contract ($2,100) shortly after the season ended, returning to Kansas City, Kansas, to live with his mother and brothers. It was written of his mother, "She is an enthusiastic reader of baseball and takes a great interest in Zack's career, reading whatever she can get about his game."[7] In late October, he played centerfield for the Smith Team in the Intercity League Championship, losing 7–6 to the Stevens Club in front of 3,000 fans at downtown Kansas City's Association Park.

Over the next few winters, Wheat trained with locals at Kansas City's Union Club. On the basketball court, he was described by Judge Benjamin Terte as "a little shy on basketball finesse," and "it wasn't considered entirely safe to be in his path when he had the ball."[8] Wheat also played endless handball. One of his frequent opponents was Ed Stilwell, president of Commercial National Bank, who described Wheat as being as "solid as a rock, quick in his reflex and had a fine temperament."[9] Wheat also played the wildly popular indoor baseball whenever possible.

Lumley was relieved of his managerial duties by the end of October 1909, but remained on the roster for 1910, appearing in a scant eight games. Veteran shortstop Bill Dahlen, recently released by the Boston Beaneaters, signed as a free agent on October 27, and was named Brooklyn's next manager. He was a member of the Dodgers' pennant-winning club of 1900, and was considered for the job the previous fall, before returning to Boston as a player-manager. A favorite of Ebbets, Dahlen—once considered one of the game's top shortstops—possessed a fiery temper aimed at anyone that contradicted him or stood in the way of what he was trying to accomplish—evident by his career ejections total approaching 70. Previously accused of meddling with his manager's decisions, Ebbets wasn't concerned he would have to with his new hire. "In Bill Dahlen I have secured a man who will not ask me to interfere. He will run the club himself," said the Dodgers owner.[10]

Wheat's surprising play had him being hyped up by many during the winter months, including managers: John McGraw, New York Giants; Fred Clarke, Pirates; and Frank Chance, Chicago Cubs. Ebbets brashly predicted that Wheat would "prove another Ty Cobb next season."[11] Now that Wheat was a known commodity, those that had dismissed him—namely the other 15 ball clubs—were befuddled by the fact that they didn't sign him. There were also those that lamented why they hadn't acquired Wheat when presented the opportunity. Stanley Robinson, owner of the St. Louis Cardinals, told his woeful tale: "Last year a St. Louis traveling man begged me to go to Mobile and see a real wonder. 'And you can get him cheap,'" he said. "I thanked him and forgot all about it as we get fifty such tips a day. The player was Zack Wheat now with Brooklyn, and in my opinion the greatest outfielder today."[12]

2. A Star in the Making, 1910–1912

Despite the praise being heaped on Wheat, there were still holes in his game. *The St. Louis Star and Times* released a scouting report of Wheat in February 1910:

> Zach Wheat, with proper coaching will make a wonderful player. He is a natural born hitter and as fast as a deer, but he has a few faults that must be remedied, to make him a big league star. There is no better player living than Wheat when it comes to fielding a fly ball, and he can throw a mile, but he is very weak on fielding safe hits to his territory, especially when runners are on. He seems to be over-anxious in his effort to get the ball in making the play at the plate and that is the cause of two-thirds of his errors. His other weakness is on the paths. Although fast as chain lightning, he stole only ten bases in 129 games in the Southern League and one in 26 in the National. Proper coaching will soon remedy these two defects and Wheat is sure to be a star.[13]

One of the few bright spots for Brooklyn during these lean years in club history was Nap Rucker, a hard-throwing, hard-luck lefty. Saddled with facing the opposition's best pitchers, the 25-year-old from Crabapple, Georgia, was seldom backed with many runs. Sportswriter Sid Mercer was once asked what team gave Rucker the most trouble.

"Brooklyn, unquestionably," replied Mercer.[14]

Rucker came to the Dodgers in 1907 from the Augusta Tourists of the South Atlantic League, where he roomed with Ty Cobb. Rucker went 15–13 with a 2.06 ERA as a rookie. The next year he threw a no-hitter against the Boston Beaneaters, setting a National League record of 14 strikeouts. In 1909, Rucker was 13–19, with a 2.24 ERA, establishing a career-high strikeout total of 201, including 16 against the St. Louis Cardinals on July 24—tying a modern-day record. He was soon the team's highest-paid player, cracking $4,000 within a few seasons. Years later, Wheat recalled, "During Nap's days our club didn't amount to much. It was a shame to see games kicked away for him." He added, "When they talk about great lefthanders don't let them overlook Nap Rucker."[15]

The feeling was mutual for Rucker. Nearly two decades later, shortly after Wheat retired, Rucker was comparing batters of different eras. "No better natural hitter ever lived than Buck Wheat and Old Buck just buried his spikes in the ground and swung."[16]

In early March 1910, Wheat boarded a train in St. Louis, heading to his first major league camp at the epicenter of spring training, Hot Springs, Arkansas. It was the Dodgers' first spring there after three years in Jacksonville, Florida. Located in the foothills of the Ouachita Mountains, Hot Springs had been a destination spot for teams to ease into the season for over two decades, ever since Albert Goodwill Spalding sent his National League Chicago White Stockings there in 1886. It was an ideal setting for the moderate training schedules of the day. Teams dispersed amongst the elegant hotels and lakefront cottages. Players took in the hiking, country clubs, hot springs, and bathhouses along Central Street, sometimes independently training in the spa city before reporting to their respective camps. Over the years, ball teams

Wheat and Red Smith (left) in a postcard sent to Wheat's mother in the early 1910s. He and Smith were teammates from 1911 to 1914, when the third baseman was traded to the Boston Braves in August (Kenny Dixon photo collection).

2. A Star in the Making, 1910–1912

went through drills and played games at a few different ball fields, including: Whittington Park (1894), Majestic Park (1908), and Fogel Field (1912).

Wheat and roughly 30 other Brooklyn hopefuls arrived in Hot Springs on March 4, 1910, checked into the Majestic Hotel, and within three hours were going through exercises at Whittington Park. For a decade-and-a-half, Whittington was the only field in the city, having replaced the original training site, Hot Springs Baseball Grounds in 1894. A second field, Majestic Park, was built as a training site in 1908 for the Detroit Tigers. John I. Taylor, owner of the Boston Red Sox, signed a five-year contract for the team to train at the more attractive Majestic Park, named after the hotel that gained its name from the Majestic Stove Company for unknown reasons. In 1910, the Red Sox shared the facility with the Cincinnati Reds, and, at times, Brooklyn.

A week-and-a-half into camp, Dahlen took his team over to Majestic Park to watch the Red Sox and Reds. The arrival of the Dodgers pushed the spectator count over 200 in the newly built grandstands. The weight was too much, collapsing underneath them. Luckily, no one was hurt, but supposedly Brooklyn shortstop Tommy McMillan ended up in Cy Young's lap. Wheat eluded injury when the grandstand toppled, but he was already hobbled. A few days into training, he hurt his foot hiking through the surrounding mountains. It didn't bother him at first, but stiffened up upon his return, keeping him on the bench for a few days. When back to health, Wheat put in hours of practice in the outfield. Among his competition for a spot was Joe Jackson, who was eventually retained by the Philadelphia Athletics, with whom he had stints over the previous two seasons.

It was a change to Wheat's hitting approach that made him stand out in camp. He had made it to the majors, finding success in limited action with a conservative game plan. That changed one morning after a batting practice session that saw him repeatedly dump balls over the third baseman. As Wheat headed back to the dugout, he heard, "Say kid, you gotta wallop 'em in this league if you expect to linger long; wallop 'em from the toes or you'll be drifting back where you came from."[17] The advice came from a trio of respected veterans seated at the end of the bench: Harry Lumley, Tim Jordan, and John Hummel.

The foursome took a bag of bats and a dozen balls to one of the corners of the field, beginning the transformation. Lumley picked out the heaviest bat and handed it to Wheat. "Grab 'er right at the end," directed Lumley. Hummel took on the role of batting practice pitcher.

Jordan modified Wheat's stance and placement in the batter's box. "As far away as you can get, Zack, my boy," he said.[18]

Over the next week the group repeated this routine, and by the end

Wheat was pulling the ball with power. "I'll never forget those days," recalled Wheat a decade-and-a-half later. "I didn't a thing about hard hitting because I didn't think that I was built for a fence-buster."[19]

Wheat remembered the kindness shown to him, paying it forward throughout his career. Sportswriter Tommy Holmes wrote, "Wheat's popularity with his fellow players and his kindness to younger players were legendary."[20]

Moving forward, Wheat was hesitant to take certain advice, particularly around hitting. The group had redirected Wheat's approach to that of his power-hitting semipro days, and he never changed it. "That's the secret of every batter's success. Every batter has a natural style of hitting," he told F.C. Lane of the *Sporting News*. "Let him follow that style regardless of what others tell him. Then, whatever talent he has will come to the surface. Advice is all right when it tends to overcome some technical fault, but advice should never go so far as to change a batter's style."[21]

During his first major league spring training, Wheat was given the nickname "Buck" by the *Eagle*, which quickly caught on. When the more menacing "Black Lightening" was bestowed, "Buck" had already stuck. Later on, Wheat would become "Ol' Zack." He was quickly accepted by Brooklyn fans, including super fan, Sheriff William Buttling, the Exalted Ruler of the borough's Elks Lodge No. 22, who made sure Wheat became a member early in the season.

The Dodgers were in the second division a week into play, where they remained for all but one game during the rest of the 1910 campaign—another sixth-place finish, 64–90. Wheat's play, particularly his batting—he was one of the team leaders from the start—was being taken notice of, leaving fans wanting to know more about the promising outfielder. On June 3, 1910, the *Brooklyn Daily Eagle* ran the first of what would be many exposés of Wheat. It gave his often repeated background story, saying that he "has the prospects of being one of the greatest hitting outfielders in the National League."[22]

That same month, Wheat was asked to write a piece for the American Press Association's *Stories of the Diamond* series. The headline read, "Zach Wheat Tells Secrets of His Great Batting: Hit Sphere in the Eye." He spoke at length of his approach depending on the type of pitch, with the common theme of keeping one's eye on the ball throughout the at-bat. To aspiring ballplayers, he offered the following advice: "Keep a close eye on the ball from the time it leaves the twirler's hand until it connects with the bat. Let your eye follow it up to the instant it connects with your club."[23]

Wheat brought an aggressive batting tactic, gaining the reputation as a first-ball hitter early in his career—and at times a bad-ball hitter. "They are harder to meet than the good ones," he said of the latter. "You can hit them safe, but it's more of a job."[24] He seemed to give little thought to the pitcher's strategy—his 80 strikeouts were second-most in the National League to the 81 of teammate Hummel. The veteran, Hummel, who played 11 of his 12 seasons in Brooklyn, spent much of his career playing several positions, but in 1910 he was the league's best-fielding second basemen. Referred to as the "prince of utility players," the Bloomsburg, Pennsylvania native only batted .244, but established career highs of: runs (67), doubles (21), triples (13), home runs (five), RBIs (74), and stolen bases (21).

"Poor batters generally try to outguess the pitcher," Wheat told F.C. Lane. "I won't say positively that is the cause of their poor hitting, but I do know that good batters generally don't try to outguess the pitcher."[25] He was particularly adept at hitting curveballs, leading John McGraw to prohibit his pitchers from throwing Wheat breaking balls. Though he was known as a moderate power hitter, home runs were never a priority for Wheat, who hit his first major league home run on August 25 off the Pirates' Lefty Leifield. "Give me a line drive single or a long one between the outfielders any time," Wheat said.[26]

Harry Grayson, longtime sportswriter for the Newspaper Enterprise Association described Wheat at the plate: "Wheat twisted the handle of a black bat until sawdust came out of it. He hit in a semi-crouch with his feet spread far apart. He wiggled his front foot digging in and when he brought the bat back to the hitting position went into a little shimmy before the swing uncoiled like a steel spring."[27]

Wheat never took up the trend of choking up and slapping at the ball. "In my own case I don't believe that applies," he said later in his career. "I have always been used to slugging the ball, and that is the only way I know. I think every man should bat according to his own style. He will do a great deal better that way than by trying to copy someone else."[28] Wheat became an anomaly for the era. He despised bunting and swung a heavy bat from the handle, something few players did at the time. He carried bats of varied weights, opting for heavier bats on a cold day, lighter on a hot one. He used lighter bats against curveball pitchers and heavier against fastball pitchers. "I plan always to have a bat that is just suited to my weight and strength, so that I can feel the ball when I hit it," he explained.[29]

By season's end, Wheat was one of just two players in the league to play in all 156 games, Mike Mitchell of the Reds being the other. The games played figured to be a career-high for Wheat (he would crack the top ten just two more times in his career), as were the 15 triples. He batted third in the lineup in all but four of those games, leading the club with a .284 average.

His 172 hits and 36 doubles (along with the triples) led the club (the first of seven times doing so—he tied another time in 1912), and were among the league-leaders.

Wheat's output placed his name with the game's best in the following year's *Spalding Base Ball Guide*, where fans could buy an 8x10 picture of him for a nickel or even splurge for one Wheat's "Model W" bat by Spalding for a dollar. He was also fodder in the burgeoning vaudeville scene amongst major leaguers in the offseason. In a skit involving Wheat's teammate George Crable, one of the biggest laughs played off Wheat's speed. "Zach laced the ball so hard one time that it hit him on the head as he touched second," quipped Crable.[30]

Brooklyn's other impact player was another rookie—a 26-year-old former coal miner from Shamokin, Pennsylvania—Jake Daubert. He began mining with his father and two brothers at age of 11, working for over a decade, before leaving in 1906 to try to make it as a baseball player. He played well enough in leagues in Pennsylvania and Ohio to sign a contract with the Cleveland Indians in 1908, but was released a short time later, finishing the season with the Nashville Volunteers in the Southern Association. He started the 1909 season back in Ohio with the Toledo Mud Hens of the American Association, before returning south to play with Memphis, where he caught the eye of Sutton, and, subsequently, the Dodgers.

In 1910, Daubert took over first base from Jordan, who twice led the league with a dozen home runs (1906 and '08). The left-handed batting Daubert hit .264, second on the club to Wheat and matched the 15 triples. Over the next several years, the quiet and reserved Daubert—nicknamed "Gentleman Jake"—was regarded as one of the game's best all-around first basemen, often compared to the great Hal Chase of the Yankees. Daubert's brilliant fielding (he led the National League in fielding percentage and double plays) was overshadowed by his batting prowess, winning back-to-back batting titles in 1913 and '14. Batting mainly from the second spot in the lineup, he had great bat control, utilizing a slashing chop style, with the ability to place a bunt perfectly. He still holds the National League record for sacrifices, 392. For the next several years, he and Wheat posed a formidable duo for Brooklyn.

The addition of Wheat and Daubert gave Brooklyn pitchers more run support, but no other starter found much success beyond Rucker, including the team's other workhorse, right-hander, George Bell, a hard-luck starter, who led the majors with 27 losses. Rucker went 17–18, but losing record aside, it was the best year of his decade-long career. He led the National League in innings pitched (320), complete games (27), and shutouts (6). He

2. A Star in the Making, 1910–1912

won 22 games the following season—despite losing his first six decisions—and lost 21 in 1912 (with a 2.21 ERA—over a full run better than the league average). He was the first Dodger to win 20 games since Oscar Jones did it in 1903, and the first to have back-to-back 20-win seasons.

The following spring, 1911, in a heavily attended Hot Springs, Arkansas series, expectations were high for Wheat. In the first exhibition game he clubbed a home run and a pair of doubles. A few days later he went four-for-four, hitting another home run, a triple, and two singles. The *Brooklyn Daily Eagle* boldly predicted, "If Zack Wheat keeps up his present all around form during the season and there is no reason to doubt it, he will be an even bigger sensation than last year. The way he is hitting, running bases, and fielding stamps him as the coming star outfielder of both leagues. Ty Cobb and Tris Speaker are expected."[31]

That spring, Brooklyn took on another name. After over a decade of being known as the Superbas, they adopted a moniker of the Trolley Dodgers, or "Dodgers" for short. It had been unofficially used for years, dating

Fielding never came easy for Wheat. Starting in the minor leagues, he worked tirelessly on his glove work. He had great range and a good arm, but had trouble with ground balls. Here he is warming up alongside fellow outfielder Hub Northern in 1912 (Library of Congress, Prints & Photographs Division [LC-DIG-gg-bain-11521]).

back to the mid-1890s, as a nod to the street Trolleys that citizens had to elude throughout the thoroughfares of the borough. A new wrinkle was also added to the Dodgers' spring. Ebbets put together an expanded exhibition schedule that had the club logging 3,000 miles heading north for the start of the season. The Dodgers also took to the field with a new look. Their logo was now an old-English "B," that was enclosed in overlapping lines that formed a diamond. The following season the diamond was enclosed with the elimination of the overlapped lines. These changes came a few years after adopting a plain home jersey with the logo on the left sleeve. On the road, the word "Brooklyn" ran down the area around the buttons.

In the third game of the 1911 regular season, Wheat fell a home run short of the cycle in a 15–2 pounding in Boston against the Braves. The run total was the most Brooklyn would score all season, and the 2–1 record was the last time the Dodgers were above .500. A season-high six-game losing streak followed, slipping Brooklyn into the second division permanently, eventually finishing with a 64–86 record in seventh place.

The pressure was on Wheat to live up to off-season expectations. After a fast start at the plate in April, it looked like he would meet them. He stumbled over the next few months, though, and, in June, had the worst full month of his career to date, batting just .216 and striking out 14 times. A trade to the Phillies was floated, but eventually squelched by Dahlen. Frustrations came to a head during a scorching July 4 doubleheader at Washington Park that saw Wheat nearly lose his temper. When Rucker asked him what he was mad about, Wheat replied, "At nothing. I guess I am just mad with the heat, for nobody has done anything to me, yet I am sore enough to bite a tenpenny nail in two."[32]

Wheat improved in July, rapping 11 extra base hits (five doubles, four triples, and two home runs—coming in back-to-back games), but by July 28, his batting average dipped to .252. The next day his season turned around with his first four-hit game of the season. It was the beginning of a stretch of nine out of ten games with multiple hits, raising his average to .282. He would finish at .287, second on the club to Daubert's .307 (his first of ten .300 seasons). The first baseman became the club's first full-season .300 hitter since Lumley hit .324 in 1906. As a team, Brooklyn was at the bottom of nearly every National League batting category in 1911.

During the season, Wheat received bags full of fan mail. One of those came from a family friend back in Kansas City, L.S. Stengel. He was contacting Wheat on behalf of his son, Charles, an outfielder who was on his way to winning the batting title for the Aurora Blues in the Wisconsin-Illinois League. He and Wheat had been youth basketball teammates. Wheat

2. A Star in the Making, 1910–1912

suggested to Larry Sutton that he should stop in Aurora to take a look at the player known as "Dutch." The scout obliged, and on September 1, Stengel, better known as Casey, was drafted by Brooklyn in the rule 5 draft. Another player of impact selected that day was George Cutshaw, a speedy infielder from the Oakland Oaks of the Pacific Coast League. The Illinois native would be one of the league's best fielding second basemen over the next few years. During his six seasons with the Dodgers, he would lead the league in putouts from 1913–16 and assists from 1914–16.

Wheat was a line-drive hitter, who was aiming for the gaps rather than over the fence.

"Home runs always were unlucky for me," Wheat said. "Give me a line drive single or a long one between the outfielders any time."[33] Otto Miller corroborated Wheat's sentiment. "It's a fact that Buck didn't want to hit home runs," said Miller of his longtime teammate. "I've seen him hit a couple in a game and come back cussing to the bench. When Wheat hit one out of the park, it meant to him that he was swinging too hard."[34] One of his five home runs on the season made club history. On August 3, he hit the Dodgers' third home run of the fifth inning against the Cubs at Chicago's West Side Grounds. His two-run shot into the right-field bleachers followed back-to-back home runs earlier in the inning from Eddie Zimmerman and Tex Erwin, propelling Brooklyn to a 5–3 win. It was the first time the feat had been accomplished in club history.

Wheat's late-season resurgence was halted for a few games by a severe ankle sprain suffered during the early August Cubs' series. He persisted for several days, but finally the injury became so painful that it caused him to be out of the starting lineup for the first time in his major league career, after starting all 288 games since being called up to Brooklyn in September of 1909. Later that month, on August 24, one of Wheat's line drives altered the career trajectory of pitcher Larry Cheney, a future teammate. On September 17, the rookie spitball pitcher was making his third career appearance and first start. The right-hander was shutting down Brooklyn for seven-and-two-thirds innings when Wheat scorched a ball back through the pitcher's box. Cheney quickly raised his pitching hand, deflecting the drive, but suffering a severe injury. "The ball broke the little finger of my right hand and jammed my thumb so hard up against my face that it broke my nose, too," he recalled.[35]

The injury changed the way Cheney delivered the spitball, which he learned from Ed Walsh during a brief stint with the Chicago White Sox during spring training in 1908. Cheney's injury courtesy of Wheat left him weakened the following spring of 1912. He opted to throw with an exaggerated overhand delivery, giving him some late movement on his pitches. It worked, as he was a 20-game winner over each of the next three seasons, reaching a high of 26 in 1912.

For the first time in his career, Wheat took on the role of run producer, leading the club with 76 RBIs—the first of seven times he did so in his career. He also showed his speed, stealing a career-high 21 bases in 1911 (equaled in 1915). He also covered a great deal of ground in the outfield and was very quick from first to third base or second to home, but the speed displayed early in his career never equated to large stolen base numbers. There were a few seasons throughout his career where he was caught stealing more times than he stole a base. Within a few years his ankles and legs began to plague him, requiring bandages and rub downs from trainers before and after games. The lower extremity problems were likely linked to the stress put on his small feet—size six—by his pigeon-toed style of running. Wheat thought the contrary. According the *Brooklyn Daily Eagle* columnist Ed Hughes, Wheat "always claimed that pigeon-toed ball players had less trouble with their pedals than others and he would go to great pains to cite examples if you hankered for them."[36]

On January 2, 1912, Ebbets announced his plans to build a new ballpark in front of a handpicked crowd at the Brooklyn Club. The estimated cost was $650,000-$750,000. It was a growing trend around the league, as three teams had new homes in 1912: Boston Red Sox, Fenway Park; Detroit Tigers, Navin Field (later Tiger Stadium); and Cincinnati Reds, Redland Field (later Crosley Field). The Giants also moved into a newly rebuilt concrete-and-steel Polo Grounds after it had burned in 1911, so Ebbets knew it was time to make a move. "Brooklyn has supported a losing ball team better than any other city on earth," said the Dodgers' owner. "No place has such loyal and cheerful fans, and no one realizes it more thoroughly than myself. Such a patronage deserves every convenience and comfort that can be provided at a baseball park, and that is what I hope to provide."[37]

Ebbets had been plotting the new structure for years. Unbeknownst to many, his architect, Clarence Van Bushkirk, had completed building plans after an extensive review of ball parks throughout the league. Ebbets had decided on the location back in 1908 while out on a walk in Pig Town, a neighborhood on the Southside of Brooklyn, bordering Flatbush. The site was literally a garbage dump, described as "four and a half acres of as squalid a tract of land that ever disgraced a civilized community," that "sent up stenches that must have reached further than Heaven."[38] It couldn't have been much worse than the rancid air from nearby factories and canals that enveloped Washington Park.

For three years Ebbets aggressively bought out claimants who owned

2. A Star in the Making, 1910–1912

nearly 30 land parcels. In all, he spent close to $200,000. The process led him to eventually go looking for financial support. After fellow owners refused to give him money, Ebbets turned to the McKeever brothers, Edward and Stephen, successful Brooklyn contractors and friends of Ebbets for over three decades. The brothers had gotten their start in the business when they landed a contract to provide the plumbing, gas, and steam fixtures for the construction of the Brooklyn Bridge. Ebbets bought out the shares of Henry Medicus, who had shared ownership of the Dodgers with him since 1905, when they had bought shares owned by Harry Von der Horst. Ebbets, in turn, sold the half shares to the McKeveers for $100,000 in August 1912, which helped finish the construction of the ballpark.

The McKeever brothers would be an integral part of the Dodgers franchise for the next quarter century—for better or worse. Steve was the larger personality of the two, calling everyone he encountered "Judge." Ed was quiet and hard to get a read on, yet more reliable and accountable with baseball matters. The parties formed two corporations. One was the Ebbets-McKeever Company, with Ed McKeever serving as president, Steve McKeever as vice-president, Charles Ebbets as treasurer, and Charles Ebbets, Jr., as secretary. This entity owned the land and stands. The other firm was the Brooklyn National League Club, with Ebbets, Sr., president, Ed McKeever, vice-president, Steve McKeever, treasurer, and Ebbets, Jr., secretary.

The McKeevers became more involved than originally planned, so Ebbets installed two long wooden benches at the lower tier of the stands. One was to accommodate Ebbets and his friends. The other was for the McKeevers and their group. The area was accessible to fans, so depending on the outcome of the game, you could find the owners either soaking in the congratulations after a win or engaging fans in loud arguments following a loss. The scene was often too much for Ed, who would flee the area before the game had ended.

Ground for the new park was broken on March 4, 1912, just a few blocks from several borough attractions, including the Brooklyn Museum, Prospect Park, and the beautiful 52-acre Brooklyn Botanic Garden. Among the onlookers were the four Brooklyn sports editors, whom Ebbets called "The Four Kings": Abe Yager, *Brooklyn Daily Eagle*; Bill Rafter, *Brooklyn Standard-Union*; Bill Granger, *Brooklyn Citizen*; and Len Wooster, *Brooklyn Times*. The owners' relationship with the quartet was complex. Frank Graham wrote, "Although they quarreled with him sometimes and blasted him in their newspapers, had supported him loyally when their support was needed most."

The park had yet to have an official name. Ebbets' lawyer, Bernard J. York, suggested it be named after his client. The motion then gained traction from an article in the *Brooklyn Daily Times*. A few days later, a reporter for the paper proposed the idea to Ebbets, who according to John G. Zinn "probably somewhat disingenuously, claimed he hadn't thought about the parks name."[39] When Ebbets admitted the idea of naming the ball yard would be stressful for him, the sportswriter asserted that perhaps the newspapers should then. Ebbets agreed and soon with input from the "Four Kings," the name Ebbets Field became official.

An opening date for Ebbets Field would be set several times during the 1912 season, but the largest crowd during the summer was when the cornerstone was put into place on July 6. Ultimately, the park wouldn't open until 1913. The Dodgers were already in Hot Springs, Arkansas, for spring training, being the first full team to arrive and begin drills on February 29. Wheat's 1912 leg problems began on the team's barnstorming tour north to start the season. On March 19, he suffered an ankle injury on a delayed steal in a game against his former team, the now Memphis Chickasaws of the Southern Association. His toe caught the bag on a slide into third base, grotesquely twisting his ankle. He was helped off the field, and the next day he was walking on the swollen ankle with the aid of a cane. It was estimated that he would be out for a week to ten days.

The team travelled to Louisville, Kentucky, for a weekend series against the American Association club, the Colonels. Rain and snow kept the Dodgers off the field for a few days. Wheat took the opportunity to visit relatives, connecting with his father's cousin Mary Davis Forsman (married to Harry C. Forsman). Wheat was met at the train depot by his second cousin, Daisy Kerr Forsman, who took him back to her parents' house for supper.

Daisy, described as a "musician and society girl," had been previously married (to Willis Hofstatter on March 11, 1904), and was currently engaged to a wealthy Louisville man. She had been initially reluctant about having to entertain Zack, but there was an immediate attraction between the two. After parting ways, they wrote to each other multiple times a day, discussing a wide variety of topics, including the recent sinking of the *Titanic*. After an eight-day courtship, the couple became secretly engaged.

Wheat played sparingly for the last month of spring training, but was in the lineup at the start of the season. In the April 11 season opener against the Giants, a crowd of over 30,000 swelled at Washington Park. Gates opened at 12:30. Within two hours they were closed, as the wooden grandstand, bleachers, standing room, and even tickets on the field, had sold out. That didn't sit well with fans that were still trying to get in, climbing over and under the fence to enter the ball yard. Nothing could be done as they openly defied the private security detail that had been hired. It

2. A Star in the Making, 1910–1912

took Mayor William Gaynor summoning numerous city police who were outside the park to come in to gain some order. Ground rules had to be made to accommodate the multitude that stood mere feet from play, and, surprisingly, crisis was averted, as no fans were injured, no major fights incited riots, and the bleachers stayed erect. Mercifully, Umpire Bill Klem called the game due to darkness, as the Giants embarrassed the Dodgers, 18–3. Wheat went one-for-two, driving in a run with a third-inning double, coming around to score on a Hummel single.

After the first few games, it was obvious that there was something more serious going on with Wheat's ankle. He was given a few days off and then limited to pinch-hitting duties, but that did little to subside the lingering pain. Finally, he was diagnosed with tendon damage and was given orders to stay off his feet as much as possible. According to the *Brooklyn Daily Eagle*, during his absence, fans in the cities the Dodgers visited made "inquiries about him coupled with the expression of the wish that he would soon be back in [sic] harness."[40]

On May 13, Brooklyn—already in the second division, where they remained for the rest of the season—was playing the last game of a three-game

Hard-throwing, hard-luck left-hander Nap Rucker was Brooklyn's go-to pitcher during the first half-decade of Wheat's career with the Dodgers (Library of Congress, Prints & Photographs Division [LC-DIG-ggbain-22997]).

series against the Reds in Cincinnati. Wheat was still a day away from returning to the lineup. Joining him at the Sinton Hotel, where the team was staying, was Daisy Forsman. The couple walked a few blocks to the Central Christian Church, where they were married. Wheat didn't want to be listed as a ball player on the marriage license, opting for civil engineer instead. Forsman was equally as secretive, listing her address as the Sinton Hotel. The fact that they were second cousins was never perceived to be an issue.

When word got out that Wheat had gotten married, his teammates congratulated the well-liked Wheat and his new bride with a "bridal suite" on the train as the team headed for St. Louis. The celebration was short lived, though, when Daisy got off in Louisville to break the news to her family—and fiancée. The nuptials changed the complexion of Wheat's career. With the confident Daisy in his corner, Wheat would find the courage to speak up for himself, negotiating for his contract, rather than accept the first one offered to him by Ebbets.

Wheat was out of shape when he returned to the lineup. His sluggish start even brought word of him being shopped to the St. Louis Cardinals. It took nearly a month for him to return to form. When he did, he hit safely in 21 of 22 games, reaching a season-high average of .339 on July 5. The only thing that could slow him down was illness. In July, he was forced to the bench with what was described as exhaustion, costing him ten games.

Late in the season, Brooklyn called up some of their minor league prospects. Among them was Wheat's old friend, Casey Stengel, who had a successful season with the Montgomery Rebels of the Southern Association. The left-handed batting and throwing outfielder reported to Ebbets' office at Washington Park, giving the owner a taste of things to come. "Do you want to go forth in uniform and be introduced to your playmates?" inquired Ebbets.

"Aw, no, I'm dead tired from traveling and think I'll look the fellow," replied the newcomer, nonchalantly. "I know some of them and Zach Wheat came from Kansas City, which is my hometown. Have somebody watch my duds while I take a peep at the show, and I'll break in tomorrow."[41]

When Stengel did start the following day, he slapped four straight singles, walked, stole a pair of bases, and drove in two runs. Wheat also had four hits, including a double and home run, part of back-to-back long balls over the right field fence in the fifth inning for him and Daubert. It was all part of a 14-hit barrage by Brooklyn to help Rucker to his 16th victory in a 7–3 win over the Pirates. Rucker was once again snake-bitten by poor run support. He finished with an 18–21 record—the only Dodger to reach double-digits. He tied the Pirates' Marty O'Toole for the league-lead with

2. A Star in the Making, 1910–1912

six shutouts. His 2.21 ERA was third-best in the National League. From September 17 to October 3, he threw 29 consecutive scoreless innings.

The Dodgers' final game at Washington Park was a 1–0 loss to the Giants on October 5, 1912. Wheat went hitless in three at-bats. Brooklyn finished 58–95, for another seventh-place finish—46 games behind the pennant-winning Giants. In the season postmortem, Thomas Rice was somewhat critical of Wheat, saying that he had "recently burdened himself with a lamentable propensity for striking out when the striking is decidedly bad."[42] Overall, Wheat's batting numbers were respectable. Hitting mainly from the fifth spot in the order, he batted over .300 for the first time in his career (.305)—the only other regular to do so besides Daubert (.308). In 123 games, Wheat was near the top of all team batting categories. He tied for the club lead in doubles (28) with third baseman Red Smith, and had a team-high eight home runs. Wheat's 65 RBIs were one behind Daubert's team-high, 66.

Rather than returning to Kansas, Wheat took in a hunting excursion in Oklahoma, then wintered with his in-laws in Louisville, a pattern he would repeat over the next few off seasons. When asked by John J. Ward of *Baseball Magazine* what he did in the winter time, Wheat responded with a wink, "My father-in-law."[43] Before the year expired, he signed a contract for the 1913 season, one of the last times there wasn't a contentious negotiation between him and the club.

3

Uncle Robbie, 1913–1915

Much of Wheat's willingness to sign his contract in 1913 was that he continued to support his mother and two brothers in Kansas City. In February 1913, Mack, a catcher with the Lawrence outfit in the Interstate League, received an invite to Brooklyn's spring training (he wouldn't play for the Dodgers until 1915). The youngest brother, Basil, a 15-year-old high schooler, was already showing his talents on the local diamonds. Zack and Mack stuck close together in the Dodgers' new training locale, Augusta, Georgia. Zack, whose salary increased to $3,300, earned the title of "champion letter writer" from the *Brooklyn Daily Eagle*, which wrote that Wheat "may be found at the writing table inditing reams of fond missives home."[1]

Wheat was hopeful of the team's prospects in 1913. "I'd like to see us finish in the first division this year," he said confidently. "We ought to, and get a start for that flag. We've got a fast team of young players that should get going and reach the top in time."[2]

The early excitement centered on Ebbets Field at 55 Sullivan Place in the Flatbush neighborhood, which would finally be opening. Designed by Van Bushkirk and built by the Castle Brothers, Inc., the grand structure's principal architectural feature was the ornate 80-foot circle-shaped rotunda. Enclosed in Italian marble, the tiling had a representation of baseball stitches and a chandelier, with 12 baseball-bat arms holding 12 baseball-shaped globes. The field dimensions were similar to that of Washington Park. Left field was a cavernous 419 feet (shortened to 410 the following year), centerfield, 450 feet, and right field an inviting 301 feet (shortened to 300 in 1914). Fences varied in size to match the divide from field to field, starting at 20 feet high in left and down to nine in right for a further advantage for Brooklyn's lefty combination of Wheat and Daubert. Wheat found a lot of success at Ebbets Field. In his 942 games played there over 14 seasons, Wheat batted .329. His totals equated to six full seasons of averaging 30 doubles, 10 triples, 12 home runs, and 86 RBIs.

The inaugural game at Ebbets Field was an exhibition match against

3. Uncle Robbie, 1913–1915

the Yankees on April 5. Besides a lack of grass in the outfield, it was realized that keys to the bleachers were forgotten, a press box hadn't been built (and wouldn't be added until 1929), and there was no flag for the flag pole. Ed McKeever's wife, Jennie, tracked down an American flag and raised it in centerfield. Wheat provided some pregame entertainment by hitting a home run over the right field fence. Ebbets' youngest daughter, Genevieve, threw out the first ball from the stands. The Dodgers scored first with an inside-the-park home run by Stengel, eventually winning 3–2, when Wheat scored from third base on a single by Smith in the bottom of the ninth inning.

The first regular season game at Ebbets Field was held on April 9, a 1–0 Dodger loss at the hands of the Phillies. The first test for the ballpark didn't go well. One of the major criticisms of Washington Park was how fans filtered in and out of the park, evident by the fiasco with the Giants on Opening Day the year prior. When New York came to Ebbets Field for the first time on April 26, a similar weakness of the new stadium was exposed when the ornate rotunda became bottlenecked with fans—a near stampede ensuing. To address this concern, two new entrances were placed in different parts of the park to divert thousands of fans away from the rotunda. Other

Early in Wheat's career, he was known for speed and daring on the base paths, which would sometimes get him into trouble. By the mid-1910s, leg problems began to plague him, likely due to the stress put on them by his small feet—size six. Here he is sliding back into first base during a rundown in 1927 as a member of the Philadelphia Athletics against the Chicago White Sox at Shibe Park (Kenny Dixon photo collection).

notable problems included a batter's eye that made it difficult to pick up the spin of the ball, and shadows that made it hard for fielders to track the ball as it passed from shadow to light and back to shadow. All that mattered from that game against the Giants was the final score, a 5–3 Dodgers victory—the first regular season win in the new park—after four losses to the Phillies in the first two weeks.

In May 1913, Wheat was listed among the nearly 300 members of the Baseball Players' Fraternity. Members wore a pin to signify their involvement. Daubert served as vice president of the controversial organization that was part of the union movement. By mid–May, Wheat was batting .350 and enjoying a power surge, hitting doubles and home runs in back-to-back games. A month later he was struggling at the plate, at .239. His stroke returned to form, soon enjoying another streak and collecting multiple hits in seven of nine games over an 11-game hitting streak. One of the highlights was the eventual game-winning home run over the would-be pennant-winning Giants in a three-hit game at the Polo Grounds on June 23 in the first game of a doubleheader. A few days later the *Brooklyn Daily Eagle* wrote that Wheat was "going like a house afire these days and he is pulling off wonderful plays every game that cause the rooters to leave their seats and howl."[3]

Usually recognized for his batting, Wheat was asked to contribute an article for the *Junior Eagle* insert of the *Brooklyn Daily Eagle* about playing left field. The first line of Wheat's lengthy piece was autobiographical: "Most boys become outfielders after they have for various reasons failed to become infielders or pitchers." He stressed how different muscles are used when playing the outfield, and that outfielders should stay in motion in between pitches, throw overhand with "a free movement" that would give it "a hop," monitor the wind every inning, and take "fungos" regularly.[4]

On July 4, Zack and Daisy welcomed a daughter, Mary Helen, born at the family home in Louisville. Wheat was said to have "swelled up like a toy balloon and discussed the obligations of a parent with great volubility," when talking about his daughter. Family was very important to the Wheats. Their son, Zack, Jr., was born in 1918 and the foursome was seldom apart thereafter. Daisy and the children were always at home games and tried to travel with the team as much as possible. The Wheats even included the children in fine dining, bringing a highchair into the Waldorf-Astoria.

Brooklyn struggled through ankle injuries to: Stengel, Hummel, Fisher, and Cutshaw—all sliding into second base—and the persistent arm troubles of Rucker, sending him to the early specialized baseball doctor John "Bonesetter" Reese. Wheat flourished, despite heat sickness, a hand injury, soreness in his legs, and a rumored trade to Cincinnati, though his

3. Uncle Robbie, 1913–1915

efforts went mostly unnoticed outside of opponents and Brooklyn fans. John J. Ward of *Baseball Magazine* said that Wheat had "long been denied that measure of public recognition which his work so clearly bespeaks."[5] In the same article Wheat was compared to Sam Crawford of the Detroit Tigers. "Both are quiet, courteous, unspoiled by their recognized abilities, hardworking and efficient. And both are dreaded at the bat by every pitcher in their respective leagues," wrote Ward.[6] Left field at Ebbets Field came to be known as Wheatville. Whenever he did something—whether batting or in the field—fans in the bleachers would give him a sustained round of applause until he tipped the brim of his cap.[7]

Roy Skelly, a correspondent for the *Brooklyn Daily Eagle*, recalled the special relationship Wheat had with the "bleacherites":

> He had a little gag that endeared him to the bleacherites. Every day as the game began the fans would yell, "How many hits today, Zach?" The answer was always the same. Wheat would smile and cross two fingers of his bare right hand across the palm of his glove. Sometimes he got two hits, sometimes he got three or four, sometimes he would be shut out. But the same cheery smile and the same two fingers again would answer the same eternal question the next day.[8]

Wheat's reputation as one of the game's good guys was growing. He dispensed advice to teammates and opponents alike and always controlled his emotions. He would go his entire career without being ejected from a game, a statistic he was proud of. That didn't mean he wouldn't let an umpire know that he disagreed with them. According to Skelly, "When Zach thought a bad one had been called against him, he'd step out of the batter's box, shake his head a couple of times, pull at the peak of his cap, give his belt the usual hitch, step back into the box and give that old familiar 'shimmy' while digging in for his cut."[9]

"I did come close once," Wheat recounted during an interview after being named to the Hall of Fame in 1959. "Bill Klem called me out on a third strike thrown by Lee Meadows in St. Louis. I threw my bat and yelled, 'no, no, no.' Klem told me later that the only reason he didn't throw me out of the game was because I didn't turn around."[10]

Wheat batted cleanup for the majority of the season and was now established as a power hitter, contrary to his line drive approach (he tied Stengel and Cutshaw for the team lead with seven long balls). The fourth spot in the lineup would be the most common for Wheat throughout his career (1,314 of the 2410 games he appeared in). He explained his strategy and those of other heavy hitters of the time to F.C. Lane:

> There are all kinds of sluggers. Those that swing from their feet; those that get their shoulders into it, and what I call arm hitters. I am an arm hitter. My wrists are strong

and my forearm is bigger than my biceps. The strength to hit as I do is in my wrists and forearms. It isn't so much the swing you give a bat as the quick snap just as you meet the ball. That's what drives the ball. It's the same as boxing. A long, roundhouse swing that come halfway across the ring and then bumps into a man will shove him out of the way, but it won't hurt half so much as a quick, short jolt from a boxer who knows how to hit. When you snap the bat with your wrists just as you meet the ball, you give the bat tremendous speed for a few inches of its course. The speed with which the bat meets the ball is the thing that counts. You can tell when the ball is going to travel by the quick, sharp crack when the bat meets it.[11]

Jack Daubert batted .350 and won the 1913 National League Chalmers Award, a precursor to the Most Valuable Player Award (MVP). He was gifted a Chalmers automobile, which he had no idea how to drive. (A few years later he taught Wheat how to drive when he purchased a Reo). Daubert was also rewarded with a rare 5-year contract at $9,000 a year.

Wheat was the only other Dodger to bat above .300 at .301, his first of nine top-ten batting performances. It didn't show in the standings, but it was by far the best lineup since he and Daubert had come to Brooklyn. Smith hit .296 and led the majors with 40 doubles. Cutshaw paced the team with 13 triples, 80 RBIs, and 39 stolen bases—all career highs. The team—second in the league with a .270 average—took on Wheat's aggressive approach, seldom taking a walk. Over the next decade the team finished last (1913, '14, '15, '18, '19, and '22) or second to last in base on balls ('16, '17, '20, and '21).

In the offseason, Daubert was put in charge of taking a squad of teammates to Cuba to partake in the American Series, where they would play a few different teams across the island. It was the first time Brooklyn had been there since 1900, when they, along with the New York Giants, became the first major league teams to play on the Caribbean island. Wheat was absent from the 1913 trip (the Dodgers went 10–5), opting to return to Polo, Missouri, where he purchased farmland for his new family.

Located south of his birthplace and in the same county, Caldwell, Polo took its name from Polo, Illinois, named after explorer Marco Polo. The Missouri incarnation of Polo had begun as a station for the railroad, thus platted six different times to accommodate the rerouting of the rails before it was finally built in the late 1860s. By the time Wheat returned to Caldwell County, Polo was a prime spot. "Not only does the land present a pleasing appearance, but it is productive, rich and rolling, with plenty of drainage and very fertile," wrote W.H.S. McGlumphy in the *History of Clinton and Caldwell Counties, Missouri*. "Along the streams and valleys the land is even more productive and the county is in a high state of cultivation."[12] Wheat enjoyed living in the area, spending the next two decades splitting time between there and homes in Kansas City and Brooklyn.

3. Uncle Robbie, 1913–1915

Wheat and Stengel played their usual slate of fall exhibition games in 1913. In one of the heavily attended contests, Stengel played a fast one on Wheat, much to the amusement of the onlookers. Late in the game, Wheat sent a drive that cleared two wire fences. As he leisurely made his way around the bases, he saw Stengel, who was coaching third base, frantically motioning to pick up the pace as he rounded third base, giving Wheat a surprising directive to slide into home. When the dust settled he saw the right fielder climbing over the first wire fence to retrieve the ball.

According to Ernie Dunn, a local ballplayer, Wheat "looked down toward Stengel at third and there was Casey laughing like mad. And so were the home folks."[13]

Shortly after the 65–84, sixth-place finish of 1913, Ebbets made it apparent that he needed someone else to manage the team. It had been a trying four seasons for Dahlen, guiding a young, inexperienced club. According to John Snyder, author of the *Dodgers Journal*, Dahlen's "fiery temper, which was exasperated by running losing clubs, placed him in almost constant turmoil with his players and with reporters and umpires," but, "to his credit, Dahlen started a youth movement that included many players who would play on the 1916 National League pennant-winning club."[14]

Abe Yager of the *Brooklyn Daily Eagle* put pressure on the replacement process by suggesting Daubert. Ebbets publicly responded that the selection process should be respected with patience. Yager retorted with a list of five more possible replacements with Roger Bresnahan of the Cubs gaining the most attention. Finally, in mid-November, Ebbets returned from the annual minor league meeting in Columbus, Ohio, to announce that he had signed former Giants coach, Wilbert Robinson, to be an assistant to Dahlen. Ebbets put out a long statement publicly thanking Dahlen for his years in Brooklyn and the intention to keep him on as a special assistant. A few days later it was announced that Robinson would be the Dodgers' eleventh manager in franchise history. For the next 13 seasons he would manage Wheat.

Wilbert Robinson was born on June 29, 1863, in Bolton, Massachusetts, growing up in nearby Hudson. He was one of seven children of Henry, a butcher, and Lucy Jane. By the age of 12, Wilbert had organized a team to travel to nearby towns to play, transporting his teammates by driving a horse and wagon he rented from a livery. He found early success as a catcher, honing his skills by rigging up a clothes line in his backyard at eye level when crouching and having his friends throw balls at it to simulate foul tips. "You see, after I had blinked at that clothes line and been bunged up by those foul tips off the line I got so I could catch any kind of a ball and the waving of a bat meant nothing to me at all," he explained half-a-century later.[15]

Zack Wheat

Within a few years, Robinson was catching for the local nine, alongside two of his older brothers. The only piece of protective equipment he used was a piece of rubber between his teeth. He earned the spot after his younger team played against the "first nine." When their catcher was injured in the second inning, he stepped in and caught the entire game for both teams—never getting a turn at-bat. Throughout his life he considered the promotion "as high an honor as I had."[16]

Robinson entered professional ball in 1885, as a member of the Eastern New England League's Haverhill Club, bringing with him an aptitude for the game and a good-natured personality that rubbed off on teammates. One of the first pitchers he caught was John K. Tener, who went on to serve as governor of Pennsylvania, before becoming president of the National League in December 1913 (shortly after Robinson took over managerial duties in Brooklyn). Robinson played well enough for Haverhill to latch on with the Philadelphia Athletics of the American Association the next year, where he spent five seasons. He finished the 1890 campaign with the league's Baltimore Orioles, when the A's went broke and folded.

For nearly a decade, Robinson was the Orioles' catcher and captain, finding the most success as a member of Ned Hanlon's notorious teams that included: John McGraw, Willie Keeler, Joe McGinnity, Hughie Jennings, Joe Kelley, Dan Brouthers, Kid Gleason, and Sadie McMahon. Robinson came into his own as a batter during those years. On June 10, 1892, he recorded a record seven hits in a nine-inning game (as well as 11 RBIs). He topped out at a .353 batting average in 1894. Behind the plate he developed the knack of snapping a finger out of joint to simulate a foul tip to deceive the umpire.

Robinson had a close relationship with McGraw, nearly a decade his junior, serving as the soothsayer to umpires for the fiery infielder. The two were opposites on many accounts, but were inseparable, even purchasing new row houses next door to each other in Baltimore. On March 9, 1900, the pair was assigned to the Brooklyn Dodgers when the National League contracted to eight teams. The next day they were purchased by the St. Louis Cardinals after refusing to report to Brooklyn. They spent an unhappy year out west with the fifth-place Cardinals, throwing their St. Louis uniforms in the Mississippi River at season's end, vowing to sign a contract with the Orioles, now part of the American League. McGraw, who served as manager and part owner of the club, was released July 7, 1902, after frequent disputes with league president Ban Johnson. Robinson finished out the season as the manager, retiring at season's end. McGraw signed with the National League New York Giants shortly after leaving Baltimore to serve as player-manager. Within two years he had developed a

3. Uncle Robbie, 1913–1915

Wilbert Robinson managed Wheat for 13 seasons. On good terms for many years, but their relationship soured during Wheat's last few seasons as a Dodger when Robinson suspected the outfielder of planning to take his job (Library of Congress, Prints & Photographs Division [LC-DIG-ggbain-18833]).

winner, taking the pennant in 1904 and 1905, and found a new best friend in pitcher Christy Mathewson.

After Robinson retired, he and McGraw stayed in contact as partners of the *Diamond Cafe*, a popular oyster bar and saloon in Baltimore. McGraw asked Robinson to help out with the Giants' pitchers during spring training. The manager did the same in 1910, and, by midseason of 1911, Robinson was serving as a full-time bench coach. According to author Alex Semchuk, Robinson's main duties were "keeping the club loose, jockeying the opposition, and developing the pitching staff."[17] With Robinson's antithetical approach to McGraw's—once described by *Brooklyn Daily Eagle* columnist as "kindliness, friendliness and confidence"—the Giants flourished, winning the National League pennant three straight seasons, 1911–13.[18] Robinson also provided a much needed bridge to sportswriters, which benefited him when he took over as manager of the Dodgers. He was instrumental in guiding New York's strong pitching staff of Mathewson, Jeff Tesreau, and Rube Marquard.

The Giants lost all three series, and there were signs of a rift between the old friends throughout the 1913 season. It came to a head at an Orioles reunion following the World Series-ending Game Five loss to the Philadelphia Athletics. A drunken McGraw, who had gained the nickname, "Little Napoleon," loudly criticized Robinson's third base coaching, to which Robinson retorted with a critique of McGraw's managerial skills. McGraw kicked Robinson out of the get-together, but not before Robinson doused him with a glass of beer. The incident with McGraw soured Robinson. Initially, he was hesitant to take another job, thinking he could bide his time with fishing, hunting, golf, and billiards, but a month later, he was Brooklyn's new manager. He would be one of a long line of managers that worked with McGraw, either as a coach or player. The list included Stengel, Billy Southworth, and Bill McKechnie—all of whom made it to the Hall of Fame on their managerial credentials.

Robinson's task would not be easy. The Federal League was challenging Major League Baseball for players, offering higher salaries, and in turn, pushing up payrolls for American and National League clubs. Expanding from six to eight teams, the Federal League claimed six future Hall of Famers. It also brought a different, batter-friendly brand of baseball that fans seemed to take to, thanks to watered down pitching and a lively baseball. The Brooklyn entry was the Tip-Tops, who played their games at Washington Park. Daubert was a prime target of the Federal League, leveraging a five-year contract from Ebbets—a rarity at the time—that not only paid him $9,000 per season, but dropped the reserve clause. Wheat was also rumored to have a three-year deal on the table. The Federal was also infringing on Ebbets' territory, but he was willing to spend money to keep his players. It was one of four leagues that challenged the National League during Ebbets' four decades with Brooklyn.

In January 1914, Robinson and Ebbets headed west on a contract "signing trip," traveling inconspicuously. They had their eyes set on Joe Tinker of the Cincinnati Reds, the shortstop in the famed Chicago Cubs Tinker to Evers to Chance infield combination that played in four World Series from 1906–10. Slated to be Brooklyn's starting shortstop in 1914, Tinker refused to sign, opting to return to Chicago as a member of the Federal League Chicago Whales. The missed opportunity was seemingly the only disappointment of the trip, as Ebbets returned to Brooklyn with most of his roster signed, including Wheat, who agreed to a one-year contract. Robinson implemented a tactic of Hanlon's from his days in Baltimore and McGraw with New York, by having pitchers and catchers report a week early. Robinson's grudge with McGraw—whose Giants had gone on a world tour with the Chicago White Sox during the offseason—didn't keep him from calling his former teammate "the best man in the business for bringing clubs north in the pink of condition."[19]

3. Uncle Robbie, 1913–1915

Weather plagued the beginning of the regular season, but the Robinson era was ushered in with an 8–2 win over the Braves at Ebbets Field on April 14. Prior to the game, Brooklyn's new manager was given an enormous floral horseshoe by a group of fans. New National League president John K. Tener threw out the first pitch from his box seats. Wheat doubled and drove in a run. A few days later, on April 18, the first of 387 games between the Robinson-led Dodgers and McGraw's Giants took place (New York bettered Brooklyn 190–197 over those 18 seasons). Wheat was the batting star of the inaugural clash, hitting a double, home run, and driving in five RBIs off Christy Mathewson, in a 9–6 win over New York to move the Dodgers' record to 3–0. The home run—of the inside-the-park variety—was thought to be the longest ball hit at Ebbets Field to date. It hit the Bedford Avenue gate on the fly, caroming off toward the flagpole. By the time Giants fleet-footed outfielder Bobby Bescher tracked the ball down and threw it in, Wheat was crossing home plate standing up.

Though he never publicly acknowledged the rift, "Robinson would always relish a ball field victory when McGraw was his adversary," wrote Robinson biographers Jack Kavanagh and Norman Macht. "In some seasons to come, beating the Giants would make up for a losing year. When the situation required a pose of mutual respect, they shook hands for the cameramen, but neither would make the first move to mend the rift."[20]

Robinson and his wife, Mary, quickly became entrenched in the Flatbush neighborhood, living alongside fans and his players, many of whom had apartments around Parkside and Flatbush Avenues. Legendary reporter Damon Runyon called him "Your Uncle Robbie," while others called him "The Round Robin." He would become "Robbie," and Mary was "Ma," who "would argue strategy and lineups with anyone she met, often exchanging views with fans while Uncle Robbie listened," wrote Kavanagh and Macht.[21] She split time between Brooklyn and Baltimore, where the couple's youngest son, Wilbert Jr., lived with them. Once a promising ballplayer, he suffered from a chronic illness that over the next few years would leave him bedridden at the Baltimore residence. He was cared for by his sister, Hannah, herself suffering from health issues. Within a few years he would pass away, devastating the family. Hannah would die from heart issues in 1929. The other two Robinson children were Mary, who married Frank Gunther, of the Gunther Brewing Company family, and Harry, who went into construction after starring at football at Baltimore Polytechnic High School.

Wheat slumped during May—traditionally his weakest month throughout his career. There was concern, but not for Wheat, who didn't put much thought into early season averages—good or bad. "These May batting averages don't amount to much," he told F.C. Lane. "The test of a good hitter comes later in the season. The morning glory average is generally a false alarm."[22]

Wheat had a well-rounded June, but by then Brooklyn found themselves struggling to stay out of the second division. A five-game slide amidst a long June homestand had them fighting to not slip into last place. In a surprising move, Ebbets rewarded his new manager with a three-year contract. The club was now frequently being referred to as the "Robins," in a nod to their manager to go along with "Superbas" and "Dodgers." The "Robins" moniker was following past trends of giving the team nicknames after their manager: "Hanlon's Superbas," "Ward's Wonders" (John Montgomery Ward), and "Foutz's Fillies" (Dave Foutz).

There was some clubhouse turmoil when a faction of players began trying to get Robinson ousted as manager and replaced by Daubert. The group was headed by Smith, who clashed with his new manager immediately. The third baseman, who had played so well the year before, slumped in '14, threatened to jump to the Federal League if a change wasn't made. He was sold to the Braves in August, helping them to the World Series. Unfortunately, he broke his ankle in the last game of the regular season, leaving him unable to play in the four-game sweep of the Philadelphia Athletics.

Playing .500 ball (42–41), the Dodgers improved in the second half of the 1914 season, enjoying an 11-game winning streak in late September. It was the most since the 101-win pennant winners of 1899 won a dozen in a row. To the satisfaction of Robinson, his club had some critical wins over the Giants, keeping McGraw from capturing his fourth consecutive National League pennant. Brooklyn's fifth-place, 75–79 record in '14 was the best win total in 12 seasons. Boston took the '14 pennant, becoming the first team other than the Giants, Pirates, or Cubs to finish first since 1900—when the Dodgers did.

As much as he was lauded for working with pitchers, Robinson's batters led the league with a .261 average. Daubert—who suffered a head injury on July 4 that nagged him for the rest of the season—won his second consecutive batting title. His .329 average bested the .325 output by Phillies outfielder Beals Becker. The next three leaders in average were Daubert's Brooklyn teammates: Wheat and centerfielder Jack Dalton tied at .319, followed by Stengel with .316. The Dodgers became the second National League club to have four of the top hitters, joining the 1908 New York Giants (Mike Donlin, .334; Larry Doyle, .308; Al Bridwell, .285; and Roger Bresnahan, .283).

After being a solid contributor in 1913, Stengel had a breakout campaign in '14. In addition to the .316 average, he legged-out 10 triples. Much of it had to do with his approach at the plate (he led the league in on-base

3. Uncle Robbie, 1913–1915

Jake Daubert taking batting practice as Wheat (squatting, third from right) looks on during the 1918 season. The pair spent the first nine years of their careers as teammates with the Dodgers (Library of Congress, Prints & Photographs Division [LC-DIG-ggbain-16225]).

percentage with .404). Some of the breakthrough came from emulating how Wheat handled spitballers. Stengel worked closely with Nap Rucker on this, the two showing up early to the park each day to drill. "It finally got to the point that I was hitting the low pitch pretty good; so good, in fact," Stengel recalled to sportswriter Ernest Mehl years later, "they started throwing me the high pitch again which used to be right down my alley."[23]

The speedy Dalton had found his way back to Brooklyn after a dazzling debut in June 1910. In the second official game of his career, the right-handed batting Dalton went five-for-five—four of them singles off Christy Mathewson—in a win over the Giants. Things quickly went downhill for Dalton, who had starred at the University of Virginia. He was beaned just above the temple against St. Louis a few weeks after the game with New York, was injured in August against the Cardinals after colliding with the outfield wall, broke his finger on an inside pitch against the Cubs a few weeks after that, and played sparingly thereafter because of illness. He didn't play again in the major leagues until Opening Day, 1914.

Ebbets had been desperately trying to find consistency in the outfield around Wheat, who had seen over 20 different players alongside him in the outfield over the past four seasons. Ebbets seemed to have found it in Stengel and Dalton in 1914, also unearthing his centerfielder of the future. Henry Harrison Hy (or "Hi") Myers joined the club in July to spell Dalton, who was slowed by injury. Obtained from the Newark (New Jersey) Indians of the International League, the two were teammates on the pennant-winning club in 1913.

Myers was not a new face to the franchise, having played a handful of games for Brooklyn in 1909 (six) and 1911 (13). Over the next nine seasons, the Ohio native would play the most games in the outfield alongside Wheat of any player. The two became roommates on the road, spending a good amount of time off the field together. The fleet-footed Myers became known for his unique running style, with his arms straight down at his side, as if running with suitcases. He signed a two-year contract and moved to a full-time role when Dalton signed a three-year contract with the Federal League's Buffalo Blues.

As a former catcher, Robinson knew that establishing a reliable target behind the plate was important to pitcher success—something Brooklyn had been lacking over the past several seasons. He found that in Lowell "Otto" Miller, who never gained the trust of Dahlen, and thus, had played sparingly, first as a backup to Bill Bergen (a horrible batter, but one of the game's best receivers), and then splitting time with inferior players. Robinson saw a lot of himself in Miller, who called a great game, was a superb defender, and had a great rapport with pitchers. The relationship was instrumental in Miller's dozen years spent with the Dodgers. "You can help me a lot," Robinson told Miller. "You're my kind of catcher, and we can do things with these pitchers."[24]

Nicknamed "Moony," for his round face and round blue eyes, Miller was lucky to make it out of spring training in 1910. It took the intervention of Rucker, who approached Dahlen when he found out the young catcher from Nebraska hadn't made the team. "He's the best catcher that ever caught me," Rucker told his manager. "Right now, he's the best—and he'll get even better with experience."[25]

Miller's admiration for Rucker was evident. "He was the easiest pitcher to catch and had the best disposition of any pitcher I ever knew," Miller told Frank Graham years later.[26]

Robinson and Miller had their work cut out for them with the pitching staff. Ebbets had acquired right-hander Ed Reulbach from the Cubs the previous August, but he was no longer the dominant force he had been during his pennant-winning heyday in Chicago. Rucker was beginning to show signs of wear after years of heavy workloads. In 1913, he had to adjust his grip to accommodate a thumb injury. His velocity waned, but

3. Uncle Robbie, 1913–1915

he developed a slow curveball (some claim it was an early incarnation of a knuckleball) that allowed him to remain effective, logging 260 innings—the last large total of his career—on his way to a 14–15 record. The change in delivery took its toll, and in 1914 and '15, he pitched sparingly due to arm troubles. By '16 he was done but for a handful of appearances. He did take to the role of mentoring younger players such as Stengel, but also was generous with pitchers, including Jeff Pfeffer, who emerged as staff ace in 1914, leading the team in wins (23), strikeouts (135), and ERA (1.97). The Illinois native started 34 games, completing 27, and finished nine other games, earning four saves. He threw a one-hitter against the Reds in September.

Pfeffer was a large, imposing right-hander (6'2", 210 pounds), who was the younger brother of former big-league hurler, Frank. Although his given name was Ed, his nickname when he started playing ball was "Big Jeff" because he resembled heavyweight boxing champion Jim Jeffries. He later shortened it to "Jeff." He had appeared in two games for the St. Louis Browns in April 1911, before returning to the minor leagues, where Sutton kept tabs on him over the next few years. When Pfeffer won 25 games for Grand Rapids of the Central League in 1913, Sutton recommended that Ebbets draft him. The Dodgers' owner did, and Pfeffer appeared in five games for Brooklyn over the last month of the season. When a rotation spot came up for grabs in 1914, Pfeffer brought an edge to the club that had not existed previously, becoming an integral part of the rotation over the next few seasons. One of the game's hardest throwers, he wasn't afraid to use intimidation, regularly throwing inside, or flat out throwing at the opposition. He would lead both leagues in hit batters in 1916 and '17. "Pfeffer was a wonderful pitcher," Wheat said years later. "A good, big strong right-hander and he had a cross fire that was really a honey."[27]

A 17-game hitting streak from late August 1914, into September, kept Wheat flirting with the batting title. "The test of a good batter is this, does he improve as the season advances? If he does, he's a good batter," Wheat said when asked what makes a good hitter.[28] He hit nine home runs in 1914—five over the fence—along with 89 RBIs, not only leading the team, but also among the league leaders. They were both the highest totals of his career during the Deadball Era and wouldn't be eclipsed until a livelier ball was introduced in the '20s. Wheat's 170 hits were tied for second with George Burns of the Giants, just one behind Sherry Magee of the Phillies. In the field, Wheat's aggressive style made his 331 putouts tops amongst National League outfielders—he also committed 14 errors.

The 1915 season got off to a rough start for several players at the team's new spring training spot, Daytona Beach, Florida. The most notable was

Zack Wheat

Wheat, who suffered a few injuries that plagued him for the rest of the season. The first was a pulled muscle in his side, likely an oblique strain, suffered when he became enamored with golf and began playing it every chance he could. The other was a calf injury that he blamed on the uneven outfield playing surface. Neither properly healed, greatly hampering him throughout the season. The combination of the two maladies caused his batting numbers to drop off significantly, equating to some of the lowest totals of his career. His .258 batting average would be a career-low, and his power numbers were down dramatically, most notably the 15 doubles. Despite that, he led the club with 66 RBIs. By all accounts, it was the worst season of Wheat's career. Those numbers weren't pleasing to Ebbets, who was now paying Wheat $5,350.

Besides his brother, Mack, finally earning a spot on the roster—used mainly as a bullpen catcher—one of the only good things that came of Zack's time in Florida was a paycheck to be a spokesmen for a Palm Beach Featherweight Suit. "A ball player particularly appreciates the advantage of hot weather garments. I am sure that no suit could give better service, or be more satisfactory, than your Palm Beach suit which I am now wearing," Wheat was quoted as saying in the newspaper advertisement.[29]

The most memorable moment of spring training came when Robinson set up a stunt of catching a baseball dropped from an airplane. He heard that aviatrix Ruth Law was dropping golf balls from a plane as a publicity for a local golf course. Recalling how Washington Senators catcher Gabby Street caught a ball dropped from the Washington Monument in 1908, Robinson thought he would try to better Street. As Law was getting ready to take flight, she realized that no one had given her a baseball. One of her crew members tossed her a grapefruit to substitute a ball before she took off. Once in position, she dropped the grapefruit to a waiting Robinson, who was hit in the chest and knocked to the ground. Covered in juice and pulp, Robinson thought he was mortally wounded, calling out for help from his players, who sat laughing at the scene.

The Dodgers did make strides during the 1915 season. In January, they added former Philadelphia Athletics right-hander Jack Coombs, who had pitched a total of 13-and-one-third inning over the previous two years. Before that, he helped the Athletics to back-to-back World Series titles in 1910 and '11, winning 31 and 28 games, respectively, relying on his big curveball. He added 21 in 1912 before typhoid ravaged his body, taking away his strength. Ebbets signed Coombs upon letters of recommendations from Athletics owner Connie Mack and former teammate and rotation mate Chief Bender. Coombs slipped nicely into the spot vacated by Reulbach, who jumped to the Newark Peppers of the Federal League, where he won 21 games. Over the

3. Uncle Robbie, 1913–1915

next few years, Coombs replaced Rucker as Brooklyn's go-to pitcher against opposing teams' aces. Like Rucker, Coombs tutored Brooklyn's young pitchers, including Pfeffer, rookies like left-hander Sherry Smith, who had a move to first base that was unparalleled, and right-handers William "Wheezer" Dell and Ed Appleton. In 1915, Coombs tallied the second-most victories for the Dodgers, 15 behind Pfeffer's 19. Coombs soon came to have an appreciation for Wheat, calling him "one of the greatest outfielders I ever saw."[30]

Wheat ran afoul with the club when he decided to head back to Missouri for a few days to convalesce as the team barnstormed their way back to Brooklyn. He only missed a few games, but it was enough to draw the ire of Robinson and Ebbets. By all appearances the rift settled down, but on April 29 it was announced that Wheat had been traded to the Giants for pitcher Pol Perritt, outfielder Jack Murray, and power-hitting, Dave Robertson. An infuriated Ebbets took the overnight from Philadelphia to dictate a lengthy, blistering denial to Thomas Rice of the *Brooklyn Daily Eagle*. "It makes me boil with rage to have to read such contemptible rot," he rebuked. "There is absolutely no truth in the story, and where it came from I cannot even attempt to guess."[31] That wasn't the end for Ebbets, who received endless correspondences from perturbed fans. He responded to as many as he could. He assured the masses that no such deal would ever be made. "Wheat does not belong to me or the Brooklyn Ball Club, but to the Brooklyn public."[32]

Two days after the errant announcement, Wheat was met with a sustained round of applause when he came up to bat in the second inning. "The crowd of about ten thousand gave Zack the ovation as if he were a successful candidate with a lot of offices to distribute," wrote Rice of the Ebbets Field mass.[33] It was soon found that at a writers' lunch, it was teased that the Giants landed Brooklyn's top outfielder. That outfielder was actually Benny Kauff of the Brooklyn Tip-Tops, one of the Federal League's best players. Alas, Ebbets was able to laugh about the mix-up when sportswriter Ring Lardner relayed the news to him.

The situation certainly couldn't have been a comforting one for Wheat. Kauff—referred to as the "Ty Cobb of the Federal League"—was transferred to the Tip-Tops after a dominating 1914 season for the pennant-winning Indianapolis Hoosiers. There, he led the league in average (.370), hits (211), stolen bases (75), and total bases (305). The coal miner from Pomeroy Bend, Ohio, found success in Brooklyn, too, but it was the way he carried himself that garnered attention. He was everything that Wheat was not. The magnetic Kauff played the game with swagger and liked to be noticed off the field, wearing eye-catching clothes and diamonds. He frequented popular spots in Brooklyn's nightlife; known to pull out a roll of hundred dollar bills and pay the tab for everyone at the bar—even though he rarely drank. Ebbets was quiet thereafter when discussing Kauff, but Robinson was not. "Jesus, I wish I had him," lamented the Dodgers' manager.[34] Kauff landed in New York the next year but never matched the successes he found in the Federal. By the end of the decade he would fall under suspicion for involvement in fixing games and then an automobile scam. The charges were enough for him to catch the wrath of Commissioner Landis, who banned him from the game before the 1921 season.

On June 1, 1915, Wheat led Brooklyn to a 5–4 extra-inning win over Philadelphia. In the ninth he hit a game-tying inside-the-park home run to left-centerfield on a two-strike, no ball count. Two innings later with runners at the corners, Wheat pulled a one-out chopper down the first baseline. Phillies back-up catcher Bert Adams, who came into the game as a defensive replacement in the ninth inning, couldn't field it in time as Ollie O'Mara raced down the third baseline for the winning run. All this excitement caused 45-year-old Chauncey Martin to suffer a heart attack, dying in the stands. When Wheat learned of Martin's passing he responded, "Had I known a home run was going to cause anything like that, I would not have hit it."[35]

Later that month, on June 26, in Philadelphia—where he always hit well—Wheat broke up Grover Cleveland Alexander's no-hitter in the eighth inning. The better the pitcher, the better Wheat was—even when he was struggling. Some of his greatest success came against those with devastating curveballs. Alexander was one that Wheat seemed to hit with ease and the great right-hander knew it. The future Hall of Famer with 373 wins to his resumé counted Wheat and Jimmy Sheckard as the best left-handed hitters he ever faced. After his career, Alexander listed Wheat as an outfielder on his personal all-time team, mainly for his hitting.

Alexander described Wheat's outwardly low-key approach. "Wheat was funny; at the start of the season he'd say 'Hello,' and in October he'd say 'Goodbye,' and all you'd hear out of him in between would be the ring of his bat."[36]

Like many batters, Wheat revered Mathewson: "He had great stuff and superlative control," but "Alexander was almost as good," as Mathewson, "and to my mind, better than Johnson."[37] Wheat faced Alexander 210 times, the most against any pitcher. He batted .303 with seven doubles and three triples. He also walked 15 times—the most against any pitcher—and struck out 16.

Wheat thrived against some of the game's best pitchers, but he also faltered against a few. The pitcher he struggled against the most was six-foot, six-inch left-hander Eppa Rixey, who pitched for the Phillies and then Cincinnati Reds. The future Hall of Famer gave Wheat fits, evident by his paltry numbers: .228 (34-for-149), with eight doubles, a triple, and 10 strikeouts—one of a handful of pitchers that had double-digit strikeouts against him. Wheat struck out the most times, 18, against George "Lefty" Tyler, who pitched for the Braves and Cubs.

The Reds pitching staff in general gave Wheat a tough time; they were the only team he batted under .300 against throughout his career (.287). Another Cincinnati pitcher, right-hander Adolfo Luque, at times baffled Wheat, particularly the Cuban's ability to throw different types of curveballs. "I'm up there with a couple of men on base. I know he'll curve me sure and I'm set for the pitch," recalled Wheat. "And instead of that cute little wrinkle he has been feeding me all afternoon, he'll throw me the best hook I ever saw in my life. And nine times out of 10 I either break my back missing it or ground out to the second baseman on six hops."[38]

Wheat once said, "I don't like left-handers any way and I'm willing to admit it."[39] Despite that statement and his noted troubles against Rixey, Wheat had success against some of the game's best lefties, including Wilber Cooper of the Pirates and Jim "Hippo" Vaughn of the Cubs. Wheat's numbers were modest over 92 at-bats (.272, one double, two triples, and a home run), but Vaughn held Wheat in high esteem. "I believe the batter I fear the most in this league is Zach Wheat," Vaughn said a few years later in 1919. "He is a left handed batter and not supposed to be good against portsiders like myself, but I know of no one that I dislike to see at bat more than Wheat."[40]

Unbeknownst to Vaughn, he was tipping his pitches. "When he raised his hands over his head to pitch a curve he would bend his left wrist as the hand went up," Wheat told Thomas Rice in 1922, the year after Vaughn retired. "He was preparing to have the wrist in such a position that it would give the twist that produced the curve. When he was going to pitch the fastball he kept the wrist straight."[41]

Another left-hander that Wheat found to be tipping pitches was his future teammate Rube Marquard. In the same interview with Rice, Wheat explained Marquard's tell: "If he intended to pitch a curve you could see him juggling the ball in his bare hand, feeling for the seams on which to get the grip that would add to the twist that produced the curve. If he planned a fast shot he did not engage in the juggling and fooling with the ball. He held it carelessly and cut loose without preliminaries."[42]

Wheat certainly observed pitchers, but rarely tried to outthink them:

> There are batters who watch the pitcher's hand and try to foretell what he is going to throw. Some of these batters claim to be able to predict from the way a man delivers the ball whether it will be a curve or a fast ball. Perhaps they can. I don't even try to do this myself. This is observation and is a little different than guessing, but I don't think it's good dope and I never try to guess what the pitcher is going to throw even when I have

a hunch that it's a fast ball, for instance. I don't like to dwell on the thought. I want my mind on the ball and nothing else. And I want to feel that I can hit it no matter what happens. If batters would concentrate on that one thing and forget all the other frills, I believe they would be better off."[43]

Wheat's biggest insecurity on the ball field was his fielding. He led the league in errors committed by a left fielder in 1914 (14) and '15 (18—the most of his career). He worked tirelessly to improve, both from observation and repetition. "Whatever I know about fielding I have picked up myself by watching other players and practicing," said Wheat. "I have spent hours at a time having fellows bat flies and grounders to me from all possible angles and at all kinds of distances, until I felt sure of handling a ball wherever it might come from."[44] He came to be known for the slight jump he'd make after running down a long fly ball. Despite his high errors committed total in 1915, Wheat finished fourth in the National League with 345 putouts (Myers led the league with 352).

The one aspect of fielding that plagued Wheat throughout his career was his inability to field ground balls—the source of most of his errors. According to Tommy Holmes of the *Brooklyn Daily Eagle*, the often uneven outfield playing surface caused Wheat to frequently drop to both knees to stop a hard hit ball from skipping past him. By 1917, perceptions had changed. *Baseball Magazine* was calling Wheat's fielding his "most showy characteristic," and even went as far as to say that he was "the finest mechanical craftsman of them all," and "the easiest, most graceful of outfielders with no close rivals."[45]

A few years later, Wheat was looked upon as an expert at catching fly balls. He sat down with Thomas Rice in May 1920, and explained different trajectories and the approaches that need to be taken. He called line drives at eye-level "the hardest kind of ball for an outfielder, and the kind that is most likely to show him up as a boob when he is using his best intelligence."

Wheat spoke of the ease of catching balls hit to one side of the fielder or the other: "They do not have the flat trajectory of the straight liners, and they do not break as sharply. The fielder can follow them with his eye, and, as he is already in motion, he can follow them with his feet better than those which start directly for him and then dip or swerve like a pitched ball."

Of balls hit over a fielder's head, Wheat said, they "are of the looping variety, and while they do not go straight, or come down straight, their variations from their original pat are usually slow and can be traced."

In a rare, candid moment, Wheat took umbrage with the cheers and jeers of the uneducated fan, saying they "will excuse us for dropping a fly after a hard run, when it was really a simply chance and the catching would

3. Uncle Robbie, 1913–1915

have been purely mechanical, will roast us in nine different languages for not catching a straight liner that has broken away several feet just when we thought we had it as safe as old wheat in the barn."[46]

Wheat's throwing arm would also come to be feared. "He could throw with any outfielder in the league, and no base runner who had been around even a little while ever took a chance on his arm," wrote Frank Graham. "Maybe a busher did once in a while. A busher who hadn't seen him throw. Once they had seen him throw, they respected him too much."[47]

The Dodgers moved within percentage points of the Phillies with a pair of wins over the third-place Cubs on August 19 and 20, 1915, the latter a 6–5 victory on a 10th inning walk-off two-run double by Wheat. Brooklyn fell back into second place, but stayed a few games behind the rest of the month. On August 31, Brooklyn prepared for a September pennant run, purchasing a pair of pitchers: former Robinson protégé, Marquard of the Giants, and spitballer, Larry Cheney from the Cubs. This was in addition to the June acquisition of the talented, yet unpredictable spitballer, Phil Douglas. The tall right-hander, late of the Reds, had a drinking problem, occasionally going missing for days at a time. He performed with mixed results for the Dodgers over a few months (5–5, 2.62 ERA), but was made expendable when the two veterans were acquired.

Both new pitchers were well established. The effectively wild Cheney (he led the league in wild pitches in six of his eight seasons) had notched over 900 innings, and a 67–42 record, with 16 saves from 1912 to 1914. A Kansas native, Cheney didn't pitch until his first year in the minor leagues, learning the spitball from the great Ed Walsh during a spring training stint with the White Sox in 1907. Cheney led the National League in wins (26) and complete games (28) in '12, and the yet to be named statistic of saves (11) in '13.

Marquard thrived for the Giants under Robinson's tutelage, when a change-up was added to compliment his fastball and breaking ball. By all intents and purposes, the Cleveland native's 201 career-wins and Hall of Fame membership can be attributed to Robinson's influence. Marquard had three straight 20-win seasons (1911–'13), led the league in strikeouts (237) in '11, and wins (26) in '12, including 19 straight—tying a league record set by Tim Keefe of the New York Giants in 1888. (Conversely, the American League record was set in 1912, when Walter John of the Senators and Joe Wood of the Red Sox each strung together 14 wins in a row).

Marquard parlayed his baseball successes into a dalliance in show business, starring in a short silent film, *Rube Marquard Wins*, as well as playing a part in a vaudeville act, which many ballplayers did at the time. Out of that came an affair with a married actress, Blossom Seeley, who divorced her husband, fellow actor Joe Kane. The love triangle inspired a book, *Marquard & Seeley: A Scandalous Ragtime Romance*. Marquard and Seeley would eventually marry in 1913. Since Robinson's departure, Marquard struggled to a 12–22 record in 1914, threatened to join the Brooklyn Tip-Tops of the Federal League, and was in the midst of another disappointing campaign thus far in 1915, but for a no-hitter against the Dodgers on April 15. One of the first things Robinson did was tell Marquard that he was tipping his pitches.

With the addition of infielder Ivy Olson off waivers from the Reds in July, Brooklyn had some key components to their pennant runs in the coming seasons. Olson would take over full-time shortstop duties from Ollie O'Mara in 1916, filling a void at shortstop that had been a weakness of the franchise for years. Olson's fielding would draw the biggest ire from fans. He had great range, leading to many chances—and his fair share of errors. The criticism at Ebbets Field got so bad that he stuffed cotton in his ears to drown out the negativity. Olson, who attended the same grade school as Stengel in Kansas City, was described by his former classmate as a "bully at the grammar school," which he lived up to on the ball field. He was known to carry a rule book in his back pocket throughout his career, sometimes referencing it in an argument with umpires. He was described by sportswriter Murray Robinson as "a spike-scarred, swarthy veteran with a barrel chest, high shoulders, a sharp nose and chin, and piercing black eyes. All he needed to make him look like a pirate of old was a bandana on his head, a patch over one eye, and a cutlass instead of a bat."[48]

Wheat's aching legs finally gave way on September 3, 1915, in Boston, when he was trying to keep the Braves' Rabbit Maranville to a single on a ball down the left field line. Team trainer Joe Quirk estimated Wheat would miss at least a week, but he was needed as the Dodgers played a series against the first-place Phillies. He was called on to pinch hit in the opening game, delivering a two-run single off Alexander to help secure a 6–3 Brooklyn victory. The win was the first in a three-game sweep that brought the Dodgers within a game of Philadelphia. Wheat started a game a few days later against the Braves but was unable to finish.

Brooklyn remained in second place, but fell a few more games behind as they set out on a lengthy road trip that would determine their season. Robinson kept Wheat out of a series in St. Louis due to the ankle injury—still causing a noticeable limp—and the sweltering heat that had overcome him in recent years. He got a courtesy pinch hit appearance, but other than that remained on the bench. He, Daisy, Mary Helen, and Mack stayed at the Wheat farm in Polo before rejoining the club in Chicago. Wheat returned to full-time action in a final push for the pennant, but it proved fruitless.

3. Uncle Robbie, 1913–1915

No member of the Dodgers had a particularly outstanding season with the bat. Myers had a 23-game hitting streak, but didn't play up to expectations. Daubert was the only regular to hit higher than Wheat's .258, with a mark of .301. Pfeffer anchored the staff, leading in wins (19), innings pitched (291-and-two-thirds), complete games (26), and shutouts (6). He threw 18-and-two-thirds innings in a 4–3 loss against the Cubs in June and had a 27-inning scoreless streak in August. Rookie left-hander Sherry Smith won 14. Coombs contributed his 15, and Dell, 11.

The Dodgers 1915 season was a success—a precursor of the things to come. They finished with a winning record (and in the first division) for the first time since 1903—an 80–73, third place finish, ten games from pennant-winning Philadelphia Phillies. It was a tight race all around, as just 21 games separated all eight clubs. The Dodgers finished in front of the Giants—who placed last—for the first time since 1902, and the only time of McGraw's decades-long tenure (between 1903 and 1914, New York finished ahead of Brooklyn by an average of 33 games, doubling up in head-to-head victories, 175–85). There was a new rivalry between the two clubs, with the press playing on the Robinson-McGraw rift. Wheat was also being pitted against the Giants outfielder George Burns, who had come into his own over the past few seasons.

In the offseason, Robinson travelled to Dover Hall, a hunting resort on nearly 2,500 acres of lush hunting and fishing outside of Brunswick, Georgia. The new destination became a respite for numerous ball players over the years. Robinson was one of them, using it as a winter home for the next 18 off seasons. There, he quickly became friends with one of the major investors, Yankees co-owner Tillinghast L'Hommedieu Huston, better known as "Cap," and New York sportswriter, Bill McGeehan. Later, the Robinsons would invest in roughly 500 acres of the property and eventually retire there. Robinson's relationship would lead to the eventual dissolution of the Huston-Jacob Ruppert New York co-ownership. Following the 1917 season, Bill Donovan was dismissed from his Yankees managerial duties. Huston, who was in Europe as part of the war effort, wanted Robinson. Ruppert didn't, so he bypassed his partner and signed Cardinals manager Miller Huggins to a two-year contract.

4

A Pennant for Brooklyn, 1916

For the first time since he took over as Brooklyn's manager, Robinson didn't have the threat of the Federal League looming over him as he headed into the 1916 season. The dissolution added almost 200 players to the market, but the only one Ebbets signed from the lot was veteran Mike Mowrey (Pittsburgh Rebels, 1915), who would play 144 games at third base for the Dodgers in 1916. Ebbets also released Hummel, the club's longest tenured player following the '15 season. For the most part, Brooklyn was able to maintain a consistent roster, while others were ravaged by the Federal League. "I have been assuming the burden of the biggest payroll I have ever been called upon to meet," Ebbets told sportswriter Frank Menke. "The Federal League wanted my stars—well, so did I. That meant I had to outbid them, and I assure you, those fellows certainly did boost those figures. But I met them. I didn't let one of my good players get away."[1]

Ebbets' other major acquisition for 1916 was picking up Christy Mathewson's personal catcher, John "Chief" Tortes Meyers, off waivers. A Cahuilla Indian from California, he attended Dartmouth for a year and didn't catch his first major league game until he was 28. He quickly became one of baseball's best all-around catchers. Adding in the 1915 late-season acquisitions, Brooklyn was looked at as a group of castoffs, rejects, and has-beens. Even with the heavy veteran presence, emerging as a clubhouse leader and foreshadowing his future success as a manager was Casey Stengel. "It was Casey who kept us on our toes," Meyers told Lawrence Ritter for the seminal *The Glory of Their Times*. "He was the life of the party and kept us old-timers pepped up all season."[2]

Aesthetically, Brooklyn uniforms took on a different look in 1916. Vertical pinstriped uniforms of the year before were replaced by a checkerboard design that was accented by crimson horizontal stripes. The Giants took the look a step farther in 1916, donning bold crimson plaid. Ebbets Field also looked different. On the right centerfield wall was a new

4. A Pennant for Brooklyn, 1916

advertisement for Tanglefoot flypaper: "In 1915, Wheat, Brooklyn, caught 345 flies. Tanglefoot caught 50,000,000,000 flies."

From the moment the team convened in Daytona Beach, it was evident that there was a cohesion that wasn't there in prior seasons. Robinson could see it, declaring, "Give me three fellows who can pitch that ball and four who can hit and I'll win the pennant."[3]

The Dodgers adhered to Robinson, and they proved successful, taking over first place on May 1 and remaining atop the standings for all but three days for the duration of the season. That didn't mean it was easy, as the '16 season proved to be one of the closest pennant race of the Deadball Era.

Thanks to Wheat and Myers, the Dodgers took on a mascot early in the 1916 season. His name was Joe Monahan, a redheaded schoolboy who had been barred from school because he was suffering from whooping cough. One day he snuck into Ebbets Field to watch the team practice. His presence was given away by a coughing fit, and Robinson was going to send Monahan out of the park until the youngster explained his situation. The team took to him, especially Myers who claimed that red-headed, freckle-faced kids were good luck. When players were slumping, they would run their fingers through Monahan's curly hair. Though he was with the team for just one season, it was a life-altering experience for him. He was given a World Series share and remained good friends with Myers and Burleigh Grimes, traveling to Ohio for hunting expeditions.

Another speedy outfielder, Jimmy Johnston, was added to the mix in 1916. He had previous major league experience—one game with the Chicago White Sox in 1911, and 50 with the Cubs in 1914. In between those two stints, the Cleveland, Tennessee native set a professional baseball record by stealing 124 bases for the San Francisco Seals of the Pacific Coast League in 1913 (in 201 games). A slap hitter, he returned to the Pacific Coast League in 1915, banging out 52 doubles for the Oakland Oaks, his sixth minor league stop. He was looking to latch on with the Federal League in 1916 before it eventually folded. As Ebbets biographer John G. Zinn noted, the Brooklyn owner was "in the right place at the right time," to negotiate with Johnston, having travelled to the San Francisco for the minor leagues' annual meeting.[4] After sorting out some legal matters with the Newark Peppers of the Federal League—who owned the rights to Johnston's contract—the two parties came to an agreement.

With Brooklyn, Johnston eventually transitioned to the infield, becoming Wheat's longest tenured teammate over ten seasons. A solid contributor, Johnston's best seasons with the Dodgers came between 1920 and '25. Though he wouldn't come close to the stolen base numbers of his record-setting season, Johnston stole 164 over his decade with Brooklyn, including swiping home 10 times. He played for the Boston Braves and New York Giants after the Dodgers. He holds the distinction of all five of his major league managers being Hall of Famers: Hugh Duffy, White Sox; Hank O'Day, Cubs; Robinson, Dodgers; Dave Bancroft, Braves; and McGraw, Giants.

Wheat and his teammates soon found that Johnston had a knack of observing nuances of the game that benefited Brooklyn. "Nothing that goes on in a ball park escapes him," said Wheat several years into their time together as teammates. "He is forever noticing little details that most players overlook but which are extremely valuable on the offense and defense. He passes the dope around our team and he applies what he learns."[5]

There was domestic strife for Wheat during the 1916 season. Daisy yearned to be in their own house as a growing epidemic swept through Brooklyn, one that threatened the health of the Wheats' daughter, Mary Helen. Since May, poliomyelitis, better known as polio, had been ravaging the country, particularly in urban areas. The Wheats were so concerned for their daughter that she and Daisy accompanied the team as they headed

Brooklyn's talented outfield during the 1916 pennant-winning season. From left to right: Casey Stengel, Jimmy Johnston, Hy Myers, and Zack Wheat (Library of Congress, Prints & Photographs Division [LC-DIG-ggbain-22985]).

4. A Pennant for Brooklyn, 1916

west, bound for the family home in Polo, Missouri, where they spent a good portion of the summer.

When back home in Brooklyn, Wheat still found ways to enjoy his time off the field, with smoking cigars being a source of enjoyment. He and Myers spent a lot of time at the cigar store on the corner of Rogers and Maple. Wheat would even occasionally smoke during games. According to Roy Skelly, "If Zach was not due at bat in the last half of an inning, he would sit between the end of the grandstand and the old bleachers at Ebbets Field, smoking his Perfecto and talking to the groundskeepers and the bleacher kids."[6]

W.R. Hoefer celebrated Wheat's batting prowess with a poem in the *Brooklyn Daily Eagle* titled "Our Coming Champions: Zach Wheat":

> The pitcher wept and tore his hair;
> His howls were loud, his grief profound;
> His sad map registered despair;
> His tears were splashing all around.
> I ambled up to him to see
> What awful thing had killed his joys,
> To offer him my sympathy
> And try to stop his doggone noise.
> "Please tell me, sir" I begged of him,
> "What makes you pull this sob stuff drear?"
> "What makes the old world seem so dim"
> "Oh, spill your trouble in my ear."
> The pitcher dried his dripping lamps
> And piped, "Kid, life to me was sweet.
> Until I met those Brooklyn scamps.
> And had to pitch to that guy Wheat.
> He busted up my gems today;
> He slugged the onion on the beak.
> He put a crusher on the fray
> And submarined my winning streak;
> He cracked our infield right in two
> And shot the grandstand full of dents;
> He maimed a fielder ere he blew
> And busted Charley Ebbets' fence.
> This Wheat is growing awful wild;
> Just hand the bloke a bat, by jing,
> And if a pitcher gets him wild
> He's apt to bust most anything"
> Now, Robins fans, preserve the fame
> Of Buck Wheat, who's swatting art
> Has busted many an old ball game
> And broken many a pitcher's heart;
> Give thanks to Wheat, the Son of Smite;

Zack Wheat

> The Grand Massager of the Pill,
> The chap whose batting dynamite
> Has blown the club toward Pennantsville.[7]

The Dodgers' first-place lead grew to five games during a season-high eight-game winning streak at Ebbets Field in late July and early August. In mid-August the club went on a grueling road trip that saw several players suffer injuries, including Johnston (broken nose) and Myers (shoulder). Wheat continued to experience leg problems, limping through games with his legs in heavy, rubber bandages. The taxing stretch of games could have dismantled Brooklyn's pennant hopes had it not been for timely pitching of the two late-season pickups from the year before—Cheney and Marquard.

There was no denying that Pfeffer was the anchor on one of the majors' best pitching staffs. Coming into August his record stood at 17–4, but he stumbled during the month with a 2–4 mark, finishing the season 25–11, with 20 complete games and a 1.92 ERA. He was backed by Cheney, who won all five August decisions, losing just one game dating back to July 4, and a stretch that included seven consecutive wins. A three-time 20-game winner with the Cubs, Cheney went 18–12, matching Pfeffer's ERA, 1.92 ERA. His career-high of 166 strikeouts was just one behind league leader, Alexander. Robinson inserted Marquard into the rotation in July when Coombs (13–8, 2.66) began to tire. It was a brilliant move, as Marquard went 4–1 with a .85 ERA in August, going 13–6, with 1.58 ERA. Robinson's other lefty starter, Smith, notched a 14–10 record and 2.34 ERA.

No injuries could keep Wheat from hitting. On August 20, he tripled off the Cubs' Claude Hendrix and then scored the only run of a 1–0, one-hit gem by Coombs. The next day, Wheat gave his legs a one-day reprieve, but returned to play on August 22, remaining in the starting lineup for the next 35 games. From August 20 to September 16, Wheat hit safely in a club-record 29-games in a row—the most since Ty Cobb's 40 in 1911. It was the longest National League streak since 1897, when Baltimore's Willie Keeler hit safely in 44 straight. The hit on September 16 was an inside-the-park grand slam in the first game of a doubleheader against the Reds at Ebbets Field. Wheat's streak was snapped in the nightcap that ended a 1–1 tie due to darkness. He claimed to have beaten out an infield single against big right-hander Fred Toney, who, Wheat said, "had five or six styles, all sorts of deceptive motions, and as good a change of pace as there is in the National League."[8]

Wheat's success was his ability to adjust. "I shift my position at the plate more often than people think," he said. "I'll shift my shoulders more than my feet so as to meet the ball at a different angle. You must vary your position with the different pitchers or they'll soon get your number."[9] He hit safely

4. A Pennant for Brooklyn, 1916

The intimidating Jeff Pfeffer was the Dodgers' best pitcher in 1916, but was used sparingly during the World Series in both 1916 and '20 (Library of Congress, Prints & Photographs Division [LC-DIG-ggbain-22409]).

in the next five games after his streak was broken, including three two-hit games, his batting average apexing at .321. The consistent pace helped put him among the league leaders. Along the way he developed the habit of tearing off his ball cap and clutching it as he raced around the bases. Alas, he would finish with a .312 average, good enough for fifth in the league. Daubert finished second at .316 behind the Cincinnati's first baseman Hal Chase, .339.

Wheat paced Brooklyn in three major batting category: doubles, 32; home runs, nine; and RBIs, 73. His 262 total bases and 54 extra base hits led the National League—the only time he did so for each category in his career—as did his .461 slugging percentage. His four four-hit games led both leagues, too. He and team captain Daubert were the only two Dodgers regulars to eclipse .300, but the entire lineup was one of the league's best. Brooklyn's .261 team batting average topped the league. Individually, Stengel hit .279, with 27 doubles and eight home runs. Myers, in his first full season as a Dodger, led the club with 13 triples. Robinson's aggressive approach continued, finishing seventh in walks (355), and second in stolen bases (187). In the field, second baseman George Cutshaw paced the National League in putouts (361), and assists (467).

Zack Wheat

In the mid–September series against the Reds, Wheat bruised his hip on a hard slide on the base paths. When he awoke the next day, he could barely move. In any other season, Wheat would have likely taken an extended rest, but between the pennant race and his streak, he gritted it out in the lineup. The situation caused him great consternation down the stretch. "I found I couldn't sleep nights," said Wheat, who would awake in the middle of the night, needing to calm his nerves with a cigar. "I was thinking and dreaming and eating pennants."[10]

Wheat's fortitude was recognized by both fans—who tried to put together a petition to purchase him an automobile in early fall—and, surprisingly, Brooklyn sportswriters, who, according to Wheat, protected him from possible pariah status. In early September, the Dodgers were swept by the defending National League Champion, Phillies, in a five-game series in Philadelphia. Brooklyn dropped out of sole possession of first place for the first time since May 27, moving into a first-place tie with the Phillies and Boston Braves, World Series champions in 1914. One of the turning points for the Dodgers was a fluke outfield play involving Wheat, who would finish second in the league with 333 assists. Years later, he recalled how one of the league's premiere power-hitters, Philadelphia's Gavvy Cravath, hit a line drive down the left field line. "Just as I was set for a stop, over near the foul line, the ball hit a pebble, or a clod, landed kerplunk on the toe of my foot and I drop-kicked as pretty a goal into the bleachers for a home run as you ever saw." Three runs scored and the Phillies went on to win. In a surprising move, the *Brooklyn Daily Eagle* made little of the play. "I could have been given the goat's horns the same as [Mickey] Owen or Fred Merkle," Wheat recalled decades later, "but Abe Yager and Tommy Rice laid off."[11]

The Braves, whom Brooklyn had its only losing record against during the '16 season, fell out of contention, but the Phillies continued to challenge the Dodgers. For much of the month, Brooklyn's lead never grew to more than two games over Philadelphia. The Giants were also threatening. From September 7 (a victory over the Dodgers) to September 30, New York won 26 games, bettering the mark set by the 1884 Providence Grays. Six of those victories came from the arm of the team's new ace, left-hander, Ferdie Schupp. It had been a set of highs and lows for McGraw, as he tinkered with his roster throughout the season, including the gut-wrenching decision to trade Mathewson to the Reds, which allowed for the emergence of Schupp. New York began the season winning just two of their first 15 games. They then went on the road, winning 17 in a row. At the end of July and early August, they won 13 of 16, then promptly lost 11 of their next 12.

The pennant came down to the last series of the season—a four-game

4. A Pennant for Brooklyn, 1916

set at Ebbets Field between the Dodgers and Giants, with Brooklyn needing two games to clinch. The first game, on October 2, celebrated "Nap Rucker Day," acknowledging the pitcher's career in Brooklyn. The Dodgers won 2–0, behind Coombs. The following day, October 3, Brooklyn clinched the franchise's first National League pennant since 1900 with a 9–6 win over the Giants. They split the final two games, finishing with a 94–60 record—the most since the 101-win pennant-winning campaign of 1899. According to author Glenn Stout, Wheat "caught the final out, he tossed the ball into the stands and the players snake-danced around the clubhouse."[12]

McGraw wouldn't allow Robinson to fully enjoy the moment. During the clinching game, the Giants' manager accused players of not following directives, before storming off the bench, and retreating to the clubhouse. He gave an explanation to reporters after the game: "Such baseball disgusted me, and I left the bench. I do not like indifferent playing of this kind after the hard work we have had this season. I refused to be connected with it."[13]

Robinson had a different perspective on the situation. His team had beaten New York 15 times during the 1916 season—the most ever by Brooklyn. "McGraw's assertions are very unsportsmanlike," said Robinson. "He knows very well that the Dodgers are superior to the Giants. The Giants were simply outclassed."[14]

Of the pennant-winning, veteran club, Meyers told Ritter, "We knew so much ball that we just outsmarted the rest of the league and walked off— or, you might say, limped off—with the pennant." He added, "It was an old, crippled-up club, and you might say, figuratively, they had to wrap us up in bandages and carry us out to play the World Series. We were done."[15]

The Dodgers' opponent was the heavily favored and ultra-confident defending World Series Champion Boston Red Sox, whose path to the pennant was just as arduous. A 91-win team—10 less than the year before— the Red Sox finished two games in front of the White Sox. Player-manager Bill Carrigan, who announced he would be retiring after the series, had done it with a pitching staff made up of dynamic left-hander, Babe Ruth (23–12, league-leader in ERA, 1.75; shutouts, nine, and starts, 40) and right-hander, Dutch Leonard (18–12, 2.36). Rounding out the rotation were talented right-handers Carl Mays (18–3, 2.39), Ernie Shore (16–10, 2.63), and Rube Foster (14–7, 3.06). F.C. Lane called them the "best in the country bar none."[16] That was without Joe Wood, who was sitting out the season after refusing to take a pay cut. In 1912, he led the majors in wins (34), complete games (35), and shutouts (10). His play had been in decline following an appendectomy in the spring of 1914. In 1915, he led the league in ERA (1.49) in abbreviated innings. By the end of that season, it was apparent there was something wrong with his shoulder, and he didn't pitch during the Red Sox World Series victory over the Phillies.

The one glaring difference between the 1916 team and the '15 champions was the absence of one of the game's great all-around players, outfielder Tris Speaker, who butted heads with Carrigan since he took over as manager mid-way through the 1913 season. Speaker was traded to the Cleveland Indians just three days before the '16 campaign began as part of the largest transactions to date. Boston received pitcher Sam Jones, infielder Fred Thomas, and $55,000. The '16 Red Sox batters were nowhere near as dominant as the club's pitching. Third baseman Larry Gardner was their only .300 hitter (he also had 19 doubles, leading the team with 62 RBIs). The regular outfielders were the other lineup threats: Harry Hooper (20 doubles, 11 triples, and 27 stolen bases), Duffy Lewis (29 doubles), and Tillie Walker (29 doubles and 11 triples), whose three home runs tied him for the club lead with part-time first baseman Del Gainer and Ruth, who hit one of his home runs as a pinch hitter. As a team, Boston hit just 16 home runs (compared to Brooklyn's 28), with just one coming at Fenway Park—a June 20 round tripper by Walker.

The Dodgers received a huge sendoff from Brooklyn as they traveled to Boston for Game One on October 7. Absent from the group was Ebbets, who was hospitalized with vertigo, an ear infection, and general head pain, but no malady could keep the owner from attending the start of the series in Boston. For the second year in a row, the game was moved to Braves Field from the Red Sox's home field, Fenway Park, to better accommodate a larger crowd. Carrigan had Shore tabbed as his starter, but Brooklyn thought that at the last minute the Boston manager would send out Ruth, which he did not. Robinson countered with Marquard.

One of the most curious managerial moves of the series was that Robinson didn't start his best pitcher, Pfeffer, until Game Five (he did see relief duty in Games One and Three). According to Wheat, the Brooklyn manager took suggestions from the players throughout the season, but called the shots throughout the series without any input. In Robinson's defense, it was Marquard's fourth World Series, having pitched in the 1911, '12, and '13 Fall Classics with the Giants. He was 2–2 in five appearances, including four starts. His best output was the 1912 series, when he threw two complete-game victories over the Red Sox, which included many players on the current Boston roster.

Batting from his customary cleanup spot, Wheat secured Brooklyn's first hit of the Series with a second-inning single past Red Sox second baseman, Hal Janvrin. Wheat then drove in the Dodgers' first run in the fourth inning with a booming triple off the right field wall, plating Stengel who led off with a single. Cutshaw followed with a low liner to right field. Boston's

4. A Pennant for Brooklyn, 1916

Hooper came racing in, ending up on his back when his feet came out from under him while making a shoestring catch. Wheat could have scored easily had he tagged up, but despite there being no outs, he had wandered several feet down the baseline towards home plate. He rushed back to third to tag up as Hooper leapt to his feet, throwing a perfect toss to catcher Hick Cady, who applied the tag on Wheat for a double play.

Brooklyn squandered a one-out triple by Meyers in the fifth inning. The Red Sox retook the lead in the bottom half, 2–1, when Hooper led off the inning with a double (lost in the sun by Hy Myers), moved over to third on a bunt by Janvrin, and scored on Walker's single to left field. The Dodgers went down in order in the sixth and seventh, and Boston opened up the lead to 5–1 in their half of the seventh thanks to errors by Olson and Cutshaw. The Red Sox added another unearned run (Stengel throwing error) in the bottom of the eighth off Pfeffer, who relieved Marquard to start the inning to push the advantage to 6–1.

The run proved crucial. Brooklyn stormed back against Shore in the top of the ninth. Daubert walked on four pitches, and Stengel singled to right field. Wheat followed with a ground ball back to Shore, who forced Daubert at third. Cutshaw was then hit by a pitch, loading the bases. Janvrin misplayed the next batter, Mowrey's bouncer to him at second base, plating Stengel and Wheat to cut the lead to 6–3. Olson then reached on an infield single to load the bases once again. Meyers popped out to first base for the second out. Robinson pinch hit Fred Merkle for Pfeffer, drawing a walk to force in Cutshaw

Wheat's base-running error in the fourth inning cost the Dodgers a run in Game One of the 1916 World Series. He is pictured getting thrown out at home plate (Cleveland Public Library).

with another run. Carrigan finally pulled Shore, bringing in submarine pitcher Mays and catcher Pinch Thomas. The change didn't help, as Myers scratched another infield single, scoring Mowrey to bring the score to 6–5 with Daubert, who started the inning to the bat. He ripped a ball to the left side that got by a diving Red Sox third baseman Gardner. Ranging far to his right, shortstop Everett Scott fielded the ball and threw it in one motion, barely getting the dead-legged Daubert's headfirst slide into first to secure the 6–5 Boston win.

The Dodgers were encouraged by their comeback. "Do you think that failure to quite come through in the ninth worried us or broke our hearts?" asked Daubert. "If you do, you are a mistaken young man, for that gave us the idea that this Red Sox team isn't made up of unbeatable men. It was just what we needed. I guess, for we feel a whole lot more confident than we did when we started the game."[17]

Two days later, October 9, the teams reconvened at Braves Field for Game Two. A pair of left-handers, Smith for Brooklyn and Boston's ace, Ruth, matched each other pitch for pitch in an epic game that lasted 14 innings—a record that stood for over 100 years.[18] In the first inning of Game Two, Ruth retired the first two batters before Myers ripped the second pitch he saw to the right-centerfield gap. Both Walker, in centerfield, and Hooper, in right, ended up on the ground in their efforts to retrieve it. Myers made his way around the bases and slid headfirst into home for an inside-the-park home run to give the Dodgers a 1–0 lead.

Brooklyn had an opportunity to add to the lead in the third inning, but ran themselves out of the inning. Smith hit a ball to the right field wall, but was thrown out by at least ten feet when inexplicably trying to stretch it into a triple. Johnston followed with a single to center that would have likely scored Smith. A hit-and-run was put on the next batter, Daubert, but he missed the pitch, and Johnston was thrown out at second base, ending what had the makings of a promising inning. Boston countered with a run in their half of the frame when Scott, who led off with a triple, scored on a ground out by Ruth to tie that game, 1–1.

It would be another 11 innings before another run was scored. Both teams threatened to do so once, each getting a runner to third. Ruth came to the plate in the bottom of the fifth with Thomas on third, after Olson was accused of tripping him when he rounded second on a two-out double to left field. Ruth was unable to capitalize, striking out on three pitches. In the eighth inning, the Dodgers got a runner, Mowrey, to third base. However, he was thrown out in a rundown after he broke for home when Smith grounded to Scott, who engaged Mowery in the rundown, with Ruth eventually applying the tag.

4. A Pennant for Brooklyn, 1916

In the bottom of the ninth, Janvrin led off with a hard liner to left field that Wheat almost made a brilliant catch on. The ball got away from him, and Janvrin pulled into second base and was awarded a double. Walker popped foul the first offering he saw from Smith while attempting to bunt. Carrigan pulled him mid-at-bat, substituting in Jimmy Walsh, who hit a soft come-backer to Smith. The left-hander tossed the ball to Mowery, who applied a tag on Walker with the ball in his throwing hand, which fell upon contact. Umpire Ernie Quigley initially called him out but reversed the call. Dick Hoblitzell hit the second pitch he saw to centerfield. Myers called off Wheat, throwing a perfect toss to Miller, who applied the tag just as Janvrin slid into home. The stunned Boston crowd gave Myers a round of applause for the game-saving play. Smith then intentionally walked Lewis and got Gardner to foul out to Miller, extending the game to extra innings.

Ruth and Smith continued on unfettered as the game extended to the 14th inning while daylight dwindled. Ruth, who hadn't allowed a hit since the eighth inning, set the Dodgers down in order. Smith walked Hoblitzell to open the Red Sox's half of the inning. Lewis sacrificed him over to second base. Carrigan made a double switch, replacing Hoblitzell with Mike McNally. He then brought in the right-handed batting Gainer to bat for the left-handed Gardner, who was 0-for-5 on the day. Gainer singled to left to score McNally, giving Boston the 2–1 win and two game to nothing advantage. "He hit the ball to me," said Wheat, recalling the game-winning hit years later. "It was a low, skipping hit down the left field line. I ran over and grabbed the ball and remember thinking, 'What's the point of throwing it?' I threw it anyway, but the run was in."[19]

"They say I pitched a good game. Let the records tell the story," said a dejected Smith after the game. "In any case, it didn't do any good—we lost."[20]

Game Three took place the next day, October 10, in Brooklyn in front of a sparse, unenthusiastic crowd of 21,087 (compared to the 47,373 that showed up for the game in Boston the afternoon before). The low turnout, what *Baseball Magazine* called "New Yorkers, Boston rooters, and folks from various other towns than Brooklyn," was due more to Ebbets hiking up ticket prices as high as $5 than the cold fall weather.[21] With his team down two games to none, Robinson opted for World Series veteran Coombs over Pfeffer. Carrigan countered with Mays.

In the bottom of the first, Wheat was intentionally walked to load the bases with one out. The Dodgers failed to capitalize when Myers was forced out at home on a groundout by Cutshaw, followed by Mowrey striking out looking. In the third, Cutshaw broke a scoreless game with a two-out single to score Daubert, who had singled (one of the first baseman's three hits on the day—his only ones of the series—after going 0-for-9 in the first two games). The Dodgers scored again in the fourth when Olson came in on a Coombs single. The following frame, Wheat drew a one-out walk and advanced to second on a groundout to the Mays. Mowrey walked, and both he and Wheat were driven in on a booming double to deep left by Olson, extending the Brooklyn's lead to 4–0.

The Red Sox countered with two runs of their own in the top of the sixth when Hooper plated Olaf Henriksen with a triple and then scored on a Chick Shorten single. In their next at-bat, Boston cut the lead to 4–3 on a one-out Gardener home run to right field. Coombs, knowing the magnitude of the game, asked Robinson to replace him with Pfeffer, who retired all eight batters he faced to solidify the Brooklyn victory (including a foul ball that Wheat nearly went into the stands to track down), putting the series at two games to one.

The Dodgers hopped out to an early lead in the first inning of Game Four, scoring two runs off Red Sox starter—the talented, yet combative right-hander Dutch Leonard. Johnston led off with a triple to right centerfield, coming home on a Myers single through a drawn in infield. Merkle—who had been acquired from the Giants in August while Daubert dealt with sciatica—walked, but was forced out at second on Wheat's groundout to third base. Cutshaw grounded to Janvrin at second base, who bobbled the ball, allowing Myers to score and Wheat (who had advanced to second base on a wild pitch) to move to third base. Brooklyn tried a double steal during Mowrey's at-bat, but Wheat was thrown out in a rundown between home and third. Mowery struck out to end the inning, but the Dodgers led 2–0. They wouldn't score again in the game.

Boston answered immediately off starter Marquard. In the top of the second inning, Hoblitzell walked, Lewis doubled to right field, and Gardner raced around the bases for an inside-the-park home run to take a 3–2 lead. Two innings later, after Brooklyn squandered a leadoff double by Cutshaw, Carrigan singled in Lewis to increase the Red Sox's advantage to 4–2. The following inning, the fifth, they added yet another run, when Hoblitzell doubled to left field to score Hooper, who new pitcher Cheney walked to start the inning. The right-hander surrendered one more run in the seventh inning when he hit Hoblitzell with his throw to first base on an infield single, allowing Janvrin to come around from second to push the score to 6–2, the game's final score. In another curious management of the strong pitching staff, these would be the only three innings Cheney threw during the series.

4. A Pennant for Brooklyn, 1916

In the last two innings, Robinson brought in Rucker to finish the game. He received a warm reception from the fans, striking out three in two innings, part of a World Series record 11 recorded on the day by the Dodgers. Despite the loss, Rucker was thrilled to finally play in a World Series. "I have got my wish: I have pitched in a World Series game," he said after the series ended. "Even if I had only pitched one ball I would have been satisfied."[22]

Game Five was played the following day in Boston on Columbus Day, October 12. Another robust crowd of 43,620 (over double the 21,622 that attended the game at Ebbets the day before), showed up. Pfeffer finally got a start against Game One winner, Shore. For the fourth time in as many games, Brooklyn scored first, when Cutshaw, who walked, came home on a wild pitch in the bottom of the second inning. Boston tied the game at one in the bottom frame when Lewis scored on Gardner's short flyball to left field, beating Wheat's wide throw. The Red Sox scored two more (unearned) runs in the next inning on an error by Olson and a single by Shorten. A two-out double by Janvrin in the bottom of the fifth scored Hooper from first base, making the game 4–1. The Dodgers, who had supposedly had a team meeting before the game to divvy up the loser's share, didn't get their first hit until the fifth inning, mustering just three hits—all singles—off Shore. The Red Sox clinched their second consecutive World Series title and third in five years (1912) with a 4–1 win over the Dodgers.

The hobbled Wheat had a miserable series, doing little after the first few games. He batted a disappointing .211 and time and again, his defensive shortcoming of fielding ground balls was exposed. He pushed some of the blame for Brooklyn's poor World Series performance on the draining pennant race. "There was a natural let-up or relaxation which isn't difficult to explain," he told *Baseball Magazine*'s John J. Ward a few months after the loss. "We felt that we had won out and we eased up a little. And the time was so short we never got going again."[23]

As quickly as the Dodgers were celebrated for winning the pennant, they were ridiculed for their poor showing in the World Series. An enraged Robinson brought his players together for some final words of encouragement upon their return to Brooklyn. "They say this is a joke ball club," he roared. "Joke ball club hey? It's a god damned good ball club! You should have won the series. If you'd had any decent breaks, you would have won it. Start that series all over again tomorrow and you'd win it."

Now at a fever pitch, he bellowed, "I'll tell what I'm going to do! I'm going to give you a dinner! I'll show them! Joke ball club, hey?"

The next night Robinson entertained the team at The Pohlmeyer, known for its beer and German cuisine. "Before the evening was over the Robins, who had been so glum on their retreat from Boston, were singing songs, laughing, making speeches and telling each other what great ballplayers they were," wrote Frank Graham. "The renewed confidence in themselves, which had bubbled out of the beer barrels, still was strong when, the following day, they disbanded for the year."[24]

Immediately after the series, rumors swirled of Ebbets being offered large sums of money for the ball club. He emphatically denied each one. Later in the fall, Red Sox team owner Joseph Lannin sold the team to New Yorker Harry Frazee, a Broadway theater producer, and his partner, Hugh Ward, for $1 million. Two years later, the Red Sox would once again win the World Series, defeating the Chicago Cubs at the end of the war-shortened 1918 season. Frazee, who had once tried to buy the New York Giants, would be vilified when he sold Babe Ruth to the New York Yankees on December 26, 1919, for $100,000, one of several sales of players to the Yankees to raise capital.

Wheat returned home to his Polo, Missouri farm with his World Series share of $2,715.40. He played in several exhibition games with other major leaguers, but none was more noteworthy than the November 29, 1916, tilt held in Kansas City with some of the game's top players. The marquee attraction was the pitching match—Walter Johnson against Grover Cleveland Alexander—the first time the pair would square off. Wheat played on the "Johnson's." The "Alexander's" had Stengel, Max Carey, and Hal Chase.

In the December issue of *Baseball Magazine*, Wheat and Daubert were named to F.C. Lane's "All-Star National League Baseball Club." Lane called 1916 "the best season" of Wheat's career. He added, "Neither Burns nor Whitted hit so well and neither Burns nor Whitted in their palmist days were ever the graceful, easy fielder that Wheat is," and "It is a sight for the fan to watch the Brooklyn outgardener on a long run for a hard catch. What Lajoie is to infielders in grace of motion, Wheat is to outfielders."[25]

Wheat's offseason activity was mainly spent tending to his livestock. "I have two professions, I am a ballplayer in the summer and a farmer in the winter," Wheat said, "and I try to be successful at both."[26] Some of his mules had even been shipped over to the battlefields of Europe. "I have an idea that shrapnel would bounce off their hides like rain drops off a duck's back, and they would thrive where an ordinary animal would die."[27]

Wheat liked to joke that dealing with the stubborn animals helped his on-field disposition. "After you've spent a winter with some tough Missouri mules you can get along better with the umpires."[28]

Training was something that Wheat did very little of intentionally

4. A Pennant for Brooklyn, 1916

during the offseason. He occasionally roller skated on the third floor of his farmhouse, but, other than that, everyday life around the farm kept him in shape. According to author Steve Gelman, "He was proud of the condition of his body, and he liked to show off by putting on his shoes while standing up and then reaching down to tie his laces without bending his knees."[29]

5

Uncertain Times, 1917–1919

In 1917, Brooklyn was set to return to Hot Springs, Arkansas, for spring training for the first time since 1912. Excitement surrounded the fact that both the Dodgers and Red Sox would be in town, playing twice. World War I—which the United States would enter in April—was on the minds of many. In a show of support for the war effort, many teams learned some military basics. Players paraded in front of fans with bats on their shoulders in place of guns. Brooklyn was one of the few teams that decided not to, but it wasn't for a lack of patriotism. Ebbets had started a fund for players called to service, deciding that any member of the Dodgers that was in the military would receive half pay. When the season began, the Dodgers returned to pinstripes at home and checkered on the road. They also became one of five teams to emblazon the United States Flag on their jersey, placing it on the chest of their home jerseys—the only club to do so.

Wheat wasn't a part of the group that voted to not partake in the marching exhibitions in spring training. For the first time in his career, he held out for more money, using the Federal League as a bargaining tool. It had come upon suggestion from Daisy and would be an annual point of negotiation—and contention—between Wheat and Ebbets each winter. "Zack just needed someone to push for him," Daisy recalled. "He was just too good for his own good."[1] Ebbets was further incensed that his two other outfielders were holding out in Ohio—Stengel in Toledo and Myers in Kensington. The latter had even gone as far as to have mock letterhead with "Myers's Stock Farm" printed up for their correspondence to show that he had other options than baseball.

Daily messages between Ebbets and the outfielders proved fruitless. According to Frank Graham, the Dodgers' owner traveled to Ohio and signed Myers, who had panicked when he found out Ebbets was coming to negotiate. Encouraged, the Brooklyn owner took the train to Polo to convince Wheat it was time to come to an agreement. Ebbets offered a small increase, which Wheat refused with a smile. "All right," responded Ebbets, "if you won't play for that salary, you can stay here."

"Suits me," Wheat replied. "I always wanted to stay home in the summer. And I won't starve, Mr. Ebbets. Not with this farm. By the way won't you stay and have dinner with us?"

"No," raged Ebbets, who expected salaries to drop after the demise of the Federal League. "All you can do for me is drive me to the station for the next train, I'm going back to Brooklyn."

When Ebbets made it to Hot Springs, he was asked when Wheat was going to report.

"I'm not interested in Wheat," he replied. "I made a very fair offer to him, and since he had not seen fit to accept it, he can stay where he is … unless of course, I have an opportunity to trade him."

Ebbets thought highly of Wheat, and the prospect of not having his best player pained him. Still, he was angered, pondering aloud what might come of the stalled negotiations. "Maybe he would like to play somewhere else. Ball player are only money grabbers. They never show any loyalty to the club owners or the fans. All they think about is the dollar." Finally, he threw the edict down that the Stengel and Wheat would be blacklisted if they didn't report immediately.

A group of sportswriters, led by Abe Yager of the *Brooklyn Daily Eagle*, caught wind of the decree and banded together to use a bit of deceit in hopes of bringing the parties together. It was a bold move to try to manipulate Ebbets, who treated the members of the Brooklyn press well, paying for what basically turned out to be a winter vacation for the scribes. Most of their print work included putting pressure on those who had yet to sign. Telegrams were sent to Wheat and Stengel to report to Hot Springs immediately.

When they checked into the team hotel, Wheat approached Ebbets with a smile, "Well, here I am, Mr. Ebbets."

"It's about time you came to your senses," said a tepid Ebbets, as the two shook hands.

"What do you mean," replied a surprised Wheat.

"Well," Ebbets responded with a shrug, "it's obvious that you realized I meant what I said when I was at your home and that you couldn't get any more money out of me."

"This is what brought me here," retorted Wheat, producing the telegram from his pocket. "What are you trying to do now—go back on your word?"

"What word?" said Ebbets, matching Wheat's tone. He put on his glasses and read the telegram.

Zack Wheat

A group formed around the two, including the sportswriters who had sent the telegram.

"I never saw this before! This is—why—this is forgery! That's what it is! A forgery!" shouted Ebbets.

"Why don't you and Zack go somewhere and sit down quietly and talk this over," said Yager, intervening before things escalated any further. "This is no place for a club owner to be rowing with a ballplayer."

Ebbets and Wheat glared at each other, before the owner finally spoke. "All right, come up to my room."

An hour later they emerged from their negotiations in a better mood. Ebbets announced to those congregated in the lobby, "Wheat has signed his contract."[2]

Ebbets called a meeting with the sportswriters and barked at them, "Who's running this ball club, you fellows or I?"

"You are Mr. Ebbets," responded the group's spokesman. "But we represent the fans of Brooklyn who want Wheat and Stengel on the team and want them now so they'll be in shape when the season starts. Let's cut out the foolishness and sign 'em up."[3]

"If I ever find out who sent that wire, I'll—I'll—well, never mind," sputtered a flustered Ebbets before exiting the room and heading to dinner with Wheat.

Graham wrote, "As they started for the dining room, Wheat looked over his shoulder at the reporters and grinned. He was sure that one of them had sent the wire, and he knew he was right when Yager winked at him."[4]

Though an agreement was hashed out, Ebbets biographer John G. Zinn called the battle waged by the Brooklyn owner on his star outfielder "poor judgment," noting that Wheat had been one of the most valuable players the year prior. Zinn also points out through sabermetrics that Wheat was "worth six more wins than his replacement player, the second-highest figure for all everyday players, with only Art Fletcher of the Giants higher."[5]

There seemed to be no hard feelings by Brooklyn fans over the holdout. When Wheat took the field on Opening Day, he received a large ovation from his loyal "bleacherites." His season did get off to a slow start at the plate, but it began to take shape on April 20 in Philadelphia when he rapped a double off the "Bull" sign on the Baker Bowl outfield wall, pocketing $50. Within three weeks he had nearly doubled his batting average, but on May 15, he suffered an oblique strain that kept him out of action for three weeks. A pinch-hitting appearance on May 21 worsened the injury.

The Wheat-Stengel holdout was only the beginning of problems for Brooklyn. Bad weather began in early spring training, lasting throughout

5. Uncertain Times, 1917–1919

Henry "Hy" Myers played the most games alongside Wheat in the outfield. The two were roommates on the road and good friends off the field (Library of Congress, Prints & Photographs Division [LC-DIG-ggbain-31069]).

the first month of the regular season. Age and injuries became the club's bugaboo in 1917. Many of the players who helped the club to the World Series in 1916 either underperformed or spent time on the bench healing a variety of maladies, including: Wheat, oblique, and, later in the season ankle; Pfeffer, back; Daubert, legs; and Myers, shoulder. Robinson also was without the veteran leadership of Rucker, who retired, moving into a role within the organization. He became one of the team's Southern scouts, helping bring a number of players to Brooklyn. His most fruitful year was 1921 when he helped acquire Hall of Fame pitcher, Dazzy Vance; catcher Hank DeBerry; infielder, Andy High; and outfielder, Bert Griffith.

Stengel was about the only position player who stayed healthy in 1917, appearing in a team-best 150 games and taking over Wheat's cleanup spot in the lineup. Stengel led the team in all power numbers: 23 doubles, 12 triples, six home runs, and 73 RBIs, as well as runs scored, 69. No regular besides Wheat batted over .300 (Daubert hit .261—his first sub-.300 season of his career). Daubert (who turned 33 the first week of the season) along with third baseman Mike Mowry, 33, and catcher Chief Meyers, 36, all showed their age. The latter was released by Brooklyn in April, finishing the season with the Boston Braves. Neither he nor Mowry played in the majors after the '17 season.

One bright spot was the reemergence of shortstop Ivy Olson. "Olson played better ball in 1917 than he ever played in his whole career, was always a dangerous hitter, and was the most useful all around shortstop Brooklyn has had since Bill Dahlen's time," wrote Thomas Rice in November 1917.[6]

Marquard was the club's winningest pitcher (19–12, 2.55 ERA), and, though Pfeffer struggled record-wise (11–15), he led the moundsmen in innings pitched (266), complete games (24), and shutouts (3). Both Smith's (12–12) and Coombs' (7–11) numbers dropped, but they played vital roles, as they often pitched in long relief, finishing 14 and 15 games, respectively. Right-hander, Leon Cadore's first complete season (13–13, 2.45) was a much-needed respite for the banged-up staff, tying Pfeffer for the most starts with 30.

The emergence of Cadore, nicknamed "Caddy," was certainly pleasing for Dodger fans. He had spent part of his childhood in Brooklyn, before being sent to live with an uncle in Hope, Idaho, at age 13 following his mother's death. He attended prep school, then college at Gonzaga University in Spokane, Washington, where he played baseball, football, and basketball. He moved back to Brooklyn in 1911 and began playing baseball professionally the following summer. He spent the next five years in different minor leagues on the East Coast and brief stints with the Dodgers in 1915 and '16. He played parts of the next eight seasons with Brooklyn, marrying

5. Uncertain Times, 1917–1919

Ebbets' daughter, Maie, during those years. A favorite of fans and teammates, Cadore would entertain with card tricks and other sleights-of-hand. He also used those skills to doctor the ball. Stengel said that his roommate, Cadore, could scuff a ball with his hand by cutting it with his thumbnail.

Wheat returned to the lineup in early June. It proved to be his only full month of play for 1917, coincidentally his best statistical month of the season: .330, five doubles, four triples, one home run—his lone round-tripper of the season. It did little to help the club, as the injuries kept them mired in the second division for the rest of the season, eventually finishing in seventh place with a 70–81 record. He kept on pace, hitting safely in 16 of 17 games from June 25 to July 10.

On July 21, Wheat singled in the second inning, followed by a Cutshaw single. Looking to go from first to third, Wheat badly sprained his right ankle. He watched the second game from the box wearing a slipper, and didn't start another game for a month. He initially didn't travel with the team when it went on a three week, 25-game road trip, opting to stay back home on the farm in Polo. Coincidentally, Brooklyn enjoyed their longest winning streak of the season in Wheat's absence—seven games between July 28 and August 3. Wheat joined the team in St. Louis and pinch hit on August 4. He spent the next three weeks as a pinch hitter, before returning to the regular lineup at the end of the month. It would be the longest stretch of Wheat's career limited to such duties. For his career, Wheat batted .239 in 75 pinch-hitting at-bats, with one double and home run. During his limited play, Wheat appeared as a pinch-hitter, drawing a walk in what would be a then National League record 22-inning game, a 6–5 win over the Pirates in the first game of a doubleheader at Ebbets Field on August 22.

Wheat's average was an even .300 heading into the last series of the 1917 season at home against the Boston Braves. He went three-for-four in each of the first three games before going hitless in the season finale. In 109 games—the lowest total of his career thus far—Wheat finished at .312 for the second year in a row, albeit in forty fewer games than in 1916. He was third in the league behind the Reds' Edd Roush (.341), and Rogers Hornsby (.327) of the Cardinals. Wheat was the only Dodger to break the top-five in any batting category. All of his statistics were a fraction of what they were in years past—15 doubles, 11 triples, the one home run. He only stole five bases after seven seasons of registering double digits. The drop was likely attributed to his injuries, but stolen bases as a whole were down throughout the league. There were 1,328 stolen bases league-wide, 183 fewer than in 1916. It was a topic that didn't go unnoticed. Some alluded to that fact that players didn't want to risk injury because of high salaries.

Zack Wheat

In an interview with the *Brooklyn Daily Eagle* in early July 1917, before his ankle injury, Wheat thought the decrease in stolen bases around the league could be attributed to two traditional factors that prohibit base stealing: a good left-handed pickoff move and a strong catcher's arm. This year he noticed right-handers getting away with a few things that were prohibited in the past. "They are bending the knee slightly as if going to pitch to the plate, but bring the arm around and shoot to first," he explained. "That bent knee used to be the signal to run, and it would be now if the umpires enforced the balk rule properly, but the umps let them give that former sign of a pitch and will not call a balk if he whirls the ball to first."[7]

By season's end, Wheat was given a clean bill of health by the team's trainer, but the prolonged absence left him off *Baseball Magazine*'s National League All-Star Team. F.C. Lane still mentioned him in the write-up. "Zach Wheat is the most graceful outfielder in the business and one of the surest," wrote Lane. "Furthermore, he is a slugger of dire potentialities. But fate was unkind to Zach this season."[8]

The Dodgers finished the 1917 season in seventh place, with a 70–81 record. It was the worst follow-up season for a pennant winner in the league's 42-year history. To add frustration to Brooklyn's regression season, the nemesis Giants had a resurgence, going 98–56, and capturing the pennant by 10 games over the Phillies. McGraw's team had few flaws; it had yet to be affected by military call-ups, and the growing micromanagement of owner Harry Hempstead. They scored the most runs in the National League behind infielder Heinie Zimmerman's league-leading 100 RBIs. Outfielder George Burns led the league in runs for the second year in a row (103), and right fielder Dave Robertson paced the league with a dozen home runs for the second time in as many seasons. A deep pitching staff was led by lefthanders Ferdie Schupp (21–7, 1.95), Slim Sallee (18–7, 2.17), and Rube Benton (15–9, 2.72). Right-hander Pol Perritt (17–7, 1.88) also played a vital role. All four threw over 200 innings. Just two years from a last-place finish, the Giants returned to the World Series for the first time since the McGraw-Robinson split, losing to the 100-win Chicago White Sox.

On January 9, 1918, Stengel and Cutshaw were traded to the Pittsburgh Pirates for infielder Chuck Ward and pitchers Al Mamaux and Burleigh Grimes. According to Tommy Holmes, "Casey's humor, verging on the caustic seemed to make both Ebbets and Robbie uncomfortable."[9] Wheat, too, though used to his old friend's antics, didn't always appreciate them. The previous spring training, Stengel accompanied some players and their wives, including the Wheats. Though friendly with Daisy Wheat, he repeatedly touched her back, which was exposed by her dress. She soon found out the mischievous Stengel had put cow itch on her. "I went out looking for Casey and if I had found him we'd have had it out," recalled Zack years later.[10]

Wheat's name had been bandied about as being part of the Pittsburgh trade as well as swaps with the Cubs and Phillies, but alas, he was not included in either. Mamaux, a talented right-hander who had back-to-back 21-win seasons in 1915 and '16, before the 2–11 mark in '17, was the central figure of the trade. He would never meet expectations, as his singing talents became a distraction when he began pursuing a show-business career. Of the three players that Brooklyn acquired from the Pirates, Grimes, a talented, but quarrelsome spitballer from Clear Lake, Wisconsin, proved to be far and away the best acquisition of the lot. The Pirates had high hopes for Grimes, but he had faltered during Pittsburgh's disastrous 1917 season. The 24-year-old, who used the bark of the slippery elm tree to lubricate his spitter, already had a reputation for scuffling with anyone—teammates and opponents alike. The most famous to-date was a knockdown, drag out brawl on a train with Hugo Bezdek, the third Pirates manager of the forgettable '17 season. Though he had lost 13 games in a row, Grimes confronted the former University of Chicago football star about why he hadn't been pitching of late. Grimes held his own against Bezdek, who was three or four inches taller than the young right-handed thrower and outweighed him by at least 50 pounds.

Grimes and Wheat would be teammates for the next nine seasons. Though Grimes squabbled with seemingly everyone in the organization over his nearly decade-long tenure in Brooklyn, the pitcher never had any notable issue with Wheat. Wheat played the game the same way that Grimes did, just at a different decibel. Of the Hall of Famer Grimes' 287 career starts for Brooklyn, Wheat would be in the lineup for 250 of them. Decades later, Grimes told baseball historian Donald Honig that Wheat "won more ball games for me than any other individual."[11]

Wheat never made it to Hot Springs in 1918 and wouldn't meet his new teammates for several weeks. He was back home in Missouri as a holdout. Ebbets threatened to replace him with Napoleon Lajoie, who last played in the major leagues in 1916, but batted .380 and managed the Toronto Maple Leafs to the International League title in 1917. However, nothing materialized with Lajoie. Wheat gained bargaining leverage when the Dodgers started out losing a franchise record nine games, but neither side budged. Wheat was absent for so long that he was threatened with being thrown out of the National League and blackballed. "Now see what you did," he said to Daisy, who was again encouraging him to stay strong until he got the salary she thought he deserved.[12]

Sure enough, the next day, Wheat received a call from Ebbets offering

Zack Wheat

Wheat played more games behind Hall of Fame pitcher Burleigh Grimes than any other player. Grimes was one of 17 spitballers allowed to throw the "trick pitch" for the duration of their careers (Charles Clark photo collection).

his 1917 salary of $5,800, below market value of comparable players. The contract did include compensation for the time he missed and expenses to join the team. Wheat promptly applied for reinstatement, which was granted by National League president, John Heydler. Wheat resented Ebbets for the whole ordeal, calling the owner "one of the most unappreciative creatures in the world."[13]

5. Uncertain Times, 1917–1919

The war was changing the complexion of Brooklyn's roster before the season had begun. Throughout Wheat's holdout, the war efforts continued to give him reason to be concerned, as it was pulling players from teams all over the league. He had originally been given a Class 1A status by the draft board in Kansas City, earmarking him for the hand grenade class. That changed in April, when the Polo draft board gave him a Class 4, delaying his call to duty because of his family obligations.

Of the 531 major leaguers under contract on October 1, 1917, 91 had volunteered for service, and another 53 would be drafted by the end of June. No players were given preferential treatment as over two dozen future Hall of Famers served in one capacity or another. Brooklyn was one of the heaviest hit. By July, 13 Dodgers were spread across the armed services and another four were in the shipyards or munitions factories; by November, 18 players were in the military. The 1918 season was a taxing one for Robinson, too, as he juggled the stress of not only managing his depleted roster, but was fraught with the grief of losing his son, Wilbert, Jr., who passed away on January 6, 1918, at the family home in Baltimore after a lengthy illness.

Wheat finally made his 1918 debut on May 7. He struggled over the next two months to find his way in the batter's box. Furthermore, he was dealing with worries associated with the July 1 "work or fight" order enacted by Secretary of War Newton D. Baker, upon recommendation of the director of the military draft, Provost Marshall General Enoch Crowder. In late June, Wheat had contemplated not making a trip to Boston, lest he be drafted, now that there was a possibility of being forced into a war-related occupation. There were even reports of him contemplating joining Mamaux at a munitions factory at the Fore River Shipyard in Quincy, Massachusetts. Also weighing on his mind was Daisy, who gave birth to Zachary Forsman Wheat, Jr., on July 16, while Zack was playing in Pittsburgh.

The birth of the Wheats' second child came right as Zack was beginning to lock in at the plate. For the second time in three seasons, Wheat embarked on another lengthy hitting streak—a 26-game stretch from July 11 to August 7. Wheat's final hit of the run came with a single on August 7. The hero of the 3–2 Dodgers victory was his younger brother, Mack. He launched a fourth-inning three-run home run—the first home run and RBIs of his career. The next day, Zack's hitting streak came to an end against the combined efforts of Cubs hurlers Hippo Vaughn and Paul Carter. Having gone through the trying 29-game streak in 1916, the end of this one was met with some relief by Wheat. He explained to Lane: "To tell the truth, I am glad it is all over. It's fine to get into a winning stride and belt that old ball. But when you have been usually lucky and come somewhere near to equaling the record, then the strain grows too great. And the farther you go the harder it is to hit safely."[14]

Wheat had his eyes on something bigger than a hitting streak: the batting title. "Tomorrow I can devote all my time to winning the batting championship," he added to Lane after the August 7 contest. "I have never had so good a chance to get it and I surely hope I'll be lucky enough to come through now."[15] As luck would have it, another hitting streak was a residual effect of his attempts at the title. The next day he started a 13-game streak, raising his average from .265 to a high point of .348 on the final day of that duration.

Wheat had a few competitors for the batting title, but as the season dwindled, it became a race between him and defending National League batting champion, Edd Roush, the feisty Reds outfielder. He had begun his career with the White Sox, spent two seasons in the Federal League, and then was purchased by the Giants for the '16 season. After a slow start, he was part of the trade that sent Christy Mathewson to Cincinnati in July of that year. Upon the recommendation of McGraw, Mathewson, the Reds new manager, immediately made Roush his everyday centerfield. In '17 he beat out Rogers Hornsby for the batting title, .341 to .327.

Seldom one to publicly compliment the opposition during his playing days, when Wheat was asked by Thomas Rice, "Who is the most troublesome batter in the National League for you as an outfielder," Wheat didn't have to think long. "I should say that for a left-fielder, about the most uncertain proposition in this league is Edd Roush of Cincinnati," he responded of his competition for the batting title. "Eddie is a left-handed batter who is usually well above the .300 mark, and so is a frequent maker of hits." In 1919, Roush won his second batting crown with .321, a World Series title with the Reds, becoming the National League's highest-paid player ($10,000/year) at the start of a new decade.[16]

Wheat slumped towards the end of the 1918 season, sitting out a season-ending doubleheader in Philadelphia. Some accused him of sitting to secure the batting title. He ended the 1918 season at .335, unofficially winning the only batting title of his career. It was one of the few bright spots for the fifth-place Dodgers (57–69). Wheat's average was .334963 to be exact, just .001630 better than Roush's .33333. There were some conflicting statistics tabulated, and the title wouldn't be verified until Elias released their official stats in the New Year.

There were several numerical oddities within Wheat's batting statistics accumulated in just 105 games. Most notably, he won the title without hitting a home run—the second (and last) National Leaguer to do so, following Pirates outfielder Ginger Beaumont, who accomplished the feat in

5. Uncertain Times, 1917–1919

1902 (.357). Of Wheat's 137 hits, only 18 went for extra bases: 15 doubles and three triples—the majority hitting cleanup (100 of the 105 games he played). His .386 slugging percentage was the second-lowest of his career and the 51-point differential between his batting average and slugging percentage

In 1918 Wheat edged Edd Roush (pictured) for the lone batting title of his career. The Reds outfielder had won it in 1917 and would win it again in 1919 (Library of Congress, Prints & Photo-graphs Division, [LC-DIG-ggbain-36159]).

was a career low. Also, his 48 RBIs were the fewest by a batting champion behind Jake Daubert's 44 and 46 in 1914 and '13, respectively. The streaky hitting (including a rare 50-hit month—53 in July) helped him capture the batting title with four separate occasions of at least 11-straight games with a hit.

Wheat's play earned him a spot on *Baseball Magazine*'s All National League team along with teammates Daubert (.308 and major-league leading 15 triples) and Grimes, who flourished as the Dodgers' only pitcher with a winning record, leading the club—which saw 17 different throwers—in nearly every category: wins, 19 (including nine in a row); ERA, 2.13; starts, 30; and shutouts, seven. He also appeared in a league-best 40 games. Johnston was one of the few position players to find any sort of success (.281, 16 doubles). Cheney was the only other pitcher to make it to double-digits (11–13). Marquard led the National League with 18 losses. Robinson was so desperate for pitching that he allowed both Pfeffer and Cadore to pitch on day passes from the military. Robinson even started a local boy sight unseen after hearing he was striking batters out by the dozen in Rochester. Harry Heitman allowed four straight hits to start the game, was removed, and never pitched another major league game again, giving him a career ERA of infinite (he would have a long minor league career that spanned nearly a decade).

For the first time in a few years, Wheat signed a contract with minimal negotiating. He did so by early March 1919, and was rewarded with title of team captain. Yet once again he reported to camp late, taking time to join the Polo, Missouri, Free Masons, Lodge 232 in mid–March, arriving in Brooklyn's new spring training site in Jacksonville, Florida, a few days into April. He seemed to be taking quickly to his new title of captain. "If any umpire or any ball team gets the idea that he or it can ride the Superbas because I figure on an even break, they are due for a surprise," he told Yager. "You may not be able to teach an old dog new tricks, but he may have some just as good stowed away that will be forced to the surface under pressure. I'm not looking for trouble, but you never can tell."[17]

Wheat's captaincy was an obvious move by Robinson, who had the unenviable task of replacing the gaping hole left by the departure of team captain, Daubert. Of great intelligence and business savvy, Daubert was so popular he had once been nominated for Alderman in Brooklyn, a race he lost. On February 1, 1919, he was traded to the Cincinnati Reds for outfielder Tommy Griffith. It was a move pushed by Ebbets, after Daubert sued him for the remainder of his 1918 contract. When players were released at the end of the '18 season, their contracts were severed, with the understanding that they would be resigned for 1919. Daubert claimed he was under a multi-year deal, and thus owed his full salary. The two parties settled out of court, but the damage between them was beyond repair, leading to the trade. Daubert slipped into the role of captain in Cincinnati and helped lead the Reds to the infamous 1919 World Series title over the Chicago White Sox.

Tragedy struck when Daubert passed away on October 9, 1924, from a later diagnosed hereditary blood disorder, hemolytic spherocytosis. According to his SABR biography written by Jim Sandoval, "A contributing factor to his death was a beaning he suffered early that season, one of at least eight in his career. He suffered from headaches and had trouble sleeping the rest of the season. In a weakened condition, Daubert began to suffer from what doctors thought was appendicitis and gallstones. On October 2, he was operated on, even receiving blood transfusions from one of the doctors. Daubert never recovered, passing away one week later."[18]

Ebbets found a replacement for Daubert the night before the 1919 season opener when he purchased veteran first baseman Ed Konetchy, who was holding out from the Boston Braves. In the early years of the decade, "Koney" was a top-ten hitter in the National League for the Cardinals and one of the best fielding first baseman in the majors. The LaCrosse, Wisconsin, native hopped to the Federal League in 1915 after a disappointing '14 season with the Pirates, enjoying one of the best statistical seasons of his career. He went so far as to say the Federal League was the "best league I have ever been connected with."[19] After three lackluster years in Boston, he had a career resurgence in Brooklyn over the next few seasons, even exceeding Daubert's output for the Reds during that timeframe. The 1920 World Series would be the self-professed highlight of Konetchy's career, but in 1919 he made his way into the record books with 10 hits in as many at-bats.

Brooklyn won nine of their first 10 games and tied another, 9–9—a 20-inning game with the Phillies that was called due to darkness. Grimes pitched all 20 innings. Wheat went one-for-eight, part of his slow start hitting. Just months after Wheat won the batting title, Thomas Rice of the *Brooklyn Daily Eagle* referred to his batting style as "awkward," picking apart his approach. Wheat's fielding was his saving grace, Rice calling it "poetic," and his fellow *Daily Eagle* columnist, Yager, heaped praise on Wheat's defensive gusto. "Wheat not only has the knack of making circus catches, but he unconsciously puts a finish on the performance that enhances it in a spectacular way and causes it to stick in the memory of fans," Yager waxed. "He is far from a poseur as could be imagined, and never intentionally sought the limelight in his life, but there is a finish and a completeness to his stunts, rounded off with a neat flourish, which reminds one of the foreign acrobatic turns, and which distinguishes those turns from those of American performances."[20]

On May 4, Wheat went hitless in Brooklyn's first legal Sunday home game, a 6–2 win over the Braves in front of 25,000 spectators. The move to allow Sunday games, known as the Walker Act, would prove to be a boon for Ebbets. Wheat's batting finally came around as the end of the month neared, including hitting in nine straight games. On May 26, Wheat ended his 196-game, 531-at-bat home run drought with a solo shot over the left field wall at Ebbets Field off St Louis Cardinal Lee Meadows, propelling the Dodgers to a 5–2 win. It came after Wheat committed an error in the seventh inning to allow St. Louis to take a 2–1 lead. According to Thomas Rice, Wheat "ranted continuously on the bench after that bobble, building up a grouch that culminated in the vicious drive."[21]

A week later, on June 1, Wheat had the first five-hit game of his career, going five-for-nine, with a double, in an 18-inning loss at the hands of a Phillies. It came a month after the two teams played to the 9–9, 20-inning tie. Wheat used the five-hit game as a springboard to a torrid two-month pace, batting .355 through June and July, becoming the first National Leaguer to have 100 hits. His overall average reached a high of .325 on August 2, following a three-hit game in a 3–2 win over the Cardinals in St. Louis.

Wheat's popularity grew to the point he could rarely get off the field at the end of the game without a caravan of fans escorting him to the clubhouse. There, they'd wait until he and other players were finished showering and then follow them home. Wheat loved to engage with fans during and after games. It was hard to avoid them, as players lived in such close proximity, but there were times when Wheat wanted to slip out of the park unencumbered. He found a way to leave alone by escaping through the side door of the clubhouse and then walking under the stands back to the outfield. Of the evasion, he said, "I beat this, to a certain extent, by cutting a hole through a far corner of the fence underneath the bleachers, leading out onto Bedford Avenue."[22] Wheat held no ill-will on their exuberance, recalling "the great loyalty they displayed towards me."[23]

Other times, Wheat tried to flag a ride from teammates who owned cars. Even then, he couldn't escape fans. He recalled the time he flagged down Jimmy Johnston. As he got in the car, a nicely dressed man followed behind him. "The three of us talked about the game and when we reached Ocean Boulevard, he said, 'Here's where I get out. Thanks for the lift, Jim. Goodbye, Zack!"

"Nice fellow, who is he?" Johnston asked.

"Don't know. Never saw him before in my life. I thought he was a friend of yours," replied Wheat.[24]

Wheat was never known to have issues or altercations with opponents or teammates, but one of the few dust-ups occurred early that summer

5. Uncertain Times, 1917–1919

between him and Pfeffer. It came as a result of Wheat's lingering insecurity about his defense. Following a bobble by Wheat that allowed a run, Pfeffer returned to the bench and was openly complaining about the miscue. "Maybe we could win a few games if we had some outfielders who could catch," said the big right-hander. Wheat sat stewing about the insults before he finally heard enough. Without changing his facial expression, he jumped over a bench and attacked the much larger pitcher, beating him bad enough where he couldn't take the mound the following inning. The incident went unreported by the press, but was legendary amongst Wheat's Brooklyn teammates for years to come.[25]

The Dodgers teetered between the first and second division for most of August. There was talk of Robinson taking over the Yankees managerial job from Miller Huggins in 1920 or leaving baseball all together. The hearsay began when Robinson let Wheat manage the team on August 11 so he could return to Baltimore for his son Harry's wedding. Wheat had a pair of hits, but Brooklyn lost to the Pirates, 5–2. The Dodgers finally fell to the lower rung for good with a 4–3 loss to the Giants on August 31. For the second year in a row, Brooklyn finished in fifth place with a record of 69–71.

Wheat's average dipped below .300 for the first time in three seasons (.297)—the only time in a ten-year span from 1916–25 that it occurred. Still, he hovered near the top three of nearly every Brooklyn batting category. In the final decade of the Deadball Era—when pitchers used all means of doctoring the ball—he had more total bases than any National Leaguer (2,121), and his 1,516 hits ranked second to Daubert's 1,535.

For the first time since winning the pennant in 1916, Robinson had a formidable batting lineup beside Wheat. As a team, the Dodgers hit .263, second in the National League. Olson led the National League in games played (140) and hits (164), and both leagues in plate appearances (636) and at-bats (590). Myers paced the senior circuit in: triples (14), RBIs (73), and total bases (223). Konetchy hit at a .298 clip and had a team-high 24 doubles. Those three batters kept the team afloat, as Robinson's pitching staff was ravaged by injuries. Marquard (3–3) was lost for the season on June 9 when he broke his leg sliding into third base against the Reds in Cincinnati. Grimes regressed (10–11, 3.47), his season ending in July when rookie Frankie Frisch of the Giants nearly severed Grimes' achilles tendon on a play at first base. Several pitchers returned from military service, and within a year would team with a healthy Grimes to help the club to a World Series appearance in 1920, specifically: Pfeffer (17–13, 2.66), Cadore (14–12, 2.37), Smith (7–12, 2.24), and Mamaux (10–12, 2.66).

6

A Whole New Ball Game, 1920

As another decade began, so did a new era of baseball. Historically, it would come to be known as the beginning of the game's "Liveball Era." This was highlighted by the Yankees acquisition of Babe Ruth from the Red Sox in December 1919 for $125,000. He transitioned to a full-time outfielder, changing the game forever. His impact would be felt immediately, as the Yankees became the biggest draw in town, evident by the attendance mark set at the Polo Grounds, that they had been sharing with the Giants since 1913. The Giants saw a spike in crowds, too, setting a National League attendance record of 929,609. They were eclipsed by the Yankees, 1,289,422. This infuriated the Giants' new owner, Charles Stoneham, so much that he sent an eviction notice. Though he withdrew it, it was evident that his club had competition for fans.

For the remainder of Wheat's career with the Dodgers, his team would be further overshadowed within the city's baseball hierarchy. Even Brooklyn sportswriters were prone to overlook Wheat's talents, instead always on the lookout for the next young player that could be the Dodgers' answer to Ruth. Wheat didn't seem bothered by this. Decades later, the Baseball Writers' Association named the greatest ball player of all-time at a banquet preceding the 1969 All-Star game in Washington, D.C. Wheat agreed, giving Ruth the nod over his close friend, Ty Cobb. "It's difficult for me, but I'd pick Ruth in a close ballot," he told Ed Rumill of the *Christian Science Monitor*. "Cobb could do more things. I've seen him steal second, third, and home in one inning. But Ruth was as good an outfielder as Cobb and he could wreck you with this bat. Babe had a better arm than Ty. And you have to take into consideration Ruth's career as a pitcher."[1]

The Giants had another outfielder that was surpassing George Burns as the player that Wheat was measured against. Ross Youngs came to New York in September 1917, quickly becoming one of McGraw's favorites. Youngs and Christy Mathewson would be the only players that McGraw

6. A Whole New Ball Game, 1920

hung photographs of in his office. By 1918, the Texan had taken over as the everyday right-fielder from Dave Robertson, to begin his decade-long career. Like Wheat, Youngs batted left, threw right, and had few weaknesses in his game. A future Hall of Famer, Youngs was instrumental in four National League pennants and two World Series championships. Tragically, his career—and life—were cut short by Bright's disease, a kidney ailment. His play slipped dramatically in 1925 and by '26 he was accompanied by a nurse. He was too weak to play the following season, passing away at the age of 30 in October 1927.

Beyond Ruth's arrival in New York City, during the 1920 offseason, team owners made several changes to the game that would have lasting effects. At the winter rules committee meeting in Chicago, the largest debate was over the abolishment of "freak deliveries." The body consisted of Barney Dreyfuss (Pirates), Connie Mack (Athletics), Clark Griffith (Senators), and William Veeck (Cubs). Also present were the league presidents, John Heydler (National League) and Ban Johnson (American League), and umpires, Bill Klem and Hank O'Day. For two days they argued about this change to the game—the impetus of Dreyfuss—that would have reverberating effects. He had been devising a plan for years, and it was one of the reasons for Grimes' exit from Pittsburgh, when he refused to return to the minor leagues to learn another pitch in anticipation of the proposal. Of the owners, Veeck, the newest to the group (he had become the Cubs' president in 1919) was undecided. Heydler stepped in, coming up with a statement that the group could agree on and put out to club owners:

> I think we shall give the old-time pitchers who are recognized as spitball throwers, a certain period to develop something to take the place of this delivery. He might be granted a year or possibly only about two months or so. Every club would have to register with the league the names of the recognized spitball pitchers. No others would be granted that extra time. No newcomers of this year would be permitted to throw the spitter.[2]

The final proclamation allowed teams to allot two pitchers to be able to throw the spitball for the duration of the 1920 season. National League owners accepted the proposal immediately, with Ebbets tabbing Grimes and Clarence Mitchell who split time between the mound and outfield. He was the only left-handed spitballer of the group, boasting a "three-way spitter," because he was supposedly able to make it break three different ways. Like Grimes, Mitchell used the bark of the slippery elm tree when wetting his spitball. Dreyfuss, who spearheaded the motion, didn't name anyone, nor did Mack and Griffith when the American League adopted the movement. In all, 17 pitchers would be allowed to throw the trick pitch. It was

Zack Wheat

thought the two leagues were playing with different balls, with the American League variety having a little more bounce than the National League's.

Years later, Grimes had a theory for why the spitball was banned: "The real reason the spitter was barred was because pitchers were roughing the

The Wheat brothers both enjoyed successful seasons in 1920. Mack (left) was acquired by the Philadelphia Phillies and set career-highs in nearly every category. Zack helped the Dodgers to the World Series (Kenny Dixon photo collection).

6. A Whole New Ball Game, 1920

ball with pop bottle caps, sandpaper, emery and whatnot, ripping a stitch or two of the seam with razor blades and such, and discoloring the ball with tobacco, licorice, coffee and in other ways."[3]

During the winter, Wheat had gained some traction as a candidate for sheriff for Caldwell County, Missouri. He seemed more interested in the

Beginning in 1918, the youngest Wheat brother, Basil (pictured), spent nearly a decade playing minor league ball. He never made it to the majors (Kenny Dixon photo collection).

prospects of donning a badge than of the rumors of being the lynchpin in a three-way trade that would see him shipped to the Phillies, Philadelphia's Eppa Rixey to Boston, and the Braves' Hank Gowdy to Brooklyn. Wheat was intrigued by the deal, particularly after his brother Mack's contract was purchased by the Phillies in January, but nothing materialized. Mack would play in a career-high 78 games for Philadelphia in 1920 and just 10 in '21, before being released on August 1 of that year. He played three games for the Los Angeles Angels in the Pacific Coast League in 1922 before retiring. Married to Ruth, with a son, McKinley, Jr., Mack worked for the Pacific Gas & Electric for years, managing their office in Los Banos, California, where he also served as manager of the Los Banos Chamber of Commerce. He passed away on August 14, 1979, at age 86.

Ebbets was intent on dealing Zack to the Cardinals before the 1920 season, even going as far as having Wheat travel from Polo to Chicago to talk contract terms with St. Louis general manager, Branch Rickey. Nothing could be hashed out, and at the end of February, Wheat signed a contract with Brooklyn. Once again, he was one of the last players to arrive in Jacksonville, Florida, blaming his tardiness on making sure his brother Basil, an outfielder fresh out of high school, got acclimated in training camp with the Birmingham Barons. He would spend nearly a decade in the minor leagues with several teams, but never reached the major leagues, as Zack had predicted.

Wheat spent the first few days in training camp watching from the stands as his teammates scrimmaged Ruth and the Yankees. Wheat eased his way into play, beginning the season on a torrid pace, hitting safely in 17 of 18 games, at a .363 clip. In the middle was a brutal three-game stretch that totaled 58 innings. On May 1, 1920, Wheat was part of the longest game in major league history, a 26-inning marathon against the Boston Braves that ended in a 1–1 tie due to darkness. Both starters—Cadore for Brooklyn and Joe Oeschger for Boston—went the entire game. "I think it hurt 'em both because neither ever had another real good season," surmised Wheat. "Both had to bear down all 26 innings."[4]

Wheat made a few terrific plays, including a shoestring catch in short left field in the sixth inning that almost resulted in an unassisted double play at third base. He went two-for-nine, with a pair of singles. "I carried enough lumber to the plate that afternoon to build me a shack," Wheat said years later.[5]

The marathon game was played on Saturday, and the two teams were scheduled to resume the series on Monday with Sunday baseball still being illegal in Boston. Newly legal in Brooklyn, the team took the midnight train

6. A Whole New Ball Game, 1920

back home to play a Sunday game against the Phillies. Wheat's one-out home run in the ninth sent it to extra innings, before losing 4–3 in 14 innings. The Dodgers took the midnight train back to Boston and played a 19-inning affair won by Boston, 2–1. Wheat went one-for-eight.

"We played 58 innings in three days with two long owl train rides in between. Now that puts us in shape to play the rest of the season," Wheat said optimistically.[6]

The marathon sessions didn't seem to have an immediate effect on Wheat. He extended another hitting streak to nine games with a pair of singles against the Giants on May 30, but tweaked his ankle trying to beat out a ground ball to second base. June proved to be the worst month of the season for both Brooklyn (12–16—the only month with a losing record) and Wheat. He returned to action for the now first-place Dodgers on June 9, but was lost upon being reinserted into the lineup.

Throughout his career Wheat rarely went more than a few games without a hit, but there were multiple stretches during June when he went three or four games without one, with a two-for-34 stretch in the nine games after returning from his ankle injury. He scuffled to a .195 average over 21 June games, with just four extra base hits. Thomas Rice pushed the team's poor play on Wheat's injury. "It is safe to say that about 8 of the 15 losses were due in part to the physical effect of Wheat not being able to hit in pinches or to start runs by hits, and in part to the demoralizing effect of his failures upon the rest of the team," wrote the *Brooklyn Daily Eagle* scribe.[7]

One of the hits during Wheat's slump was a memorable home run that drove McGraw to fits. When he entered the league, he found modest success against the Giants and was always able to hit well at the Polo Grounds. By the 1910s he was hitting at such a clip, particularly against curveballs thrown by New York pitchers, that McGraw finally banned his staff from throwing any breaking balls to Wheat, especially at the Polo Grounds. For the next five years, Wheat didn't see a curveball from Giants hurlers— and it worked. He batted just .145 there over the past two seasons, but that changed during this June swoon.

On June 30, 1920, New York was hosting Brooklyn at the Polo Grounds. Coming off a two-hit game in Boston the day prior, Wheat had already tripled, driving in a run in the first inning, part of the Dodgers 2–0 lead. Still, his recent struggles were fresh on the mind of Giants 20-game winner Jesse Barnes. With two men on, Wheat worked the count to two-two. "As Barnes started his wind-up, I noticed a peculiar gleam in his eye," Wheat recounted to Tommy Holmes. "I had a hunch on the curve." Wheat ripped the pitch into the right field bleachers. As he jogged to first, McGraw went ballistic, screaming expletives at the mound. "That pitch costs you two hundred," he shouted to Barnes.[8]

There were suggestions that Wheat needed to change his approach at the plate. Wheat felt the contrary, explaining to Lane that batters must do what they feel comfortable with:

> There are batters who watch the pitcher's hand and try to foretell what he is going to throw. Some of these batters claim to be able to predict from the way a man delivers the ball whether it will be a cover or a fast ball. Perhaps they can. I don't even try to do this myself. This is observation and is a little different than guessing, but I don't think it's good dope and I never try to guess what the pitcher is going to throw even when I have a hunch that it's a fastball, for instance. I don't like to dwell on the thought. I want my mind on the ball and nothing else. And I want to feel that I can hit it no matter what happens. If batters would concentrate on that one thing and forget all the other frills, I believe they would be better off.[9]

Wheat's July made up for his poor June. He batted .355, swatting 17 extra-base hits (nine doubles, six triples, and two home runs), and driving in 17 runs, while scoring 30 times, and enjoyed a 14-game hitting streak. He helped propel Brooklyn into sole possession of first place on July 9, spending the next month atop the standings, but their lead was never more than four games (July 17). It was amazing they held onto the lead during a testing western road trip in the unforgiving July heat, winning 16 of 22 games over 19 days. When the team returned to Brooklyn, Ebbets rewarded each player with a hundred dollar bill.

The Dodgers stumbled to a 14–13 mark in August, spending several days in second place. Brooklyn pulled out all the stops in their race to the pennant, including calling back Joe Monahan, their good luck mascot from 1916, so that players could rub their hands through his red hair. They battled the Giants and the Reds for first place, both of whom were dealing with off-the-field legal matters. McGraw was in the midst of defending himself over a nightclub brawl at the Lamb's Club, which he owned a part of. Complicating matters were the possession of multiple bottles of whiskey—problematic during the Prohibition Era. The Reds were under much greater strain. There had always been gambling in baseball, but there seemed to be more than ever. During a trial in Cook County, Illinois, for the alleged fixing of an August 21 game between the Cubs and Phillies, there was discussion of tampering with the 1919 World Series. The aftermath would become known as the Black Sox Scandal.

Brooklyn took over sole possession of first place on September 9. Wheat was instrumental during the late-season run, hitting safely in 15 games, and 22 of 23 overall from August 31 to September 20. As one of the longest-tenured players in the league, he was enjoying another pennant

6. A Whole New Ball Game, 1920

race. He was asked to reminisce on his journey, and what it took to get where he was: "When any boy asks me how I got into big baseball, I tell him by work. But I was able to make my work count because I really love the game, just as every player must do to make a real success. It is the same in baseball as in any line of business—you have to like it and enjoy it thoroughly before you will be able to get along very far. It is a clean, healthful sport. I am proud of it."[10]

Brooklyn's 1920 team batting average was .277, second in the league, but they didn't stand out in many other categories beyond leading the league with 99 triples. Wheat ended as the team's top hitter, pacing the club in batting (.328), runs (89), hits (191), and home runs (nine). He also added 26 doubles, 13 triples, and 73 RBIs. Myers wasn't far behind in production, batting .304 and leading the majors in triples (22), and the club in doubles (36) and RBIs (80). Konetchy batted .308 and Johnston played in a major league-best 155 games—the majority of them at third base—a position that had been unstable for Dodgers over the past few years. With arguably the league's best, if not deepest, pitching staff, Robinson used just nine pitchers in 1920. At times, he used a six-man rotation, consisting of Grimes (23–11, 2.22 ERA), Pfeffer (16–9, 3.01 ERA), Cadore (15–14, 2.62 ERA), Mamaux (12–8, 2.69 ERA), Smith (11–9, 1.85 ERA), and Marquard (10–7, 3.23 ERA).

For a team to win a pennant, they can't simply rely on their stars. There needs to be players that come out of nowhere with a contribution. It may be for a two-week stretch, a month, or the entire season. Robinson had several on his most veteran roster to date. Miller had the highest average of his career (.289) and led National League catchers in putouts (418) and fielding percentage (.986). Olson and Pete Kilduff, who was traded to Brooklyn in June of 1919, solidified the middle infield. A Kansas farm boy, Kilduff had the best season of a career that spanned half-a-decade, batting a modest .272 with 26 doubles and eight triples. He was a fan favorite and the cheer of "Hit her on the nose, Petey," became a rallying cry throughout the season.

The Dodgers clinched the pennant on September 27, an off day, when the Braves beat the Giants 3–2 in the second game of a doubleheader. In 1916, Boston had helped Brooklyn clinch with a sweep of the second-place Phillies. The Dodgers went 20–5 during the month, finishing the 1920 season with a record of 93–61. It was the franchise's fifth pennant. Brooklyn's success helped establish an attendance record of 808,722, ranking second in the league. A celebration was held at the local YMCA, where rousing tributes were given for each of the team members. Robinson received a silver loving cup on behalf of the team, and the players were presented with inscribed watches. It was a satisfying moment for the veteran holdovers from the 1916

Zack Wheat

World Series team: Johnston, Marquard, Miller, Myers, Olson, Smith, and Wheat. "I have been connected with nine pennant-winning teams and this is the gamest team I have ever had anything to do with," expounded Robinson.[11]

The celebration was short-lived, as rumors swirled of members of the Dodgers being approached about throwing the series. They were to be questioned by King's County (Brooklyn) district attorney, Harry Lewis. During the Reds' trial, it was brought up that Olson had wagered money on the tainted 1919 series. Still, Wheat was surprised by the hearsay: "No one has ever approached me and it would not be well for any that had. I am sure that none of the other players have been approached. If any persons have doubts about the game they had better come out and see us perform. Perhaps we will be beaten in the series, but we will play the best game that we can." He added: "Even the hint that there is anything wrong is bound to affect the fielding of the men. We have always played clean ball and were in the fight up to the finish."[12]

John Heydler wasn't as gracious: "Anyone who ever insinuates that the 1920 World Series has been 'fixed' ought to be shot, for such reports are just deliberate attempts to hurt baseball."[13]

Ebbets and Robinson aided Lewis's investigation by sending Wheat, Mamaux, and backup catcher Zack Taylor to make an official statement. The District Attorney seemed satisfied that the players were "strictly on the level," and his purpose for speaking with them "was simply to find out of any attempt had been made to approach them."[14]

The Dodgers now looked ahead to their opponent, a Cleveland Indians team who won the club's first pennant in franchise history (98–56) by two games over the highly scrutinized Chicago White Sox, with the Yankees not far behind at three games. It was the closest pennant race since 1908, when the Detroit Tigers beat the White Sox on the last day of the season. The Tigers were a half-game better than the Cleveland Naps (later Indians) and one-and-a-half games over Chicago. Cleveland's 1920 pennant finally came after consecutive second-place finishes behind Boston in '18 and Chicago in '19. Cleveland was managed by Tris Speaker, in his first season as a player-manager. "The Grey Eagle" did it by utilizing a platoon system, rallying the team after the death of star shortstop, Ray Chapman, whom they would honor by wearing a black band around their left arms throughout the series.

On August 16, Chapman stepped to the plate in the fifth inning on an overcast afternoon at the Polo Grounds. On the mound for the Yankees was Carl Mays. When the disagreeable submarine-style pitcher noticed Chapman shifting his back foot to slap the ball to right field, Mays threw the ball up and in. Chapman failed to move. The ball hit him in the temple. Thinking it hit the bat, Mays fielded the ball, throwing it to Wally Pipp at first

6. A Whole New Ball Game, 1920

base. Chapman fell to his knees, blood coming from his ear. He was able to get up on his own accord and began walking to the clubhouse, but he collapsed on the way. He was rushed to St. Lawrence Hospital where surgery was performed to relieve the pressure in his skull. It didn't help. He died the next morning.

The situation was eerily similar to a spring training incident when Pfeffer beaned Chick Fewster in the temple. The Yankees third base prospect claimed to have never seen the pitch. He suffered a fractured skull, and surgery was needed. He returned to play in early July and in a few years would be playing for the Dodgers, but he was never the same player.

"It was a terrible wallop," Wheat told *Baseball Magazine* in June 1920, a few months before Chapman's death. "He lay there like an ox that has been felled with a blow from an axe, quivering all over, and, of course, insensible." Wheat added, "I know something of how he felt, for I was hit on the head by a baseball myself once, and I was crazy as a bed bug for two weeks."[15]

For the second consecutive year, the World Series was a best-of-nine format. The first three games were to be played in Cleveland, then four in Brooklyn, and then back to Cleveland for the remaining two, if necessary. Indian's owner, Jack Dunn, approached Ebbets about swapping venues to allow Cleveland's League Park to be better prepared to accommodate a World Series crowd. With the prospect of possibly one more game in Brooklyn and the revenue that might occur, Ebbets agreed. Furthermore, Ebbets graciously allowed Dunn to add shortstop Joe Sewell, though he had joined the Indians after the August 30 eligibility deadline. He had been called up after Chapman's replacement, Harry Lunte, was injured in early September.

At 32 years old, Speaker was still one of the league's best centerfielders and managerial duties didn't have any adverse effects on his game. He played in 150 games, batted .388, had 214 hits, scored 137 runs, drove in 107, and led the majors with 50 doubles. There were five other regulars that hit over .300: catcher, Steve O'Neill batted .321 with 39 doubles; outfielders, Charlie Jamieson (.319), and Elmer Smith (.316, 37 doubles, 10 triples, 12 home runs, and 103 RBIs), and third baseman, Larry Gardner (.310, team-high 118 RBIs). Chapman was batting .303 at the time of his death, and Sewell batted .329 in his stead. First baseman, Doc Johnston hit .292. He was the older brother of Jimmy Johnston, making them the first brothers to play in the same World Series.

Cleveland relied heavily on three right-handed starters. Jim Bagby led the majors in wins (31–12) and games (48), and the American League in complete games (30). He was followed by a pair of spitballers: future Hall of Famer Stan Coveleski (24–14), who led the junior circuit in strikeouts (133), and Ray

Caldwell (20–10). In September, left-hander John "Duster" Mails, who played briefly for the Dodgers in 1915 and '16, was obtained by Speaker from Sacramento of the Pacific Coast League upon recommendation from former big-leaguer, Frank Chance. Over the last month of the season, Mails went 7–0 with a 1.85 ERA, including a key 2–0 shutout over Chicago on September 24 to give Cleveland a one-and-a-half game lead with just a few games left.

As one of the faces of the World Series, Wheat was offered an opportunity to write a column throughout the series, or at least have his name attached to one. If he was, in fact, the one who wrote them, Wheat was very confident. "We are going to win," he began his first article. "Our pitching staff is superior to the Indians and it is an accepted fact that pitching is 75 percent of the battle." He thought the difference maker was Robinson, whom he called "the greatest leader of men in baseball history."[16]

One of the problems of the 1916 World Series was Robinson's usage of pitchers, particularly Pfeffer. The relationship between not only the player and manager, but also club management (Ebbets), had been strained since then. Following the fallout from the Fewster beaning, much of the 1920 season was spent trying to get rid of the big right-hander. Despite the rumors, Pfeffer performed incredibly well during the pennant run, winning nine consecutive decisions between July 2 and August 31. But, once again, he would see the mound sparingly during the 1920 series. This time, Robinson made a peculiar move with his rotation for Game One, starting his favorite, Marquard, who was the weak link in the six-man rotation, over his ace, Grimes. It may have been a sentimental decision by Robinson, as Cleveland-native Marquard, had spent a part of his childhood serving as a bat-boy for the Cleveland Broncos, who would eventually become the Indians.

Game One was on a blustery October 5 at Ebbets Field. Speaker sent one of his spitballers, Coveleski, who had suffered his own personal tragedy in late May when his wife of seven years, Mary, passed away unexpectedly. Wheat battled the swirling winds to run down a certain extra base hit off the bat of Indians second baseman Bill Wambsganss in the top of the first inning. Speaker did the same thing to Wheat in the bottom of the second, making a shoestring catch after Cleveland had taken a 2–0 lead in the top of the inning, taking advantage of a rare throwing error by Konetchy and a double by O'Neill. The Indians added an insurance run in the top of the fourth on another double by their catcher. In Brooklyn's half of the inning, Wheat hit a fly ball that got knocked down by the wind and blown back towards the infield. Runners were on first and second, and had it fallen, the Dodgers would have likely scored and put them in a good spot for more.

Wheat led off the seventh inning with a double to deep right-centerfield.

6. A Whole New Ball Game, 1920

Wheat was a fan favorite at Ebbets Field, particularly among the left field "bleacherites," pictured during Game One of the 1920 World Series (Library of Congress, Prints & Photographs Division [LC-DIG-ggbain-31275]).

He advanced to third on Myers' groundout to the shortstop and scored what would be the Dodgers only run of the game on a groundout to first by Konetchy. Coveleski's spitball baffled Brooklyn, as he threw a complete game in Cleveland's 3–1 win. In a column for the *Cleveland Plain Dealer*, Wheat pinpointed the second O'Neill at-bat as the one mistake he could recall. "We should have passed O'Neill and nailed the pitcher," he wrote, adding, "That is the only flaw I can pick in our game, the rest was pure luck."[17]

Brooklyn countered with their own spitballer, Grimes, for Game Two, the next day. Wheat got the scoring going in the first inning, when he lined a ball to centerfield off Bagby, driving in Johnston. Wheat caught Sewell not paying attention on Speaker's throw and took second base for a double. That was the only run Grimes would need, as he scattered seven hits in a 3–0 shutout, allowing just one runner to third base. Wheat once again made another nice catch, tracking down a long fly ball from Doc Johnston after his brother, Jimmy, instructed Wheat to play shallow.

Game Three came the following day, October 7, and would ultimately be the high point for Wheat and his teammates. The Dodgers won, 2–1, behind another strong pitching performance, this time by Smith, who gave up just three hits and the one unearned run. Once again, Wheat opened the scoring in the first inning, slapping one between third base and shortstop, scoring Olson, who had walked to start the game. Wheat went three-for-four—all singles. He did play a role in Cleveland's only run. In the top of the fourth inning, Speaker made the Indians' first hit, a liner down the left field line. As Wheat pursed it, the ball bounded away from him. The Indians manager continued running. By the time Wheat tracked it down in the left field corner, Speaker was rounding third, headed for home. It was scored a double and error on Wheat, who thought it should have been scored an inside-the-park-home run. "The ball took a nasty hop just as I was about to catch it and I never got a hand on it," he said after the game.[18]

Besides family, in the stands was Wheat's coach from his Enterprise days, R.W. Hoffman, and a few acquaintances as guest for the series. They were given the full treatment, including daily access to club headquarters and box seat for the games in both Brooklyn and Cleveland. They also traveled with the team between cities. C.A. Case, who accompanied Hoffman, was wowed by Wheat's popularity. "He is a great hero of the Brooklyn kids," he said. "One day coming out of the headquarters there were 2,000 of them waiting for him and they followed him for blocks."[19]

The Series moved to Cleveland for Game Four on October 9. The Indians were 51–27 at League Park, but Wheat was confident. "There's no reason why we shouldn't keep up this winning brand of baseball in Cleveland," he wrote in the *Cleveland Plain Dealer* following the Game Three win. "We're started now and I don't think they can head us. We outhit them today two to one, and our infield and pitching were certainly superior. We've seen all their most vaunted pitchers already, while we still have got some good ones that haven't started."[20]

Robinson decided not to dip further into his six-man rotation. He confidently went with a rematch of Game One, with Marquard once again going against Coveleski. Several Dodgers felt the spitballer wasn't as talented as what they saw during the regular season in the National League. Wheat was one of them, telling Thomas Rice that the Coveleski's spitter "did not break as well as Doak's and did not have as much speed, nor did Coveleski have the fast ball to switch in among the spitters and cross the batters that Doak had shown for several years and particularly this year."[21]

Marquard never took the mound, instead finding himself under arrest for scalping tickets. The night before Game Four, he and teammates were joking about what they could get for their allotted tickets. A conversation between Marquard and Mamaux was overheard by a nearby reporter, who reported the scheme to police. The next morning, Marquard went out

6. A Whole New Ball Game, 1920

looking to sell his tickets. An undercover officer followed him, offering to purchase them. When the Dodgers' pitcher went to complete the transaction, he was arrested. He was released under his own recognizance, with an arraignment scheduled for the following day.

Robinson started Cadore in Marquard's place. He gave up a pair of runs and didn't make it out of the second inning. Mamaux couldn't last through the third inning, replaced by Marquard, who held the Indians scoreless for three innings, and then Pfeffer, in his only appearance of the series pitching the last three, allowing a run. Wheat went hitless for the first time in the series, and his teammates didn't have the success they anticipated against Coveleski. Cleveland's spitballer scattered five hits in the 5–1 Indians victory to tie the series at two games apiece.

Grimes went to the mound to take back the lead in Game Five, but it was a much different experience than his last outing. Towards the end of his masterful Game Two appearance, Jack McCallister, a Cleveland scout, supposedly noticed that whenever Grimes threw a spitball, his catcher, Miller, tossed a handful of dirt in front of him. On a fastball he threw it in between his legs, behind him. After the series, when this came to light, several Brooklyn teammates defended the catcher, even Grimes, who didn't get along with Miller. Years later, it was learned that second baseman, Kilduff was the source. He'd pick a handful of dirt up on each pitch, keeping it in if it was a spitball, dropping it on a fastball—all in view of the batter.

Regardless of the culprit, Cleveland was all over Grimes from the start of Game Five. He allowed singles to Jamieson and Wambsganss, and a bunt single by Speaker that the usually sure-gloved Grimes misplayed, loading the bases for Elmer Smith. The left-hander was one-for-seven in the series, including zero-for-four against Grimes in Game Two. Smith let a fastball go by for a ball before watching two spitball strikes. Grimes tried to throw a high fastball, but Smith wasn't fooled, sending the ball over the 45-foot screen in right field for the first grand slam in World Series history, and a 4–0 Indians lead.

In the fourth inning, Grimes' mound adversary, Bagby, hit the first World Series home run by a pitcher, a three-run blast that grew the lead to 7–1. One more World Series first was a fifth-inning unassisted triple play by second baseman Wambsganss on a line drive by Grimes' replacement, fellow spitball Mitchell. Wheat had a pair of late-game singles, coming around to score the Dodgers' only run of the game in the ninth inning on Konetchy's single to right field. The game ended an 8–1 Cleveland win to make the series three games to two. "Everything was against us today," wrote Wheat.[22]

Game Six, the following day, was a tough 1–0 loss, pushing the

Indians to the brink of a title. It was a frustrating day for Wheat, who would again go hitless. The entire team had a difficult game against Duster Mails, who allowed just three hits. It was another tough-luck World Series loss for Smith, who was on the losing end of the 14-inning game against Babe Ruth and the Red Sox in the 1916 series. Wheat showed a rare bit of emotion when he briefly argued with home plate umpire, Tom Connolly, when he was caught looking at strike three to start the second inning. In the sixth inning, Neis led off the inning with a walk to bring Wheat to the plate. Twice he was unable to bunt Neis to second. On the second attempt, O'Neill threw down to first behind the Neis, catching him far enough off the base for the first out. Olson hit a one-out double in the eighth inning, but the Dodgers were unable to capitalize.

Down to the final game, John Heydler talked with several Dodgers to motivate them. He told Wheat, "Just play the game that you did in winning the championship. Remember the strain of today's game is on the Indians. Get the jump on them today and then you can go back home and win the series. This is Cleveland's hardest game."[23]

Robinson went back to Grimes for Game Seven, pitted against Coveleski. Though he pitched two days earlier, Grimes faced just 19 batters and was ready for some redemption. Both spitballers were in command, until a fourth inning error by Grimes on a double steal. The Indians scored two more runs—one in the fifth on a Speaker triple and a seventh inning single by Jamieson. Brooklyn was unable to solve Coveleski. Wheat was thrown out in the top of the fourth inning trying to stretch a single to right field into a double and added a single in the top of the ninth inning. The game ended 3–0, giving Cleveland their first World Series title, five games to two. Coveleski won all three games he started, allowing two runs on 15 hits and two walks in the 27 innings pitched.

In Wheat's final article for the Universal Service, he was complimentary of Cleveland, calling Coveleski "some pitcher" and giving Speaker "the bulk of the praise for his handling of the Cleveland team." Wheat "was a little disappointed" in his team's batting in Cleveland, but in the end said, "We have no excuses. The other team won. That's all there is to say."[24] After his paltry numbers in the 1916 series, Wheat led Brooklyn regulars with a .333 averaged (nine-for-27) and a pair of doubles. He returned to Polo, Missouri, where he was greeted by a parade. He declined an offer to join the Casey Stengel All-Stars in the integrated California Winter League.

Less than two weeks after the World Series ended, eight members of the White Sox were indicted by a grand jury in Chicago. In November, Judge Kenesaw Mountain Landis was named baseball's first commissioner,

6. A Whole New Ball Game, 1920

replacing the three-man National Commission that had been in place since 1903. The Chicago-area federal judge signed a seven-year contract at $50,000 per year, and would begin his duties in the New Year. He was given the power to act in the game's best interest, which he did—suspending the eight White Sox awaiting trial the following spring.

7

Captain Wheat, 1921–1923

Wheat intensified contract negotiations in the 1920–21 offseason. In late January 1921, he received an offer from Ebbets, matching his 1920 salary of $8,000. Wheat responded with a counter offer of $15,000, an increase of $7,000, nearly doubling his take-home from the year prior. Ebbets countered with a 10 percent increase to $8,300, plus a $500 captain's bonus. Wheat had every intention of spending the year manning his large cattle ranch, adding an additional 160 acres in February, which increased his total to 325. He kept in shape chopping wood, walking amongst the hills, hunting, and playing on an indoor baseball team with his brother, Mack, and Casey Stengel. Wheat also made frequent trips to Kansas City, Kansas, to visit his mother and brothers, and conduct business.

"If I don't get an increase over last year's salary, I will not play ball this year," Wheat told Alpert Hager of the *Kansas City Kansan*. "I like to play baseball, but I can keep the wolf from the door without pastiming in a Brooklyn uniform."[1]

Wheat figured he had some bargaining leverage when Al Munro Elias released his updated career statistical records for current players. A veteran of 11 seasons, Wheat's name was featured throughout. He was third in hits (1,738), triples (120), and total bases (2,435). He was fifth in home runs (60), doubles (277), and at-bats. The numbers meant little to Ebbets, and as March progressed, the two parties had yet to come to an agreement. Wheat was not alone in his holdout negotiations. Three pitchers ignored Robinson's orders to report to Hot Springs, Arkansas, with pitchers and catchers. Per usual, Grimes was holding out in Minerva, Ohio, threatening to remain there to work at his rapidly growing auto garage business.

Grimes had somewhat of an advantage on past contract negotiations. In addition to the stellar 1920 season to refer to, the rules committee stepped back on the spitball ruling from the year before. Rather than the cessation of spitballs being thrown altogether, teams were allowed to allot two pitchers on their roster to throw the spitball for the duration of

7. Captain Wheat, 1921–1923

their career. Each league adopted the new ruling. Some teams chose not to name anyone, while others took full advantage. In all, 17 pitchers were "grandfathered" in as spitballers.

Other holdouts included Sherry Smith and Hy Myers. Abe Yager of the *Brooklyn Daily Eagle* alluded to that fact that there was some sort of collusion between roommates, Myers and Wheat, but predicted that the two would be there a week before the exhibition series with the Yankees. Not much had changed by mid–March as the Dodgers congregated in New Orleans, Louisiana, for spring training. On March 11, Wheat sent a telegram to the Brooklyn press with an update on contract negotiations:

> Mr. Ebbets has refused to meet my demands and I have positively refused salary offered.
> Have been in employ of Brooklyn Club for 12 years and have always played a brand of baseball that should earn me the right to demand a good salary.
> It is not fair to myself that I should continue playing ball for Brooklyn or anyone else for compensation received in past seasons.
> Know nothing of trade rumors, but it does not matter who I play ball for as long as am satisfied in regard to salary.[2]

Time away from camp brought about trade rumors for all of the absent players. The Boston Braves and Chicago Cubs were said to be ready to negotiate, willing to part with catchers, which the Dodgers needed. The Cardinals were also mentioned. Perhaps in a ploy to lure Wheat into signing, there was speculation that Ebbets was working on a swap of Smith to the Phillies for Stengel. Stengel had never been happy since leaving Brooklyn, first in Pittsburgh, then in Philadelphia. Robinson wrote to his holdouts every day, urging them to come to a compromise and report to spring training.

Wheat was beginning to grow antsy on the farm. He soon dropped his asking price to $9,000, a $200 increase from the Ebbets offer, to cover the mortgage on the land that he added to the Polo farm. Ebbets stood firm, as Wheat countered with the $8,800 plus a $1,000 bonus if the club finished in first-, second-, or third-place. Robinson accepted the contract with a bonus on behalf of the team via telegram. When Wheat showed up in Alexandria, Louisiana, he talked at length with Yager, touching on his dislike for training in New Orleans, who was going to be the front runner for the National League pennant, and his strategy for contract negotiations with Ebbets, about which he was very candid. With basically the same roster as the 1920 pennant-winners, Robinson was confident entering 1921. The only major roster move came in December 1920, when Marquard was shipped to Cincinnati for big left-hander, Walter "Dutch" Ruether. He was a 19-game

The Wheat family: Mary Helen, Zack, Daisy, and Zack, Jr., in the early 1920s (Kenny Dixon photo collection).

winner for the 1919 World Series champion Reds, but would have mixed results for the Dodgers over the next four seasons.

During the war years, a cheaper quality of wool was used in baseball composition, but in 1921, a livelier ball was introduced, leading to bloated

7. Captain Wheat, 1921–1923

batting numbers. Also affecting offensive production was the implementation of more baseballs into the game. Leading the pack was Babe Ruth, who had arguably his greatest season, establishing several records. He hit .378, with 59 home runs, 168 RBIs, 177 runs, and 145 walks. St. Louis Cardinals second baseman Rogers Hornsby dominated the senior circuit, leading the league in batting average, .397; runs; 131; hits, 235; doubles, 33; triples, 18; and RBIs, 126.

In 1921, another Giants player emerged that the press could compare to Wheat. His name was Frankie Frisch, an energetic switch-hitting infielder, who was quickly becoming a favorite of McGraw. A native of the Bronx, he was a four-sport star at Fordham University in New York City, earning the nickname "The Fordham Flash." With a slashing style, Frisch hit .341, had 211 hits, and stole a league-high 49 bases. The future Hall-of-Famer had few shortcomings in his game and would eventually be named team captain, helping the Giants to four consecutive National League pennants from 1921–'24. Wheat and Frisch formed a friendship that lasted throughout the rest of their lives.

Brooklyn had mixed results to start the 1921 season, opening 1–5, before winning 11 in a row. The one-and-a-half games behind the Pirates was as close as the Dodgers came to the pennant. There was infighting throughout the season. Kilduff and Olson came to blows in the clubhouse, and Johnston supposedly had to be forcibly restrained from going after Ebbets at Clarence Mitchell's wedding. No one would admit to the incidents, but Ebbets sent a message that no one was safe. He traded Pfeffer to the Cardinals in June for former Giants left-hander, Ferdie Schupp, and infielder, Hal Janvrin. In July, Konetchy was put on waivers and claimed by the Phillies. Neither move helped, as Brooklyn toggled between the first and second division, ending in fifth place with a 77–75 record, 17 games behind McGraw's World Series champions. Robinson infused similar tactics that had driven Brooklyn to the pennant the year before—rather than jump on the new hitter-happy techniques being used elsewhere—but they didn't equate to repeat success.

Wheat was enjoying the new batting trend. He always despised bunting, but his stance was emboldened by the power numbers that were being put up around the league. "Can't see any sense to it," he said referring to the bunt. "Can't see where a fellow should get up there and hit the ball so that maybe he'll get one base on the hit—and maybe none at all—while he passes up the chance to hammer the ball out of the lot."[3]

Bunting just didn't sync with Wheat's aggressive approach. "Perhaps if I would bunt oftener I would be better off," he admitted. "There is something to be said for a diversified system of attack. These fellows with nimble feet, who bury the ball in the dirt just in front of the plate and then beat the throw to first are all right in their place. They bat with their feet. I bat with my shoulders and wrists and eyes. Every man for his own style is my motto."[4]

Myers thought not bunting was to Wheat's detriment. "Zack Wheat has bunted twice in five years," said Myers. "If he would bunt oftener he would be a much better hitter. He could mix bunting with straight away hitting and give his batting average a twenty point boost."[5]

Robinson didn't seem to mind Wheat not bunting, even when he disobeyed a directive to do so. According to longtime *New York Times* sportswriter, Arthur Daly, once late in a game when it was obvious that a bunt was needed, Robinson "stood flat-footed in the coaching box, two hands in front of him in the unmistakable gesture of a man dropping a bunt." Along with the entire stadium, the pitcher saw this, subsequently throwing a fast one to hinder the bunt attempt. Wheat took a full swing, launching the ball onto Bedford Avenue. As he rounded third, Robinson gave a congratulatory slap to Wheat's backside and shouted, "Attaboy, Buck, that'sa way to hit 'em"[6]

There were instances when Wheat's disobeying of Robinson's orders ended in failures, but Wheat liked to tell about another time a directive wasn't followed—albeit unintentionally—resulting in a home run, this time on an instruction to put on the hit-and-run. "I hit an inside ball and it went over the right field fence for a home run," Wheat recalled with a laugh. "I came back to the bench and remembering the hit-and-run order, I said to Robbie: 'How was that?' Robbie replied: 'You should have hit behind the runner.' I said: 'I did, Robbie but I got it a little too high.'"[7]

By June, attendance was waning, attributed to the increase in batting. The ball was affecting fielding, too, as Wheat told Thomas Rice of the *Daily Eagle*:

> It's a joke to claim that the ball this year in the major leagues is no more lively than in the past. Outfielders this year are lying back 30 to 40 feet further than they ever did. They have to do that if they do not want the ball knocked over their heads. It goes with such a swift flight that if they stood where they stood last year they would be chasing extra base hits all the time. As it is, a great number of hits get away from us, no matter where we stand. You will notice that many long drives are made between center fielder and right fielder. Of course, there are the ideal shots anyhow, but this year we are missing many a fly or long drive that we would have gotten last year because the outfielders cannot get to the ball when it is shooting so fast. The other angle is also true. A number of pop hits are carrying away from the infielders and the outfielders are so far back that they cannot get in to take them. Fans are blaming a lot of infielders for missing balls that sail over them. They are panning the outfielders for not catching those short flies. They are not remembering that the outfielders are so far back that it is comparatively simple now for a sliced fly to come down between the outer and inner defenses and hop away for extra bases.
>
> We are so far out yonder that it is almost hopeless to nail a runner at the plate. I bet

7. Captain Wheat, 1921–1923

there are fewer men nabbed at the plate this season than ever before. Believe me, the ball hops. The outfield hit nowadays bounds high when it touches the ground, and seems to take on new life by meeting the dirt. The hit that we used to cut across on and block on the first bound now bounces so blamed high you can't reach it. Any outfielder in the big leagues will tell you he is missing blows that should have been nice long singles last season but in this day are skipping to the fence.

As for trying to trap a ball. It is almost suicidal. In addition to the risks always assumed in trapping we have now the difficulty that the ball has such speed on the first bounce that even if we get our hands on it the ball will generally tear through, or be deflected to one side. A trapped ball that gets away is pretty nearly always a sure home run on a large field, and we can't take the gamble. In former years we would play a first bounce close in a pinch, figuring to block it down with our bodies if we did not grab it in the hands. But no more. Even on the second or third bounce the ball has such speed that if it strikes a clod as big as your thumb it rises again and is over the head.

The lively ball has completely disarranged the outfield defense without the fans being aware of the fact. Doping out throws to the plate is almost a thing of the past, while even the safe precautionary throw to the base ahead to hold up the batter is dangerous because the ball may scoot by the infielders. I have seen more balls shoot through the third basemen this season than I ever hope to see again. It is happening on all teams.

An outfielder has always been taught to throw in on the first bounce. This year the first bounce is so hot that the odds are the man at the bag will have it flop out of his hands and so miss the runner, even when the throw is perfect. A throw may be perfect, and still, because of the English unconsciously put on the ball, or because of a people in the soil. It may rise over the baseman's head and wind up in the next State.

That keeps us guessing. With two or three men on bases and the score anywhere near close, we always wonder whether we will do more harm than good by making a logical throw that last year we would not have hesitated to make.[8]

It wasn't only the home runs that were disturbing, but also the velocity at which balls were going back through the pitcher's box. Grimes had a few close calls before suffering a thumb injury on his pitching hand on June 5, when he was protecting his face from a ninth-inning line drive off the bat of the Cubs' Turner Barber. Grimes missed one start and went on pitching with what was later diagnosed as a fractured thumb. It didn't show, as he led the National League in wins (22), complete games (30), and strikeouts (136).

A different baseball was supposedly introduced in July. Power numbers dropped as a whole, but Wheat continued on, hitting six home runs during the month. He was on his way to establishing a club record of 14, becoming the first Dodger to reach double digits since Tim Jordan hit a dozen in both 1906 and '08. Wheat took advantage of the remodeling of Ebbets Field over the next several years. The fences were being moved in as the balls were flying out of the park. In 1921 and '22 the right field fence was moved in to 296 and then 292 feet, respectively, before being moved back to

301 in '26. Left field was also modified, having dropped from 410 to 383 feet in 1920.

Wheat had also changed bat models, opting for a new make with a thicker barrel. "These bats with large ends, but with handles no larger than the ordinary, have a larger hitting surface. They are made for slugging by free swingers," he explained to the *Brooklyn Daily Eagle* in May 1922, as his success continued. "I have had the new model for two years and get good results, because it is suited to my swing."[9]

Wheat's teammates were also enjoying the deluge of growing batting numbers. At 31 years old, Jimmy Johnston began a three-year run of impressive batting numbers, and five years of consistent production, with the 1921 season being the high-point. He became the first Dodger to reach 200 hits since Willie Keeler's 202 in 1901, bettering him by one with 203. In 152 games, Johnston set career highs in average (.325), doubles (41), triples (14), home runs (5), and stolen bases (28)—all but the home runs led the club. He enjoyed a 20-game hitting streak from late May into June. In 1922 he hit for the first cycle in team history, in '23 matched both his 203-hit-.325 average of '21, and established career marks in runs (111) and RBIs (60). "Batting is the first thing a player thinks about when he crawls out of bed, and it's the last thing on his mind when the lights go out," Johnston once told F.C. Lane.[10]

Johnston was the batting standout, but Wheat put forth another solid season. In 148 games he hit .320 average, with 31 doubles, 10 triples, 14 home runs (12 coming at Ebbets), and 85 RBIs—the latter two led the team. He also topped the National League, drawing eight intentional walks. Fellow outfielder Tommy Griffith swatted a dozen home runs and batted over .300 (.312) for the first time since he hit .307 in his first full season in the big leagues in 1915. A star in the field, the speedy Griffith was a strong-armed right fielder, leading the National League in assists (27) and double plays (six). Part-time first baseman Ray Schmandt batted .306 in 95 games.

Grimes was by far Brooklyn's best pitcher, tying Pirates lefty Wilbur Cooper for most wins in the National League, 22, and was the sole leader in complete games, 30, and strikeouts, 136. Providing mound support to his gutsy performance were starters Cadore (13–14) and Ruether (10–13). Mitchell logged 11 wins going back and forth between starting and a relief role. In fact, spitballers were some of the most successful pitchers in 1921. The Cardinals' Bill Doak was tops in ERA (2.58) and winning percentage (.714). In the American League, the St. Louis Browns' Urban Shocker led in wins (27), while Red Faber, of the White Sox paced with a 2.47 ERA.

One of the few bright spots for the Dodgers was another winning record (12–10) over the pennant-winning Giants—the only club to

7. Captain Wheat, 1921–1923

do so. Wheat had a fruitful August against New York, collecting seven hits in 10 at-bats (four singles, two doubles, and a triple) in an August 11 double-header split, and four walks a week later. It did little to slow down the Giants, who wrested their first pennant since 1917 from the Pirates during a 10-game September winning streak. New York went on to win over their Polo Grounds co-tenant Yankees in eight games after falling behind 2–0. Ruth missed the final three games of the last best-of-nine series due to an infected arm and bad knee. The series held several firsts, including the Yankees first pennant, first subway series, first series to be played in its entirety in one ballpark, and the first to be broadcast on the radio.

Wheat once again declined an offer to play offseason ball. This time, Grimes put together a barnstorming team comprised of several Brooklyn teammates and a few St. Louis Cardinals that took the team to the Midwest, before heading to Cuba as part of the American Series. The trip further widened the growing divide between Grimes and his teammates (particularly his catcher, Otto Miller) as he pocketed a hefty purse at game in Austin, Minnesota, where he had played semi-pro ball a decade prior.

At the winter National League Meeting in New York City at the Waldorf Hotel, Ebbets was openly fielding offers for Wheat. Reports were that the owner was willing to sell or trade his veteran outfielder. Word had gotten out, and Ebbets knew that he would be confronted by fans, but he hadn't made it out of the hotel when two boys who had travelled from Brooklyn challenged him. "Please, Mr. Ebbets, you are not going to sell Wheat, are you?" pleaded the older boy.

"Or trade him, either," added the younger boy.

Ebbets smiled, "Why not?" he asked.

"Oh, because we like him better than anybody," responded the boy.[11]

Despite heavy off-season rumors of a trade to the Pirates and Reds, for the first time in years, Wheat signed his contract before the end of February. According to Len Wooster of the *Brooklyn Times Union*, Wheat "never reported in the spring, not even in his salad days looking better."[12] Had it not been for a surgical procedure that Daisy underwent, which called for his presence at home, Wheat would have been one of the first players to report to camp in Jacksonville, Florida, where the club last trained from 1907–'09. Holdouts were few compared to last year, but two of Brooklyn's top players—Grimes and Johnston—squabbled over salary with Ebbets, delaying their arrival. Grimes was nursing the sore thumb that was eventually diagnosed as a fracture. Unknowingly, he pitched the entire '22 campaign with the injury.

Johnston's absence allowed for the emergence of another Southern Association player—21-year-old infielder Andy High—who put up big numbers for the Memphis Chickasaws in 1921. The youngest of three major league brothers from Ava, Illinois, the diminutive High (five-foot-six, 155 pounds) earned a spot for himself amongst the proven Brooklyn veterans in 1922. When Johnston signed, Robinson found playing time for High at shortstop, before moving him back to third base and Johnston to shortstop, where he split time with Olson.

Robinson invited an abundance of pitchers to camp, including a 31-year-old minor league journeyman, whose career had been plagued by arm troubles. Charles Arthur "Dazzy" Vance had had brief stints with the Pirates and Yankees in 1915 and again with the Yankees in 1918. In between, the redhead kicked around the minor leagues, with so many stops that he once insisted, "I'll bet a hundred bucks that if I dropped in on every minor league camp in the country—and I wouldn't care how small the league was—I would know at least three men on every one of them."[13]

Vance finally found his way back to the majors when Larry Sutton—who had returned to Brooklyn as a scout after a few years with the Reds—signed 28-year-old catcher Hank DeBerry in early 1922 as a replacement for the aging Miller, who would retire at the end of the season. Vance and DeBerry, who left the University of Tennessee to play professionally and had some major league experience—40 games with the Cleveland Indians in 1916 and '17—had been battery mates with the New Orleans Pelicans of the Southern Association. DeBerry boldly insisted that the Dodgers sign Vance, too, or else he wouldn't play for Brooklyn. Ebbets was well aware of the pitcher, having passed on him numerous times. He initially scoffed at the minor leaguer's proposal, but finally conceded. It would be one of the greatest moves he ever made. Like his fellow Hall of Famer Burleigh Grimes, Vance had the utmost respect for Wheat, calling him "the hardest hitter I ever pitched to."[14]

When Wheat, who managed a few games in Robinson's absence during the trip north, arrived in Brooklyn to start the season, he went house-hunting, placing an ad in the *Brooklyn Daily Eagle*. Daisy had been pushing Zack for larger living quarters, having grown tired of apartments and hotels. He obliged, purchasing a 14-room house. Soon, Wheat was bringing home teammates and the occasional opponent after games. They were often met by large meals prepared by Daisy, who didn't think twice of setting six to eight extra places at the table. Some players took an extended stay or even made residence at the Wheats' abode. Zack Taylor lived there for three years. When he and his wife married, they moved in with the Wheats. "Our place, somehow, was just like home for the boys," Daisy fondly recalled a few decades later.[15]

Batting numbers, especially home runs, skyrocketed at the beginning

7. Captain Wheat, 1921–1923

of the season. The livelier baseball was called into question last year, but in 1922 the thicker barrel bats—like Wheat had begun using in '21—were getting a once over as usage increased and home runs continued to fly out of parks throughout the major leagues. Not surprisingly, the major league

Dazzy Vance changed the complexion of the Dodgers—both on and off the field—when he arrived in Brooklyn as an unheralded 31-year-old in 1922. Two years later, he would win the inaugural National League MVP award (National Baseball Hall of Fame and Museum).

ERA ballooned to 4.10, and the Phillies and Cardinals became the first National League teams to exceed 100 home runs with 116 and 107, respectively. According to Wheat, "The sluggers are deliberately trying for home runs this year more than they ever did before as Kenneth Williams of the Browns has admitted. With the new bats, and with the new policy at the plate by so many men who heretofore have regarded a home run as merely incidental, it is natural that there should be more long-distance hoists that get clear away for four bases."[16]

Wheat felt the playing field had been leveled. "Last spring we outfielders played out so far, even for notoriously weak batters that we had to telephone in to find whether men were on base. This year we are playing the regulation distance," he said.[17]

Batting statistics suggested something was going on, whether it be bat or ball. In addition to the home run influx, the National League batted .292. St. Louis's Hornsby had one of the greatest seasons in league history, putting together a Triple Crown campaign: .401 average, major league-leading 42 home runs, and National League leading 152 RBIs—the latter two National League records. The right-hander's 250 hits and 141 runs topped both leagues, and his 46 doubles were best the National League. The future Hall of Famer also hit safely in 33 straight games.

The American League wasn't far behind, batting .285. The junior circuit instituted a most valuable player award (yet to be known as such) to replace the Chalmers Award that was discontinued after the 1914 season. Voted on by eight writers, St. Louis Browns first baseman George Sisler won the award, leading the majors with a .420 average and 51 steals. He paced the American League with 134 hits, 18 triples, and 134 runs. For his efforts he was gifted a bronze metal and a cash prize.

Wheat was part of the league's early season power surge, hitting five home runs during the month of May. In June, he batted .375 with nine doubles, and was among the top home run hitters through the end of the month. On June 23, he tallied his 2,000th hit with an eighth-inning home run off the Giants' Phil Douglas at the Polo Grounds—the same place he got his first hit almost 15 years earlier. Wheat was the only active National Leaguer with 2,000 career hits, setting a lofty goal of Honus Wagner's record, 3,420. A few days later, on June 27, Wheat's three-hit effort helped pull the Dodgers into second place, five-and-a-half games behind New York. Things quickly dissolved during a western road trip, and, within a few weeks, Brooklyn found themselves in the second division, from which they never emerged.

In July, rumor floated of Wheat and Johnston to the Pirates for amongst others, catcher Walter Schmidt. Pittsburgh had been after Wheat

7. Captain Wheat, 1921–1923

dating back to the offseason, and Ebbets was looking for an infielder, but he denied wanting to trade two of his best players. Towards the end of the month, the Dodgers slipped to sixth place, where they would finish 76–78, 17 games behind the Giants, who were on their way to their second consecutive World Series title over the Yankees—this time a four-game sweep.

On August 8, Wheat was knocked unconscious in a home game against the Cubs. He took an inadvertent elbow to the chin by Chicago third baseman Marty Krug, was knocked out, and hit his head on the ground with what was described by Thomas Rice as "dangerous force." Wheat was out cold for "several minutes" but walked off on his own power, continued playing, and even hit a single later in the game. The next day he suited up "with a bruise on his chin and a bump on the back of his dome."[18]

During the season, Wheat was part of an advertisement campaign for Nuxated Iron, touted as an energy supplement. Created by E. Virgil Neal, a former hypnotist, the tablets consisted of iron and nux vomica, a derivative of the strychnine plant. Wheat was among a bevy of big-name athletes giving their endorsement, including Babe Ruth, and heavy-weight boxer Jack Dempsey. Wheat's testimonial read:

> Nuxated Iron has filled me with vim, energy and vitality, and I am sure that without it I would never have succeeded in some plays which have helped win games. I have never been a believer in taking anything except plain outdoor exercise, but the use of Nuxated Iron has convinced me that no matter how well a person may feel, they can get increased health and strength by taking it. I like to be on a winning team and next season earnestly advise all my brother players to use Nuxated Iron for the purpose of getting themselves in perfect condition.[19]

Wheat continued his pace, legging out a triple in three consecutive games from August 31 to September 2. A week later, September 9, he had the first multiple home run game of his career in a 6–5 extra-inning win at Ebbets Field over the Braves. There was some controversy behind one of Wheat's long balls, when it became caught in the crease of a flag that was flying from a staff in the center of the right field wall. Instead of going over the wall, it fell back into play, and Boston's outfield played it as a live ball. As Wheat circled the bases, the Braves put a tag on him, claiming he was out. The umpire-in-chief ruled it a home run. Boston countered that it should have been a double, but the home run stayed. Braves manager Fred Mitchell played the game under protest, but when the matter was put to National League president, John Heydler, he upheld the home run, after Ivy Olson pointed out that the location of the flag was such that the ball would have cleared the wall had it not been for the obstruction.

Wheat played through a painful thumb injury and back pain for much of the last two months of the season. He had an outstanding September, including nine multi-hit games over the final two weeks. He appeared in 152 games, the most since he played 156 in 1910, when he was 22. Batting the entire season as the cleanup hitter, Wheat reached 200 hits for the first of three times in his career (201), establishing career-highs and club records with 16 home runs and 112 RBIs—becoming the first Dodger to drive in 100 runs. He also led National League outfielders with a .991 fielding percentage. After the season, future Hall of Fame middle infielder Rabbit Maranville said of Wheat: "That guy has robbed me of more hits than any player in baseball," calling him one "of the smartest outfielders I have ever played against."[20]

Wheat led the club in every batting statistic except runs scored (Johnston, 110). Despite his consistent success throughout his career, pitchers seldom threw at Wheat to try to intimidate him. "For one thing, he was nobody's enemy," wrote sportswriter, Dan Daniel. "For another, it was dangerous to get him angry."[21]

Most managers followed the example of Branch Rickey, then general manager of the St. Louis Cardinals, who instructed his pitchers, "Don't get Zack mad. Just let him be."[22]

That didn't mean pitchers placated Wheat at the plate. Johnny Cooney used his hesitation pitch with success against Wheat. The left-handed thrower, who would transition to a full-time position player later in his career, first with the Dodgers, struck Wheat out the first time he saw it. Cooney began a long deliberate wind-up, went through his motion, planted his left foot and stopped, with the ball behind his ear. Wheat relaxed, and with the bat on his shoulder, Cooney threw the ball by him for the final out of the inning.

"What was that?" asked a miffed Wheat to home plate umpire, Hank O'Day.

"I guess it was strike three," replied O'Day, removing his mask.

"How about a balk?" Wheat argued.

"Don't be silly," retorted O'Day. "He motioned to throw the ball to the plate, didn't he? And he did throw to the plate, didn't he?"

"But he hesitated," responded Wheat.

"There ain't anything in the rules against that," said O'Day, getting the last word.[23]

As a team, the Dodgers batted .290 in 1922, which was only good enough for sixth in the National League. Behind Wheat was Johnston (.319, team-high 18 stolen bases), Myers (.317, 89 RBIs), High (27 doubles, 13 triples), Tommy Griffith (.316), and Bert Griffith (.308), the last two of whom, unrelated, split time in right field. Ruether and Vance were Brooklyn's most consistent pitchers. Rebounding from his disappointing first season with the club, Ruether

7. Captain Wheat, 1921–1923

was the staff's only 20-game winner (21–12). His 25 complete games also led the team—both would be career-highs. Vance (18–12), led the National League with 134 strikeouts (the first of seven consecutive seasons doing so), and his five shutouts topped the majors. He was aided by an undershirt that drove batters, managers, and the press to fits. Vance wore an old long-sleeve shirt that he had cut into slits. When he threw, a pinwheel of fabric hid the ball, making it difficult for batters to decipher between his fastball and biting curve.

An aging ball club, the Dodgers saw extended injuries to several players. It was a wonder Grimes accomplished much of anything. The fractured thumb, which he unknowingly pitched with, not only caused him to modify his delivery, but it left him unable to throw his spitball effectively. His relationship with nearly everyone in the organization continued to deteriorate, from Ebbets, to Robinson, to teammates. It got to the point where he was communicating with very few people, including Miller, who would leave the Dodgers to manage the Atlanta Crackers of the Southern Association.

Grimes wasn't alone in drawing the ire of members within the organization. In late September, a front-page article of the *Brooklyn Daily Eagle* called out three of the Dodgers high profile players, including Wheat: "Three stars—namely, Burleigh Grimes, Hi Myers and Zack Wheat—all troublemakers, have been placed on the block for sale or barter. All three gave differences with the club from time to time regarding salary. It is part of the program to rid the club of those who are likely to cause dissension in the ranks, and replace them with players who are not a troublesome disposition so as to provide perfect harmony."[24]

Ebbets shopped all three during the winter in New York City at the Waldorf-Astoria, with the Cardinals and Pirates once again vying—and eventually passing—on Wheat. When it was reported that Wheat was once again threatening to retire if his contract demands weren't met, Ebbets didn't seem concerned. "If he wants to quit he is at liberty to do so," he told the *Brooklyn Daily Eagle*. "The Brooklyn Club will not permit Mr. Wheat or any other player to dictate to it."[25]

A smear campaign about Wheat's deteriorating skills had been quietly started, likely circulated from within the Brooklyn organization, claiming that he was past his prime. In late December, a lengthy article was written by James J. Murphy in the *Brooklyn Daily Eagle* about the absurdity of such statements. Taking a sarcastic tone, Murphy wrote, "The old war horse is so feeble and his underpinning so crippled that he stepped out last season and led the entire array of talent, old and young in the National League in fielding." He added, "The veteran is slipping so fast that he is still able to set the pace for his teammates in all branches of offense, too."[26]

Zack Wheat

For years, Wheat was the Dodgers' de facto power-hitter, a label he never felt comfortable with. In February 1923, Ebbets finally acquired what he thought was a bona fide long ball hitter in St. Louis Cardinals first baseman Jack Fournier. He was traded for Wheat's close friend and roommate on the road, Hy Myers, and first baseman, Ray Schmandt, a St. Louis native who never reached expectations in Brooklyn, and would never play another major league game again. After years of chasing him, the Cardinals could have had Wheat, but opted for Myers instead. The speedy outfielder, slowed by injury, played in just 96 games, batting .300 with 18 doubles in 1923 and hitting .210 in 43 games in '24. He was out of the major leagues by May 1925, after a three-game stint with the Reds. During those seasons, Wheat would enjoy some of his best years at the plate.

The Dodgers were the fourth team for the 32-year-old Fournier. Born in Michigan's Upper Peninsula, his family moved to Washington state when he was a toddler. It was on the West Coast where he began his minor league career in 1908, at age 15, with Aberdeen-Seattle in the Northwest League. He joined the Chicago White Sox in 1912, had back-to-back .300 seasons in 1914 and '15, struggled in '16, and within the first month of the '17 season was put on waivers. When no one signed him, his contract was sold to the Los Angeles Angels in the Pacific Coast League. He spent the next three years back on the West Coast, but for a 27-game stint with the Yankees in 1918, when first baseman Wally Pipp joined the Navy.

Charles Comiskey filed a grievance that he still had the rights to Fournier, but when that was denied, he joined the Cardinals in 1920. Fournier had his best year to date in 1921 (.343, 16 home runs, 103 runs), but he faltered in 1922. His play suffered to the point of being pulled from the lineup down the stretch as the Cardinals battled for the pennant. When it was apparent that future Hall of Famer, Jim Bottomley was the club's first baseman of the future, Fournier became dispensable. The trade looked to be a flop the day after completion, when Fournier asked Commissioner Landis to place him on the voluntary retired list in order to work full-time as an insurance salesman in St. Louis. The decision to retire left Brooklyn with nothing to show from the trade.

Ebbets appeared to have ulterior motives for the transaction, as Fournier was the only remaining player for the Players Union presidency and was in jeopardy of being sent to the minors (Wheat was in the running for vice president and was the club representative for the executive board). The Dodgers' owner hoped acquiring Fournier might provide some grace with the Union, which he had been grousing about throughout the offseason. "It's a fine situation when a lawyer from the middle West tells

7. Captain Wheat, 1921–1923

our players to take part in a hold-up for more money and tries to run our affairs," he complained in February.[27] Ebbets singled out Wheat, who was holding out for $10,000, saying he had been with Brooklyn "too long."[28]

The Dodgers stayed in Florida for spring training, but Ebbets moved the club to Clearwater. The 1922 season had been one of transition for the Dodgers' owner. He looked for a change of venue, and the Gulf Coast town experiencing a real estate boom held great appeal. Early in the year, his divorce from Minnie, his wife of over four decades, was finalized after over three years of deliberation. By May, Ebbets married Grace Slade, nearly 20 years his junior, whom he had been involved with for years. His health issues mounted as the season progressed. Clearwater would prove some respite for his ailments. He and Grace would soon build a home there on Druid Road.

The Dodgers would also take a liking to Clearwater. Frank Graham wrote, "So many Brooklyn fans trekked down every year to watch them that after a while the town took on the aspects of a little Brooklyn, and many of the sights and sounds of Ebbets Field were duplicated in the Clearwater ball park."[29] The Dodgers remained in Clearwater until 1932, before moving on to other locations, including stops in Cuba (1941–'42) and Ciudad Trujillo, Dominican Republic (1948). The Clearwater locale was the longest running until Vero Beach (1948–2008).

Wheat saw very little of the new location, as he continued to hold out in Polo, asking for an increase or a two-year deal. Robinson begged Ebbets to telegram Wheat, and the veteran's teammates considered raising funds to make up the mere $500 difference in pay. Ebbets curiously allowed the *Brooklyn Standard Union* to run the telegram volley between him and Wheat. "His object in doing this is rather obscure," wrote the *Standard Union*, "as the missives fail to show any reason the club's leading hitter should not get the raise he asks."[30]

Ebbets did everything but give into Wheat's demands. He threatened to pull the present contract and not renew it, but Wheat stood firm. The Dodgers' owner then threatened to not only make Wheat relinquish his title of captain, but said if an agreement wasn't reached, he could go on the voluntary retirement list. Ebbets also explained that he tried to trade Wheat, but his salary was too large for other teams, and those that did have players with similar contracts didn't want to swap them for Wheat. Finally, when Ebbets questioned Wheat's loyalty and the fact that this matter could affect his contract for years to come, the outfielder wired that he was leaving for Florida at once. He still held out, working out independently at local diamonds, but his demands were never met. Finally, on the last day of March he signed.

Zack Wheat

Fournier was also beginning to have a change of heart. He had signed on to manage a semi-pro team in Centralia, Illinois, but reached out to Brooklyn officials, reporting that he had been working out frequently and was interested in entering contract negotiations. He was in the lineup by early May, far exceeding expectations. On June 19, he went six-for-six against the Phillies and had a chance for a seventh hit in the ninth, but Robinson sent a runner who was thrown out at second. Fournier was irate, suspecting that Robinson did it to preserve his record of seven hits in seven at-bats set in 1892 as a member of the Orioles.

Fournier's bat was feared, but his defense was atrocious, driving both Brooklyn fans and teammates—particularly pitchers—to fits. It was one of the reasons he had been shuttled to the minor leagues mid-career, and he seemed to have no intentions of improving his glove work. In the Cardinals' first series at Ebbets Field in mid–May, Ruether looked to Fournier for a scouting report on Hornsby. The first baseman told the lefty to pitch one of the game's premier batters inside. He did and Hornsby hit a shot down the left field line for an easy double. Ruether returned to the mound after backing up second base.

"You said he couldn't hit ball on the inside," quizzed the pitcher.

"No," replied Fournier. "I didn't say that. I just said to pitch to him on the inside. Son, I have a wife and family to look out for. You don't think I'm going to tell you to pitch outside to him and have him hit one of those line drives at me, do you?"[31]

Wheat and Fournier were both batting forces, but they had different approaches, especially with their bats. According to Brooklyn's clubhouse man, Dan Comerford, Wheat was tough on his bats as opposed to Fournier. "Jacques Fournier, the heaviest slugger of the club, is one of the easiest man on bats I ever saw. He had but two all one season. He's very fussy about his bat. He calls it 'his baby' and won't let anyone else touch it," said Comerford. "Zack Wheat, the other slugger, a couple of dozen during the season. Besides, he doesn't object to other batters using his bats, but rather encourages them to do this."[32]

A weight of the bat didn't mean much to Wheat either. "The weight of a bat is of no particular consequence in my style of hitting," he told F.C. Lane. "It's the snap that you get into your wrists that drives the ball and naturally you will get more snap with a lighter bat. I once used a bat that weighed 46 ounces. I now prefer a bat that doesn't weigh over 40."[33]

Wheat, along with former teammate Jake Daubert, came into the 1923 season as one of the elder statesman of the National League. Wheat had a career average of .307 and his career numbers led all National Leaguers:

7. Captain Wheat, 1921–1923

at-bats (6,917), hits (2,121), doubles (337), triples (142), and total bases (3,012). Wheat picked up where he left off in 1922. He hit safely in all 13 games in April, but it wasn't enough to keep the Dodgers—who started the season 4–12—out of last place by May 1. In a month's time, they climbed to second place, thanks in part to Wheat's 20-game hit streak from May 7 to May 30.

Between Wheat, Fournier, and Johnston, who had the last great season of his career, the three veterans supplied plenty of run support. Fournier provided the lineup with a power threat never seen before in Brooklyn. In 1923, the first of three straight years of huge batting numbers, he batted .351, topping the club in doubles (30), triples (13), home runs (22), and RBIs (102)—the first of three straight seasons reaching triple figures. He also went over 300 total bases in each of those campaigns. Even with knee troubles, Johnston eclipsed 200 hits (203), including 29 doubles, and 11 triples. He also led the club with 16 stolen bases.

During the summer, the *New York Morning Telegram* ran a "Baseball Popularity Contest" amongst the three New York teams. The winner would take home a Stephens Foursome automobile. Ruth withdrew from the contest after declaring that the publicity he frequently received would skew the voting, but fans still wrote his name in. Early tabulations had Reuther as a surprising leader, and by the end of the month, it was a three-way contest between the left-handed pitcher, Wheat, and Frisch of the Giants. Envelopes of signatures were sent to the *Telegram* in support of players, with fans coming out in droves for Wheat. Letters to the editor were frequent, touting both his on-field exploits and off-the-field congeniality. "Zack Wheat is a gentleman at all times and all places. He is known for his hospitality and good nature and always has a hearty welcome for his friends in his home," wrote Clyde Sid Jones, editor and publisher of the *Polo News-Herald* in a letter to the *Morning Telegram*.[34]

Wheat was still batting over .400 in the third week of June and was leading the National League in batting into July. During a July 7 doubleheader split at Ebbets Field against the Cardinals, he injured his left ankle, and the next day he had to be removed mid-game. Limited to pinch-hitting duties over the next few days, his ankle failed to respond to treatments. Wheat was referred to a doctor in Brooklyn, whose x-rays revealed torn ligaments, a bone chip, and an old fracture that hadn't healed properly resulting in overlapping bones. A cast was put on his ankle, and he was sent home to Polo for two weeks of recovery, set to rejoin the team when they were scheduled to be in St. Louis at the end of July.

Wheat was visibly unstable upon his return against the Cardinals on July 30. "It may be some time before Wheat can field," reported Thomas

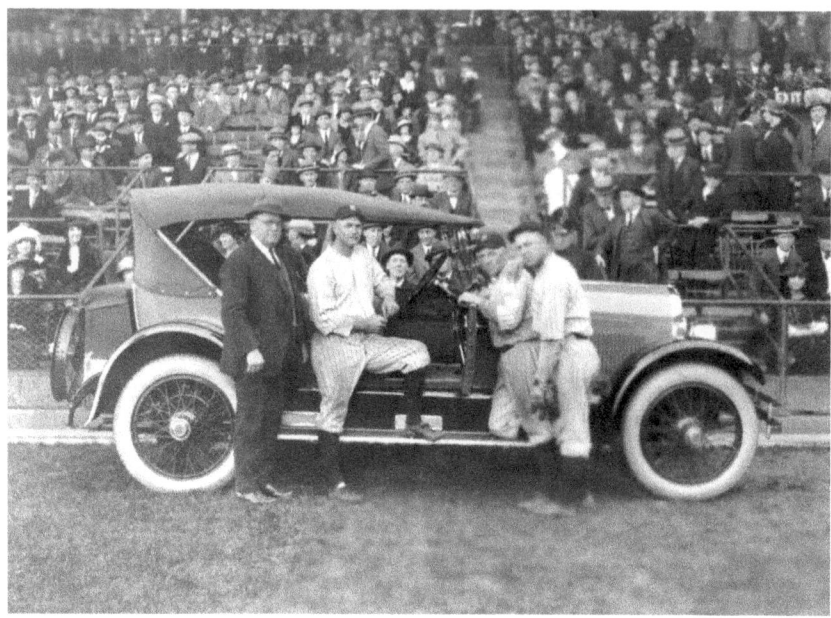

(From left to right) Robinson, Wheat, Johnston, and Grimes posing with Wheat's prize Stephens Foursome automobile awarded for being named most popular player in New York City in a poll done by the *New York Morning Telegraph* during the 1923 season (Kenny Dixon photo collection).

Rice after Wheat flew out as a pinch hitter. Two days later he was called on again. He limped to the plate in the ninth inning, pulling the first pitch he saw from spitballer Bill Doak into the right field stands for a two-run home run. It gave the Dodgers a 6-5 lead—the lone pinch-hit home run of Wheat's career. The Cardinals countered with a run in the bottom-half of the inning and eventually won 7-6 in 14 innings. Wheat's ankle was put back in a cast, and he was once again advised to convalesce in Polo. Rice wrote that if the injury didn't heal, "Wheat's baseball days will be over."[35]

Wheat rejoined the team in Pittsburgh a week later and was summoned to the hotel room of rookie pitchet Leo Dickerman. The right-hander had jumped out to a 5-1 record by the end of May, but struggled since, with a 2-8 record. Earlier in the day, he was saddled with yet another a loss, after being knocked out of the game after just two innings. When Wheat arrived, Dickerman was furious, venting to catcher Zack Taylor about what he saw was indifference by his teammates. "From now on it's every man for their self!" shouted Dickerman. Taylor took offense to this and went after his roommate.

7. Captain Wheat, 1921–1923

Dickerman ran around the room, eluding the enraged Taylor. "You're the captain, DO something!" shouted Dickerman to Wheat.

Wheat did do something. Without a word, he walked over, locked the door and put the key in his pocket. Dickerman showed up at the park the next day with a black eye.[36]

A few more setbacks with his ankle kept Wheat on the bench until September, as the Dodgers finished with the same record as the year before—76–78, resulting in another sixth-place finish. When he did get in the lineup, Wheat never played more than a couple days in a row, followed by consecutive days of rest. It was apparent that he was hurting. "At this writing it looks as though it would for the best interests of all concerned if the silent granger was sent back to Polo, Mo., to pursue the peaceful life of the agrarian for the rest of the season," wrote the *Brooklyn Standard Union* in late August.[37]

Wheat appeared in just 98 games, starting a scant 18 after the early July ankle injury. It was the first time he appeared in less than 105 (1918) other than the 26 appearances in 1909. He did hit .375, but was bested for the batting title by Hornsby, who batted .384 in 107 games. The Cardinals' second baseman was plagued by marital problems, accusations by St. Louis management of faking an injury, and a painful rash, but he still collected his fifth consecutive batting crown, besting teammate, Jim Bottomley's .371. Wheat and Fournier became the first Brooklyn teammates to hit over .350 and were one of three duos to do so in '23 (Bottomley and Hornsby on the Cardinals and the Cleveland Indians' Tris Speaker [.380] and Joe Sewell [.353]).

Once again, Robinson's pitching staff struggled besides pitching stalwarts, Grimes and Vance. In his second year of a two-year contract, Grimes had much less turmoil in his season. He returned to the 20-win mark (21–18), led the majors in complete games (33), and the National League in games started (38) and innings pitched (327). He and Vance (18–15)—who enjoyed a 10-game winning streak—tied for the league lead in hit batters, 11, and the latter led the majors in strikeouts (197). The only other Dodger to record double-digit wins was Ruether, with 15.

During his time away from the lineup, Wheat observed a shift in ballplayers' approach. The following year, in a lengthy expose in the *Kansas City Star*, Wheat mentioned how he noticed that players "are taking their game more seriously now than when I broke in." He added, "Larger crowds attend, salaries have increased and a fellow can make a comfortable living and save enough to tide him over when he steps down by hitting around .350 each year."[38]

This, in turn, changed Wheat's attitude. "You might say that I did not wake up until living thirteen years in the National League," he expounded.

"I decided that I could improve myself with a little more care by taking my time at the plate and trying for a base hit every time I faced a pitcher."[39]

The *Morning Telegram*'s popularity contest concluded in mid-September, with Wheat taking the honors. He tallied 860,926 votes, well ahead of Frisch (540,681) and Ruether (148,899). Wheat sent a telegram from Cincinnati:

> I am happy to know that I have been judged by the fans as being the most popular ball player on the three Greater New York clubs. Through *The Morning Telegram* I wish to express my sincere thanks to each and every fan who voted for me. I want them to know that I heartily appreciate their feeling toward me as I value it highly. It is a great pleasure to know that at the end of this, my fifteenth season with the Brooklyn club, my playing has won many friends for me. I regard the Stephens car more than a prize. To me it is a gift from those to whom I have always endeavored to give my best efforts. I also want to thank *The Morning Telegram*. But for it the friendship existing between the fans and myself would not have been fully disclosed.[40]

On September 30, Wheat was presented with his Stephens Foursome automobile before the game against the Phillies. He was driven around the field to show it off. Frisch, who had led the National League in hits (223) and total bases (311), paid Wheat a high compliment. "You can talk about Hornsby and Ruth, but Wheat drives a ball through the infield about as powerfully as anybody I ever saw," said the Giants second baseman.[41]

The Dodgers finished 19-and-a-half games behind the pennant-winning Giants. New York was led to a third straight World Series by a roster that included eight future Hall of Famers, all position players: High Pockets Kelly, Frisch, Travis Jackson, Hack Wilson, Youngs, Billy Southworth, Bill Terry, and Fred Lindstrom. Over the past few years the aging McGraw, still at the height of his managerial powers, had changed his approach. He stopped wearing a uniform, opting instead for a suit. Lee Allen wrote that McGraw "remained in the dugout shadow, still yapping at the umpires but letting his aides, Hughie Jennings and Jesse Burkett, pals who went so far back in time with him, relay his signals to the players."[42]

Wheat stayed in New York City to watch the Yankees beat the Giants in six games for their first World Series title. Wheat then drove his new vehicle west, making it as far as Macon, Missouri, before rain and muddy roads halted the trip. He stored the car in a garage in Macon for the winter and made it to Kansas City, Missouri, in time to play with the Casey Stengel All-Stars alongside Bob Meusel, Irish Meusel, and Dazzy Vance against the Kansas City Monarchs, champions of the Negro Leagues. It was a team that had future Hall of Famers pitcher, Jose Mendez, and pitcher/outfielder, Bullet Rogan.

The most popular player honor was a great bargaining tool for Wheat. Ebbets would do all he could to keep Wheat's pay the same, while still

7. Captain Wheat, 1921–1923

dangling him to other teams. "Zack is slipping as a fielder, but he still wields a wicked war club and would be snapped up by the opposition," said the owner in November during negotiations and trade baiting. "And by the same token, Zack would not object to going either to St. Louis or Chicago, as either is nearer to dear old Polo, MO., than Brooklyn."[43]

Wheat might have been intrigued by either St. Louis or Chicago, but as his success at Sportsman's Park continued, there was an appeal to playing there, especially as Browns owner Phil Ball continued to make renovations. He replaced the old wooden bleachers in the outfield with concrete stands and added a covered pavilion that ran from the right-field foul line to the centerfield bleachers. The second deck was also expanded down both foul lines. Wheat certainly would have been attracted to the short right field stands, measuring just 310 feet.

Ebbets' efforts to squelch a raise were hurt when his son, Charles Ebbets, Jr., offered Hornsby a reported $275,000 cash offer at the winter meetings in December. Wheat would threaten to join the Simmons (IL) Bedmakers of the upstart Midwest League, but, in the end, nothing materialized, and Wheat would see his salary increase from his 1923 take of $10,000 to $14,000 for what would be a memorable '24 campaign.

8

A Season to Remember, 1924

In February 1924, Wheat sold his farm and livestock in Polo, Missouri, via auction. He soon purchased a 160-acre plot of land nearby, building a modified colonial home designed by a Brooklyn architect. He adorned it with rocks from different ballparks. "I am a ballplayer in summer and a farmer in winter time," he told F.C. Lane. "I aim to be a success at both."[1]

Wheat arrived in Clearwater, Florida, in good shape. A loose atmosphere permeated as Robinson let the veteran team do as they pleased. Players raved about the conditioning benefits of walking several miles while play golf, but Wheat declined, opting to save on his legs and other injuries, such as the oblique strain he suffered in training camp while playing golf in 1915. "I've spent most of my time between and after workouts sitting in rocking chairs in front of the hotel, talking and reading," he said. "The idea of walking five or ten miles for the sake of exercise appealed to me not at all."[2]

The tenor of the 1924 season was upbeat from the start. Attendance was up for the first time in years. Ebbets and Steve McKeever soaked in the adulation and arguments that came their way from their benches in the back of the stands. From the get-go, it was evident that Wheat was playing some of the best ball—at least hitting-wise—of his career. He had one of two five-hit games of the season—all singles against the Phillies on April 19. A fast start carried over into May, when he batted .404 over 25 games, rapping seven doubles and five home runs. On May 3, he clubbed a pair against Philadelphia during a four-hit effort—the first multi-home run game of his career. The second home run was the 100th of his career, making him the 12th player to accomplish the feat. In a four-game stretch between May 3 and 6, Wheat went 11-for-17, with a double and four home runs. Three weeks later, on May 23, Wheat celebrated his 36th birthday at Forbes Field, with a solo blast off the Pirates' Johnny Morrison, in a 3–1 Brooklyn win. Wheat was shifted to the third spot in the order after a dozen years as the cleanup hitter (now occupied by Fournier) and flourished.

8. A Season to Remember, 1924

Robinson could see that his veteran-ladened club had a chance at the pennant but needed more of a pitching staff than Vance, Grimes, and a mediocre supporting cast. On June 14, Ebbets bolstered the rotation by acquiring spitballer Bill Doak from the St. Louis Cardinals for Leo Dickerman. At 33 years old, Doak, the two-time National League leader in ERA (1914 and '21), had been struggling over the past year-and-a-half. Grimes helped rejuvenate Doak's spitball, and after a 1–3 start for Brooklyn, he went on a ten-game winning streak that lasted for over two months (July 15 to September 22). Vance had a 15-game winning streak of his own during that time (July 11–September 18), throwing complete games in all but one of the starts in that span—a no decision against the Phillies on September 2 when he was pulled after allowing four earned runs in the first inning. Along with Grimes, the triumvirate's pitching kept the Dodgers in the pennant until the final days of the season.

Wheat showed no signs of slowing down. When asked by Joseph H.

Once best friends, former teammates Wilbert Robinson (right) and John McGraw are pictured in 1915. The two had a falling out while coaching together for the New York Giants in 1913, leading to Robinson taking over Brooklyn Dodgers managerial duties in 1914. The two managed against each other for 18 seasons, with the 1924 season being one of the most memorable (Library of Congress, Prints & Photographs Division [LC-DIG-ggbain-16227]).

Zack Wheat

Applegate of the *Brooklyn Daily Eagle* what the secret to his longevity was, the thoughtful Wheat pushed (mostly) sober living:

> In order to be successful in baseball or any other line of athletics a man must lead a good, clean life. Late hours and other forms of dissipation in athletics make for a short life but a merry one. If a ball player keeps himself in good condition his chances for success are increased. It has always been my idea to keep myself in good shape and to give the best in me. I am not boasting when I say that I believe I am always in pretty fair shape, and because of my physical condition I am able to judge accurately the balls offered to me when at bat. If I did not keep myself in good condition I do not think my eye sight would be as good as it is. Condition means a great deal in baseball.[3]

Wheat's statement might have been a warning to the team's growing unruliness off the field. He was in the minority in his good, clean way of life, as Brooklyn's famed Daffiness Boys were starting to take shape in a group that was known as the "4 for 0 club," a wink to the 0-for-4 they would have at the plate after an eventful night out on the town. It provided a camaraderie that hadn't been seen in years, creating a loose environment that equated to winning. Vance, in the middle of an MVP season, was the ringleader of a group that in the next few years would include: Fournier (who served as the group's bookie for horse racing); outfielder, Dick Cox; infielder Cotton Tierney; and pitchers, Jesse Petty and Rube Ehrardt. As the troop grew, so did their exploits. Vance put forth the motto: "Raise all the hell you want but don't get caught."[4]

Just because Wheat didn't participate in the hijinks didn't mean he had immunity from the wrath of teammates. During the 1924 season, his son, Zack, sometimes travelled with the team during East Coast trips, sitting in the dugout wearing a specially made Brooklyn uniform. The Dodgers were in Boston for a game, and young Zack was along with the team. Wheat caught the last out of the game. With the clubhouse in centerfield, closer to him than the dugout, he motioned for his son to come out to him. Zack, Jr., sat motionless on the bench. Irritated, his father ran toward the dugout. When he got to him, the elder Wheat asked, "Did you see me waving for you?"

The boy nodded.

"Then why didn't you come?" Wheat inquired.

"I couldn't," the boy replied.[5]

A vexed Wheat pulled his son off the bench. There was a ripping sound, and it was quickly apparent why he didn't go to his father—he was nailed to the bench. The culprit was Grimes.

For the first five months of the season, the Dodgers were nestled comfortably within the first division, never more than six-and-a-half games

8. A Season to Remember, 1924

from the front-running Giants. It seemed to be a foregone conclusion that McGraw's club would win their fourth straight National League pennant. That began to change the last week of August. On Sunday, August 24, Brooklyn was embarrassed, allowing a season-high 17 runs to the Cardinals in St. Louis (a total matched in another loss to the Cardinals on September 16). The next day, the Dodgers began a club-record 15-game winning streak that carried them from third place, to a first-place tie, to a half-game behind the Giants in the standings on September 6.

The next day, Brooklyn oversold tickets to the game as another 6,000 crashed through the Ebbets Fields gates with the aid of a telephone poll, stampeding into the park. "It was madness on and off the field as the throng heaved back and forth in the stands and spilled into the outfield as hardly a spectator watched the game from the seat he was supposed to be in," Glenn Stout wrote of the pre-game pandemonium. The Giants won a wild contest, 8–7, dropping the Dodgers one-and-a-half games back. Wheat had one of 11 ground-rule doubles that were lost in the throng.

Wheat's aggressive approach served him well when batting numbers spiked in the 1920s. Sportswriter Harry Grayson said Wheat's swing "uncoiled like a steel spring" (National Baseball Hall of Fame and Museum).

Zack Wheat

Wheat enjoyed the best month of his career that September. He slugged 19 extra base hits, including nine doubles, four triples, and six home runs, including a thrilling two-out, game-winner, in the bottom of the 12th inning of the first game of a doubleheader against the Cardinals on September 18 at Ebbets Field. Wheat topped 200 hits (212, including a league-high

St. Louis Cardinals second baseman Rogers Hornsby, who beat Wheat in the batting race in 1923 and '24 even though Wheat batted .375 both seasons (National Baseball Hall of Fame and Museum).

8. A Season to Remember, 1924

149 singles) for the second time in three seasons, and had his fourth hitting streak of at least 20—a 24-game run that spanned from August 21 to September 10. He became the second National Leaguer to reach that many over 20, matching Hugh Duffy, and third major leaguer, trailing Tris Speaker's five. During the streak, Brooklyn enjoyed the 15-game win streak, that included four doubleheaders sweeps in four days against the Phillies on September 1, 2, and 3, and Braves on September 4. Wheat played all six games in Philadelphia at the Baker Bowl, where he had great success throughout his career. For the series he went 13-for-27, with a pair of doubles and triples, three home runs, and 14 RBIs. A bulk of that came in the second game on September 3, when he went three-for-four with a double, two home runs, and a career-high six RBIs.

The batting totals were vindication for Wheat as other parts of his game continued to draw more criticism. "Fielding is good and so is base running, but the manager will overlook a lot of faults in the player who bats for .375," he told F.C. Lane.[6] For the second time in as many years, Wheat was beat out by Hornsby's .424 for the batting title—his fifth consecutive batting crown. The 49-point differential was the largest in National League history, trailing the 75-point American League record set by Philadelphia Athletics Nap Lajoie (.426), over Baltimore Orioles Mike Donlin (.347) in 1901. Wheat had the utmost respect for the St. Louis second baseman. "There have been a lot of nice hitters, but there has been only one Rogers Hornsby," said Wheat.[7] Wheat's other batting numbers included 41 doubles (team high), eight triples, 14 home runs, 97 RBIs, and 92 runs scored.

With the pennant in the balance, tensions were at a fever pitch, exemplified by a heated series with the Cubs in late September. Brooklyn was incensed by questionable pitching choices by Chicago in a game with the Giants a few days earlier. In the first game of the Cubs-Dodgers series—a 2–1, 12-inning Brooklyn victory—one of the Dodgers was spiked by a member of the Cubs, infuriating them even more. The next day, Brooklyn shortstop Johnny Mitchell gave the culprit a hard tag on the head during another extra inning affair, a 10-inning, 5–4 Chicago victory.

The Dodgers were desperate for a win, and Robinson badly wanted Grimes to pitch the next day. The only problem was that the pair were no longer on speaking terms. Robinson feared that Wheat was after his managerial job, but he turned to his captain—one of the few teammates Grimes was friendly with—to talk the petulant pitcher into moving up his start day. Grimes initially declined Wheat's proposition before agreeing under one condition—that he would be able to address only the eight other players in the lineup during a closed-door meeting. Wheat relayed Grimes's wishes to Robinson, who in turn let Wheat gather the team together. When the position players arrived in the locker room, they found Grimes waiting for them with a leg up on a bench.

"I'm gonna pitch this game tomorrow," Wheat recalled Grimes saying. "Anybody who doesn't wanta play had better get out now."[8] No one said a word. The game was intense from the start. The first time around the Cubs order, Grimes knocked down each batter with the first pitch, even buzzing his mound adversary, Grover Alexander, whom Grimes held in high regard. The next time Wheat came to the plate, Alexander returned the favor, throwing at the back of his head. "We finally won the game 8–6, but I was never in one that was as bitterly played," recalled Wheat. "Everyone was ready to fight if you just happened to look at them a little too long."[9]

After the contentious game, which was sponsored by the Brooklyn Chamber of Commerce, the Dodgers were transported via automobiles to the Chamber of Commerce building for a banquet to recognize their performance during the season to date. Following a meal and some tributes, the players were taken to the 160th Armory at Bedford and Atlantic Avenue to be further celebrated with gifts of a hat and gold watch with the player's initials engraved in the back with the inscription: "From the citizens of Brooklyn to the Brooklyn Baseball Club of 1924."

Thomas Rice of the *Brooklyn Daily Eagle* called the "most stirring event" of the evening when Wheat received his watch. Rice went onto say that Wheat "has been famous for his willingness to take pains to make changes, decisions and to the like, clear to the fans. He has done it not only willingly, but cheerfully—because he was built that way. He has grown upon the fans until he is a sort of fixture, more so than any other player in the club's history; and justly so."[10]

The celebration was earned, but premature, as the Dodgers still had to win their last two games over the Braves, and the Giants had to lose a pair to the Phillies. Weather forced Brooklyn to wait three days, but Robinson kept his three-man rotation of Grimes, Doak, and Vance. He sent out Doak, owner of a 10-game win streak. He was unable to extend it to 11, as Boston came away with a 3–2 win. Across town, New York wrapped up their fourth consecutive pennant.

It was clear that it was one of the more memorable seasons in franchise history to date. Nearly 819,000 filed into Ebbets Field, ranking them second in the National League. During the season, fans were even more hopeful as they noticed that it seemed that there might be a pattern of winning the pennant every four years (1916, 1920), which also happened to be election years. Alas, the Dodgers' magical season came to an end. They finished

8. A Season to Remember, 1924

one-and-a-half games behind the Giants with a 92–62, second-place finish. New York was the only team Brooklyn had a losing record against—8–14, with six of the losses coming at the hands of Giants left-hander, Jack Bentley. New York lost the World Series in seven games to the Washington Senators and American League MVP, pitcher Walter Johnson. It would be McGraw's last World Series appearance. He tallied ten National League pennants, but won only three of the nine World Series he managed in—he refused to play the 1904 World Series due to disagreements with the American League.

In 1924, the National League instituted a Most Valuable Player award (the American League's began in '22). Awarded in December, Wheat finished tied for third in the inaugural prize with Frankie Frisch of the Giants, with 40 points. Vance, who voiced motivation from the outset of winning the $1,000 cash prize that accompanied the award, finished first in front of Hornsby (74 to 62). Vance did so thanks to some astonishing pitching numbers during an otherwise batter-friendly year in both leagues. Vance led the majors in: wins, 28; ERA, 2.16; complete games, 30; and strikeouts, 262. The strikeouts were the most since Mathewson's 267 in 1903, and the first of seven consecutive years leading the league in the category. He tied a major league record by striking out seven Cubs in a row on August 1. Three weeks later he set a National League mark when he struck out 15—including six in a row—against the same team. Vance also made a side bet with Fournier that he would collect more wins than the first baseman would hit home runs. Vance's wins total bettered Fournier's total by one, 28 to 27. The voting committee also named an All-Star team that included: Vance, Grimes, and Wheat.

Fred Lieb, longtime sportswriter and one of baseball's first historians, was chairman of the voting committee and in charge of presenting the winner with a bag of gold coins equaling the cash prize. Shortly after Wheat passed away in early 1972, Lieb wrote a letter of condolence to Wheat's daughter, Mary. He told her that when he presented Vance the MVP cash prize at Ebbets Field, he whispered to the Brooklyn pitcher that he "should give half of that to Zack Wheat."[11]

Brooklyn's success of 1924 was an all-around team effort by the veteran-laden roster. Other Dodgers to receive MVP points included Fournier (21), High (9), Grimes (5), Johnston (3), and DeBerry (1). Fournier was in the top ten in several batting categories, but slumped down the stretch. Despite that, he led the National League in games played, 154, and home runs, 27—seven of them against the Giants. He was the first Dodger to lead the league in long balls since Tim Jordan hit 12 in 1908. High set career marks in: batting (.328), runs (98), hits (191), and triples (13). He was second to Hornsby in walks (89–83) and struck out just 16 times in 654 plate appearances. High would break his ankle during spring training in 1925, playing in just 44 games, before his late July release and acquisition by Boston. He ended up in St. Louis, where he was instrumental in the Cardinals' pennant winners in the late 1920s and early '30s. He remained in baseball in one capacity or another for nearly four more decades, retiring as chief scout with the Los Angeles Dodgers in 1963.

Johnston suffered through an injury-filled campaign in 1924, but his veteran leadership was invaluable, and he was rewarded with a Paige Automobile on the last weekend of the season. For the second year in a row, Grimes (22–13) led the National League in starts (36) and innings pitched (310.2), and both leagues in complete games (30). Doak and Art Decatur both reached double digits in wins with 11 and 10, respectively.

Similar to 1920, Robinson had several players that performed unexpectedly, nearly bringing another pennant to Brooklyn. Highly-touted outfielder, Bernie Neis, finally met some expectations (.303) and Eddie Brown far exceeded his. The right-handed outfielder, who played briefly for the Giants in the first few years of the decade, was obtained from the American Association on June 4, where he was having his third-straight dominant batting season for the Indianapolis Indians. He was fast, but a weak throwing arm had kept Brown from returning to the majors. His batting for the Dodgers in 1924 more than made up for his defensive short-comings: .308 with 30 doubles. He had a 20-game hit streak from August 26 to September 13. Brown wouldn't be a flash in the pan, as he would lead the majors in games played in 1925 for Brooklyn (153) and Boston in 1927 (155), and have the most hits in the National League for the Braves in 1926 (201).

Wheat opted to once again bypass an off-season barnstorming tour—this time led by Fournier—in favor of returning to Polo and playing exhibition games around Missouri with his brothers. His Dodger teammates, including Neis, Johnny Mitchell, Brown, and Milt Stock, were thrown in jail after assaulting William Weaver, a bellboy at the Elham Hotel in Wenatchee, Washington, after he was late delivering ice to their room. The group, who had been drinking, had to be bailed out by Ebbets, who paid each of their $200 fines, reimbursed the hotel $100, and paid $750 for Weaver's medical bill and personal damage.

Legal problems were the least of the franchise's worries, as health issues took the forefront of off-season news. Ebbets, who had been on a steady decline for the past several years, worsened. He had ignored doctor's orders to give up team ownership and move to Florida full-time. Shortly before the New Year, Robinson ended up in Baltimore's Union Memorial

8. A Season to Remember, 1924

Hospital complaining of shortness of breath and major chest pain. He was diagnosed with an attack of pleurisy, and a lesion was removed from his lung, followed by an extended hospital stay. Robinson's illness began what would ultimately be the downfall of his relationship with Wheat. Wheat became a favorite to take over managerial duties to begin spring training if Robinson's health didn't improve.

9

Calm Amidst the Storm, 1925–1927

The success of 1924 had several players holding out for more money in 1925, the 50th anniversary of the National League. Besides Wheat's and Grimes' usual extended contract negotiations, Vance, Fournier, and Doak held out, too, as did pitcher, Dutch Henry and catcher, Zack Taylor. In the end, all of them but Doak signed larger contracts, making Brooklyn the highest-paid club in the league. The spitballer would sit out the next two seasons, returning to the Dodgers for two seasons (1927–'28), accumulating a record of 14–16, and finishing with the Cardinals in '29. His lasting impact on the game was his signature glove model from Rawlings, which featured a groundbreaking adjustable web.

After years of being underpaid compared to market value (just an $800 raise over the first five years of the decade), Wheat received a hefty increase of $5,700 to put his 1925 salary at an even $14,000. Once he arrived in Clearwater for spring training, much of the talk was of his ability to continue to be one of the game's best hitters. In camp, Tiny Osborne, entering his first full season with the Dodgers after being acquired from the Cubs in May 1924, said he'd rather pitch to Hornsby than Wheat because of the latter's ability to remain so consistent. "He is always dangerous," said Osborne of the Dodgers' veteran outfielder, who had six hits—all singles in 18 career at-bats against the tall right-hander. "If you get away the first time he faces you in a game, you can bet your glove that he'll sock you the next time. Hornsby, on the other hand, seems to have off days—or you have good days against him."[1]

Osborne didn't stop there in his praise of Wheat. "Lots of folk don't give Wheat the credit for being the hitter he is because he hasn't a flashy style," he continued, having seen Wheat perform first as an opponent, then daily as a teammate. "He is quiet and seems sort of slow in action. But he can lay on that ball. Anybody who has had them batted back to him in the pitcher's box will back me up in that statement."[2]

Wheat felt that adjustments at the plate were essential. "I shift my

9. Calm Amidst the Storm, 1925–1927

On April 18, 1925, the Dodgers and Giants gathered together at home plate of Ebbets Field to remember Charles Ebbets, who had died that morning. Wheat is at the center of the picture, with his cap at his waist (Kenny Dixon photo collection).

position at the plate more often than people think," he explained to F.C. Lane. "I'll shift my shoulders more than my feet so as to meet the ball at a different angle. You must vary your position with the different pitchers or they'll soon get your number."[3]

Ebbets' health continued to worsen during the spring trip. He returned to New York City from Florida a few days before the team, quarantined to a suite at the Waldorf-Astoria. He died on April 18—the league opener—from a heart attack. The league flew flags at half-mast, and there was a discussion of halting play. However, National League president, John Heydler, who called Ebbets "probably the best beloved man in baseball," and the McKeever brothers decided to play the day's games, canceling those scheduled for the day of Ebbets' funeral.[4]

Though Wheat and Ebbets had their differences when it came to contract negotiations, the owner's death was a blow to Wheat. "Mr. Ebbets always liked me, and I always felt that he intended to make me manager of the club," Wheat said years later.[5]

Ed McKeever was expected to be named Ebbets' successor. He may have had the late owner's wishes in mind when he called Wheat into his office shortly after taking over as owner, asking, "How would you like to take over this club?" A stunned Wheat agreed. "It's all set then," replied McKeever. "Why don't we go down on the field and you can point out whatever changes you'd like to have made for next season." The pair went down to the field, where Robinson was working out with team. His suspicions of Wheat only grew. "I didn't want it that way but there was nothing I could do about it," Wheat explained nearly a quarter century later when he was inducted into the Major League Baseball Hall of Fame. "I know Robbie thought I was trying to get his job and it was out of the question for me to go to him and explain that Ed had come to me first."[6]

In assessing Ebbets' legacy, Lee Allen later wrote the Brooklyn owner was "one of the most able and least appreciated of the game's builders. The public, which did not understand him at all, often subjected him to ridicule, some of it friendly but much of it libelous and inexcusably abusive."[7]

Ebbets' funeral was held at Brooklyn's Episcopal Church of the Holy Trinity. The funeral motorcade travelled through the borough, passing by the now boarded-up Washington Park and then the ball park that bore his name. The group's destination was the Greenwood Cemetery, where he was to be buried next to Henry Chadwick, considered the "Father of Baseball." Ebbets had decided on the spot during his tradition of bringing flowers to Chadwick's grave on April 20, his birthday. When the casket was transported to the plot, they realized the grave hadn't been dug wide enough.

9. Calm Amidst the Storm, 1925–1927

A large crowd sat in the rain for an hour-and-a-half, waiting. Among the group was Ed McKeever, who developed a cold the next day, which turned to pneumonia. He was dead a few days later.

The successive deaths left team ownership in a state of chaos. Team shares were divided in a confusing manner due to Ebbets' personal life. He was divorced, remarried, and was estranged from his son, Charles, Jr., whom Ebbets had been training for years to take over as owner. An initial board meeting was monopolized by Steve McKeever and the Ebbets family squabbling over who would succeed as owner. Neither had a suitable replacement. Joe Gilleaudeau, Ebbets' son-in-law, wasn't active enough for Steve McKeever's taste, and McKeever wasn't serious enough for the Ebbets clan. It was decided that a new owner would be named at a shareholders meeting in May. When neither side would budge, they elected Robinson as the new president. McKeever was furious, calling Robinson "a bumbling manager who'd blown two World Series," and saying he "hadn't even shown he could get his team to the park on time."[8]

Robinson was rewarded with a raise and new three-year contract. He would keep his title of manager and return to the bench at some point, but for the foreseeable future, the board of directors wanted him to focus on his duties as president. He was ordered to name Wheat manager, an act that pained Robinson. Wheat's captain duties went to Fournier. Robinson never fully took to the president label. At first, he was perched in the press box, but the razzing of fans got to be too much for him. According to Abe Yager, "Robbie disguised himself as a spectator and removed himself to a grandstand seat in the close vicinity of the Bedford aye [sic] exit."[9]

It was one of the worst times for Robinson to take on this sort of responsibility. Not only did he suffer the health scare, but he also had a new investment that was occupying his thought—over 500 acres of land and duties at his winter home, Dover Hall, in Georgia. Robinson's fears were met when Wheat took to the new job with a successful 11–5 May home stand. He voiced that over the past few years, he began to contemplate what it would be like to manage. Robinson begrudgingly stayed in the stands during a western road trip in June and much of July at Ebbets Field. The Dodgers lingered in third- and fourth-place, but it was noticeable enough for Wheat to be mentioned as taking over the Chicago Cubs job in 1926. Despite managing the team, the ambiguity of the situation led to Wheat's managerial record not being officially recognized.

Wheat's rising profile likely pushed Robinson's abrupt return to the bench in late July, when the club slipped into fourth place. Robinson gave his side of the story to Tommy Holmes a few years later: "I wanted to let

Wheat finish the season. But the board of directors wouldn't stand for that. They wanted immediate results. So I had to go back to the bench and try to get results."[10]

Though Robinson said he was merely there to provide support to the team, Wheat submitted to him for the most part. "I didn't feel I was the man to issue orders in a tough situation when the president of the ball club was on the bench," he said years later.[11]

Wheat finally had to confront Robinson about the confusing situation. "Nobody knows where I stand, including me," said Wheat. "Who's running the ball club on the field, anyway?"

"You are, and, hell, you're right. We don't need two managers," responded Robinson. He returned to the stands, but would soon be back managing, pushing Wheat aside for good.[12]

Confrontation was just not something that Wheat was ever comfortable with, whether it be negotiating with Ebbets, challenging Robinson, or arguing with an umpire. Roscoe McGowen, who covered the Dodgers for the *New York Times* for years, recalled an incident when Wheat decided not to challenge an unnamed rookie roommate, who, thinking the veteran was asleep, went into his wallet and stole money. Wheat quietly waited until the player had fallen asleep and retrieved it. The matter was never spoken of between the two players.

Managerial drama overshadowed the season Wheat had at the plate. By the second week of the season, he was locked in. On April 24, he tallied his first of two five-hit games on the season. It came in Philadelphia at the Baker Bowl in a 10–8 win over the Phillies. The home run and four singles were off former teammate, left-handed knuckleballer, Clarence Mitchell.

At age 37, amid talk that his career was coming to a close, Wheat was more popular than ever, as amateur borough ball clubs where naming themselves after him. He played in 150 games, the third highest total of his career. He batted .359, setting career marks in at-bats (616), runs (125), hits (221), doubles (42), and went over 100 RBIs for the second time. The hits and doubles total were club records that stood until 1930, when Babe Herman tallied a still-record 241 and 48, respectively. Wheat's 1925 batting totals remain one of the best for a 37-year-old. "The only way I kept him off me was with my bat," recalled Wheat of his rift with Robinson.[13]

For the first time since 1916, Wheat hit better away from Ebbets Field—.387 on the road, against .327 at home. He had some of his best games in Chicago that year. On June 5, he hit a pair of home runs (he also lined into a triple play), and in early August he collected nine hits in nine official at-bats during a series at Wrigley Field. His overall average of .359 dipped to third

9. Calm Amidst the Storm, 1925–1927

in the league behind Hornsby's .403, putting him between two young, emerging players that would become Hall-of-Famers, too: Bottomley (.367) of the Cardinals and Kiki Cuyler (.357) of the pennant-winning Pirates. Wheat and Fournier (.350) were one of four teammate duos in the majors to each eclipse .350. The other National Leaguers were St. Louis's Bottomley and Hornsby. In the American League were Al Simmons (.384) and Bill Lamar (.356) of the Philadelphia Athletics, and the Detroit Tigers' Harry Heilmann (.393), Ty Cobb (.378), and Al Wingo (.370).

Batting numbers were up all over the league in 1925. Wheat took advantage of a new style of baseball that was jumping off players' bats. Now referred to as a "rabbit" ball, the composition had all the makings of being to the batters' benefit. The new ball had a cushion-corked center made of a sphere of cork, surrounded by a black-semi-vulcanized rubber, surrounded by yet another layer of red rubber. Wheat was unsure the lasting effects the new ball and changing approach would have on the game. In late June, Wheat partook in an extensive interview with Thomas Holmes of the *Daily Eagle*—one of the most in-depth during his playing career—as he touched on a number of topics surrounding it:

> I don't know whether the lively ball is a good thing for the game or not. Sometimes I think the public likes the burst of heavy hitting. Then again, I don't know. Are all the balls lively? Well, again, I don't know. Sometimes you see a team knock one ball after another out of the lot. The next day they may be shut out or held to a low score. That may mean that they are hitting comparatively dead balls, or that they are not hitting the lively balls just right. But there's no doubt whatever in my mind that there is a lively ball in general use today. Long flies come out to me harder and sharper that they used to. Furthermore, how often do you see a runner from second thrown out at the plate on an infield single, nowadays? Not very often. The fielders have to lay so far back anybody can score from second on any kind of a single that gets through the infield. The only time an outfielder can play in is when a comparative tapper is at bat. Even then there is a big chance that the ball will be walloped over his head. One of the big objections to the "rabbit" is that it results in two kinds of baseball—one kind at the larger parks and another at the bandboxes such as Philadelphia, Chicago and St. Louis. In these smaller parks you never know when you have a game won. Somebody gets up, with men on base, hits a fly and, if the wind is behind it, there goes a big lead to smash. A home run is something that should be earned. It used to be something of a rarity. There is no doubt that the fan doesn't get as much kick out of a base hit out of the lot as he used to. I believe that the lively ball does produce sharper fielding. The outfielders have to hustle like Old Nick. Of course, many more hits get through the infield than formerly. An infielder cannot get a fast ground ball unless it's right in front of him. But the chances they do accept are hard hit balls and look good to the crowd. The new ball has speeded up fielding, to a certain extent. But it has taken most of the base running, bunting and scientific hitting out of the game. It doesn't pay to try to steal bases these days, or to sacrifice a man along, or to attempt the hit and run play. It's too easy to make long hits

though it is taking more of a gamble. Pitchers and infielders dislike the present day ball, the pitchers particularly, which is natural. Every once in a while one is hit right back at the pitcher so hard that he has barely time to duck. It is possible that the majority of ball players make some sort of a kick to make against the "rabbit," but if you ask me, I don't know whether the fans like it or not. We seem to be getting the crowds in to just about as great an extent as we used to.[14]

The ball was discussed by owners at the National League's annual midsummer meeting held at the New York office of league president John Heydler in July. The group, including Robinson, heard testimony from Harold Fales, a Columbia University chemistry professor, who tested balls from the 1914, '23, and the current season. He came to the conclusion that the ball now being used was "larger in size, weighs more, and gives the pitcher much less control in that the seam of the ball is much smoother and the thread of same almost completely countersunk so as to be flush with the leather of the seam."[15] Fales also noted that the amount of balls now being put in play was affecting statistics. A few years earlier, 12 dozen balls were used in a week at the Polo Grounds. Now there were 90 dozen a week.

Julian Curtis, president of the A.G. Spalding Company, supplier of baseballs to the National League, gave his word that despite the evidence from Fales, little had been done to the ball over the years other than using better wool yarn. He surmised that it was the swing-from-the-heels batting approach that began with Babe Ruth's emergence as a power hitting outfielder that was affecting batting numbers. In the end, the owners sided with Curtis' explanation, doing nothing to change the ball. The one concession made (by both leagues) was allowing a rosin bag to be placed behind the pitcher's mound.

Wheat's batting numbers didn't show it, but his legs were beginning to permanently hinder his play. It appeared first in the field, where his once expansive range dwindled, leading the league in left field errors with 13 (he would also have the most in '26 with 10). The new baseballs weren't helping either, and he lamented as much to Holmes. "Long flies come out to me harder and sharper than they used to," Wheat explained. "Furthermore, how often do you see a runner from second thrown out at the plate on an infield single, nowadays? The fielders have to lay so far back anybody can score from second on any kind of a single that gets through the infield."

Though confidence in the field seemed to waver, Wheat never lost faith in his batting, as expressed to Lane:

> The man who can hit ought to grow better until his eyes go bad. Why shouldn't he? He doesn't lose the power to hold the bat or to take his swing. He may lose some speed of foot, but he ought to hit just as hard until his eye sight fails. Besides, experience counts.

9. Calm Amidst the Storm, 1925–1927

He knows the pitchers better. He knows how to handle himself better. All the tricks at batting that it took him years to learn he now uses unconsciously.[16]

Wheat also had developed a new approach in recent years that gave him an edge. "I developed a contempt for pitchers," he told Lane. When Lane mentioned this to Ty Cobb, the Detroit Tigers star called it "the best short definition of batting ability he had ever heard."[17]

One of the pitchers that drew the ire of Wheat late in his career was right-hander Jack Scott, then with the Giants. Wheat found success against the big-knuckleballer (27-for-74 and a .365 average), but despised that Scott was known for scuffing the ball with his belt buckle. During a bench-clearing brawl between the Giants and Dodgers, Wheat recalled prowling the rim of the pack, looking to take on Scott. "If I could have found him, I'da twisted his arm off," said Wheat three decades later.[18]

In early August 1925, Robinson met with Commissioner Landis while the Dodgers were in Chicago playing the Cubs. The result was a statement from Robinson deeming himself manager for the remainder of the season, with Wheat serving as assistant manager. On August 8, Robinson called a press conference to announce that Wheat would succeed him as manager when he retired. Robinson's contract was set to expire at the end of the 1926 season, but he wouldn't commit to that being his last year as manager, pending what happened with the team president title he was currently holding. "You can make it plain that so far as I am concerned, when I cease to manage the Brooklyn team, I want Zack Wheat to be my successor," said Robinson, adding that Wheat's assistant manager job was "not an empty honor."[19]

Wheat seemed nonplussed by the announcement. He was in the middle of a power-filled month at the plate. During August, he batted .400 with 13 doubles, six home runs, 25 RBIs, 36 runs, and the second 50-hit month of his career with 54. He also scored a run in 13 straight games. All of that propelled him to robust batting numbers. "I have hit uncommonly well all season and the exact cause might be hard to find," he told Lane. "True, I have felt well physically, but I have been in even better physical conditions other seasons. Somehow I seem to have developed a lot of confidence. I felt like elbowing a pitcher out of the way when I met him. I could hit anything he had. I knew it and he knew it. That's the real explanation."[20]

The other person that was shuffled as a result of Ebbets' death was Fournier, who wasn't finding the same peace that Wheat seemingly was. The first baseman was being harassed more than ever by emboldened Brooklyn fans. Though his batting was a crowd pleaser, fans had glommed on to his lackluster defense. It got so bad in September that he confided to several sportswriters on the long train tide from Pittsburgh to St. Louis that fan behavior had him contemplating stepping away from the game. "These fans have no respect for the women around them, nor for themselves, and they think that by paying the price of admission they have acquired the right to throw filth upon a professional player," he said. "My wife long since quit going to the games because she could not stand the attacks on me, and now I can no longer stand them."[21]

Fournier didn't let it affect his output at the plate. In addition to his .350 average, he collected a career-high 310 total bases on 21 doubles, 16 triples, and 22 home runs to go with his 130 RBIs. He and Wheat led the team in most batting categories, but as a team, the Dodgers hit .296; placing them third in the National League. Other notable contributors were: outfielders, Eddie Brown (.306, 39 doubles, 11 triples, and 99 RBIs) and Dick Cox (.329); infielder, Milt Stock (.328, 202 hits, including a record four consecutive four-hit games), and catcher, Zack Taylor (.310). Johnston, who, like Wheat, had little left in his legs, hit .297 before being traded to the Boston Braves in a package deal in the offseason. He ended his career with the Giants in September 1926.

The Dodgers remained in the first division for most of the 1925 season in spite of the uncertainty, but fell to the bottom division over the last few weeks of the season. Brooklyn lost 17 of their last 19 games, landing in sixth place with a 68–85 record, tied with the Phillies. They finished a half-game ahead of the Cubs. The last-place finish allowed Chicago to draft Hack Wilson, who through an oversight by the Giants, had been left available after being optioned to Toledo. Robinson was disappointed but set his eyes on Paul Waner of the

Jack Fournier was a liability in the field but was one of the National League's top power hitters during his four seasons as a Brooklyn Dodger (National Baseball Hall of Fame and Museum).

9. Calm Amidst the Storm, 1925–1927

San Francisco Seals. He offered the outfielder a contract but couldn't guarantee it without the okay from McKeever and Gilleaudeau. When he finally received the go-ahead, the Seals had already sold the future Hall-of-Famer to the Pirates for the same amount Robinson had put forth.

Robinson blamed his inability to right the 1925 season on resistance from the club. "Zack was popular with the players and they hated to see him fail," he told Holmes. "Rather than show him up by winning for me, they played indifferent ball for the rest of the season."[22]

Robinson couldn't win. Bill Corum of the *New York Times* wrote about sitting in the stands at Ebbets Field and asking Dodger fans about the difference between Robinson and Wheat as managers. While they were talking, Bill Terry of the Giants hit a fly ball that Wheat ran down at the wall. "That settles it," said the fan. "Zack is a better manager. Robbie would have never caught that ball."[23]

Pitching, or the lack thereof, proved to be the team's downfall in 1925. Vance was the only Dodgers pitcher who weathered the 1925 batting onslaught with an above .500 record. Grimes never got on track after a testy back-and-forth contract negotiation with Ebbets in the months leading up to his death. Grimes' ERA ballooned to 5.03 and he had a league-worst 19 losses. Doak wouldn't return to pitching until 1927, and the supporting crew from the year before never materialized. Vance's 22 wins led both leagues, as did his 221 strikeouts. He finished fifth in the MVP voting (Wheat finished 15th), narrowly missing out on becoming the first pitcher to throw back-to-back no-hitters—both against the Phillies in Philadelphia. On September 8, he faced the league minimum in a 1–0 victory, allowing a second-inning single to Nelson Hawks, who was erased on a double play. Five days later he threw a no-hitter, this time in a 10–1 Brooklyn win. It was the first franchise no-hitter since Nap Rucker on September 15, 1908, over the Boston Doves.

In the offseason, Wheat talked at length with Lane about his training regimen. His perspective had changed a bit since he had talked about it a few years earlier with the *Brooklyn Daily Eagle*:

> I don't pay much attention to the rules for keeping in physical condition. I think they are a lot of bunk. I have always worked hard all my life and am in the open air practically all the time. Let a man do that at my age and he can forget all about medicine and not even keep a speaking acquaintance with doctors. They say, for example, that tobacco hurts a person. I don't believe it. I smoke as much as I want and chew tobacco a good deal of the time. I don't believe that a ball player ought to go out and get soused. But during the active season I take a drink when I feel like it and I drink anything I want to drink. Generally I have a couple of drinks after the game is over. I believe a little stimulant is good for a player after a period

of exhausting physical exertion like a ball game. I don't believe it hurts a player in good condition, no matter what the Life Insurance Companies claim about it. At least it hasn't hurt me. During the off-season I practically never take a drink. I don't even have it in the house. I don't feel that I need it. I am working on a farm and sometimes I do hard work. When I am not working, I go hunting. I think the Prohibitionists are crazy. I have known ball players for twenty years. Very few of them refrain from taking a drink now and then, and outside of a few old soaks who sopped it up by the keg, I have never known drink to hurt any ball player. Anything in moderation is my motto. The less you worry about the effect of tea and coffee on the lining of your stomach, the longer you will live and the happier you will be.[24]

The subject of Wheat taking over as manager in 1926 wasn't spoken of publicly in the winter, but it was apparent that Robinson had no intention of stepping down. When Wheat demanded a two-year contract worth $16,000 a season, Robinson battled McKeever to counter with one-year offer of $16,000, a $1,000 increase from the year before. "We finished seventh with both Wheat and Stock last season and we can finish seventh this year without them," said Robinson, making reference to the team's two notable holdouts.[25]

After Wheat finally accepted the one-year deal, Robinson made efforts at any opportunity to undermine the veteran, including letting Fournier keep the title of captain. No one's job was safe, as Robinson looked to rebuild. He focused on his infield, which would be in flux over the next several seasons. He picked up shortstop Rabbit Maranville off waivers from the Cubs in November 1925. Once considered one of the game's best fielders, his appetite for alcohol had begun affecting his play. His penchant for the night life found him a quick place on Brooklyn's fraternal 4-for-0 Club. Before the Dodgers had departed from Clearwater, Florida, he was finding mischief—and nearly getting shot.

According to Maranville, Wheat, who was sick, contacted him about finding a quart of whiskey for medicinal purposes. Maranville obliged and went out for the evening with a few members of the Boston Braves. The group returned to the team's hotel intoxicated, with Wheat's booze in tow. Maranville delivered the bottle to his new teammate's room, and when he returned to his, one of the players with whom he had been out on the town—former Dodger, Bernie Neis—was riffling through Maranville's roommate, Fournier's, unlocked trunk. Neis pulled out a pistol and jokingly pointing it at Maranville, threatening to shoot him. Maranville played along, saying, "I'm a Navy man, I'm not afraid to die."[26]

Maranville, who managed the Cubs for 53 games in '25, played a part-time role. When Robinson informed the veteran infielder that he was

9. Calm Amidst the Storm, 1925–1927

being released in late August because he was making too much money, he was relieved. "I'm tickled to death," he replied to the Brooklyn manager. "I never was on such a screwy ball-club in my life."[27]

The Dodgers' high-priced pitchers struggled immediately. Vance was distracted from the get-go. He spent most of spring training fishing and dealing with real estate. He would eventually buy what would become his sportsman's camp at Homosassa Springs on the Florida Gulf Coast. When he finally got around to pitching, he had painful boils on his abdomen, a severe flu, and a sore arm, all of which limited him to 22 starts. He didn't win a game until June, finishing 9–10. He still led the league in strikeouts for the fifth straight year with 140. Grimes was having his second consecutive sub-.500 season (12–13), and certainly wasn't happy with the return of Otto Miller as third base coach.

Brooklyn's best pitcher was left-hander, Jesse Petty, who went 17–17. He was part of the 4-for-0 Club, but broke the group's cardinal rule of not getting caught, when Robinson found him breaking curfew. The club made a big scene of humiliating Petty in a mock ceremony. Word of the hazing reached other teams, who used it as fodder for jockeying Petty whenever possible. The joke was lost on *New York Sun* sports editor and columnist, Joe Vila, who felt Petty was being mistreated. Vila had the *Sun*'s sports cartoonist, Feg Murray, do a send up of the highly paid and underperforming Vance and Grimes. Under a cartoon of Petty, it read, "Jess Petty is winning while the higher-priced Dazzy Vance and Burleigh Grimes are losing. How much is Petty being paid?"[28]

Robinson didn't find the humor in the cartoon, especially from Vila, with whom he had been friends since his days in Baltimore. Robinson complained to the *Sun*, demanding an explanation. When he was told it was a motivational tool for Grimes and Vance, Robinson refused to accept the explanation, continuing to argue until he was hung up on. From then on, the *Sun* stopped contacting Dodger players, never wrote Robinson's name when writing about the team, and referred to them strictly as the "Dodgers" rather than the "Robins."

McKeever, who had been seething since being bypassed for the ownership position, now took the opportunity to question Robinson's abilities. According to Tommy Holmes, McKeever would berate Robinson to his face, and if the manager had the audacity to react, "McKeever reached threateningly for his blackthorn stick, indicating that he needed little more incentive to crash the heavy gold cane head against Robbie's skull."[29] McKeever brought the feud into the Ebbets Field office. He took the only office, pushing Robinson's desk to a balcony cubbyhole. To get there, Robinson had to walk past McKeever's desk, which usually ended in a verbal confrontation. From then on, Robinson conducted presidential business from the clubhouse or his suite at the Hotel St. George.

Robinson's fued with McKeever was affecting the president-manager's standing in the clubhouse and dugout. A distracted Robinson was absent-minded and became a target of hijinks from his players, who would nail his shoes to clubhouse floors or throw his clothes from a train. Robinson frequently argued game strategy with fans in the stands. On-field mental lapses and off the field pranks were escalating as the "4 for 0 club" was morphing into a group that would become known as the "Daffiness Boys," thanks to a column written by syndicated sports columnist Westbrook Pegler. The combination created an image of the Dodgers as an unhinged team. During times of success, the club was looked at endearingly, in the midst of struggles, disdainfullly.

Robinson tried to create some accountability by creating the short-lived "Bonehead Club," with players paying fines for mental errors during games. The players agreed. "The way we're going, you'll each get as much money as the fellows who get in the World Series," he joked.[30] However, in the first game with the club in effect, Robinson erroneously gave a different batting order to the umpire than he did to the team. The Dodgers lost, and the Bonehead Club was promptly disbanded. "The manager of the Dodgers formed a Bonehead Club before yesterday's game and promptly elected himself a charter member," snipped Eddie Murphy of the *Sun*.[31]

On August 15, in the seventh inning of the first game of a doubleheader against the Braves, rookie Floyd "Babe" Herman hit a ball to right field, scoring DeBerry easily from third base. Vance wandered a few feet off of second base. When Braves right fielder, Jimmy Welsh, was unable to get to the ball, Vance hustled to third, making a wide turn before retreating to the bag. Fewster took off from first, barely hesitating as he rounded second base and headed for third. Not far behind him was Herman, who decided to try to stretch a double into triple. The end result was three Dodgers trying to claim third base. Herman jogged towards second base. Fewster thought he was automatically out and stepped off the base. Boston third baseman Eddie Taylor tagged him out for the second out. As Herman leisurely made his way back to second, Braves second baseman, Doc Gautreau, called for the ball and tagged Herman out for the third out.

It was easy for Robinson to overlook Herman's blunder. Born in Buffalo, New York, and raised across the country in Glendale, California, the 22-year-old was one of the few bright spots for the Dodgers manager during the trying 1926 season. Herman broke into the lineup as a replacement at

9. Calm Amidst the Storm, 1925–1927

first base for Fournier, who struggled with leg injuries for much of the year, limiting him to 87 games (the highlight of his season was a three home run game in St. Louis on July 13). Herman's glove work was equally as inept, if not worse, than his predecessor (Herman finishing last in fielding percentage in '26). Things didn't get any better when he moved to the outfield, either, but his bat was undeniable. He had played for eight teams in six leagues over the previous five seasons (most recently for the Seattle Indians of the Pacific Coast League), and had trials with the Tigers and Red Sox. He hit well wherever he went. For a short time in July, he led the league in batting, but injuries took hold as the season wound down. He still paced the Dodgers in several categories: batting average (.319—the only regular to bat over .300), hits (158), doubles (35), triples (11), home runs (11), and RBIs (81). It was enough to garner a few MVP votes.

Wheat's legs completely failed him in 1926. According to Frank Graham, Wheat "had to hit them so far he could walk down to first base."[32] His batting eye came into question, and he was occasionally benched against left-handers. "Not only is Buck not grinding base hits out of the old mill at his former rate of production, but he isn't hitting in the rallies and is driving comparatively few Brooklyn runs across the pan," wrote Holmes.[33]

Despite that, Wheat remained otherwise healthy, playing in all but a handful of games into early August, leading the National League with 31 doubles to that point. On August 2, he suffered yet another leg injury—one of the more serious of his career—that would lead to him being out for nearly a month. Against the Cubs he slid hard into second, once again twisting his ankle badly. When he limped to the dugout to tell Robinson that he couldn't return to the game, the manager snapped, "It's just a mosquito bite, you can go out and play."[34]

Wheat played out the game and skipped getting his ankle examined. After an off day, Wheat played in obvious pain, going hitless in an 8–4 loss to the Cardinals. Robinson gave him the next day off, but with the Dodgers trailing 11–7 in the 10th inning, he was called on to pinch hit. Wheat hobbled to the plate and promptly smacked his fourth home run of the season off the Cardinals' Jess Haines onto Bedford Avenue. In the process, Wheat lost his balance, fell backward, stumbling over a loose board covering a hole that umpires kept extra balls in. Limping out of the batter's box, he hobbled around first base, before collapsing onto second base. The umpires and managers convened to figure out what to do. They decided to bend the rule that states a runner must complete the circuit of the bases for the home run to count. Maranville was announced as a pinch hitter, but before he made it to second, Wheat arose, traveling the final 180 feet at a slow pace with the sparse crowd cheering him on.

The injury, initially reported as a "Charlie horse" by the press, was in fact another devastating injury for Wheat. The Cardinals team physician, Dr. Hyland, examined him and determined Wheat had broken a bone in his right heel and ripped several ligaments. Robinson took Wheat's extended time on the bench convalescing to wonder aloud if his longtime leftfielder's passion for the game was dwindling. Of the fateful home run, Wheat said, "I think that Robby decide to fire me right at that moment."[35] Though his numbers were drastically down, Wheat's presence in the lineup was sorely missed. The Dodgers lost 11 of their next 12 games, putting to rest their pennant hopes once and for all.

Wheat's value to Robinson became even more apparent in August when Max Carey was claimed off waivers from the Pirates. One of the game's best outfielders for over a decade, the fleet-footed Carey had fallen out of favor in Pittsburgh after some clubhouse turmoil. He proved to be the scapegoat when, as team captain, he tried to get former manager and current team stockholder, Fred Clarke, banned from the bench when he began questioning decisions made by current manager, Bill McKechnie. Carey was seen as a replacement for Wheat, not only in the outfield, but as a managerial candidate. Robinson bypassed Wheat, asking Carey to mentor the young outfielders, particularly Herman, who was transitioning to the outfield from first base.

Nearly three decades later, in a 1955 article for *Esquire*, Carey named Wheat one of the 20 greatest ball players of all-time: "Wheat was a ballplayer's ballplayer; he could do everything well and never stopped trying. At bat or in the field he was always dependable, made hard plays look easy, an indication of a player who knows what it is all about."[36]

Besides Herman, the other Dodger to earn some MVP votes was surprise 33-year-old rookie infielder, Johnny Butler. Other than serving in World War I, Butler had been playing in the minor leagues since 1914. He led Brooklyn in games played in 1926 (147), and was near the top of several Dodgers batting categories. His game did have some shortcomings. Baseball historian Bill James called the double play combination of Butler and Fewster "probably the worst of all time."[37] The duo completed only 95 double plays, when the average was 148 per team.

In 1926, Wheat's batting average dipped below .300 for the first time since 1919. Even though his skills were a shell of what they once were, he hit .290 in 111 games, with 38 extra base hits, all on failed legs. Still, Wheat was led to believe that he would succeed Robinson as manager in 1927, despite little being said about it. Robinson's contract was up, and McKeever looked

9. Calm Amidst the Storm, 1925–1927

to take over ownership of the club and insert Wheat as player-manager. McKeever fell gravely ill with an intestinal issue that required surgery, leaving his life in the balance. A decision was made in haste by his lawyer, Frank York, and Gilleaudeau. They offered Robinson a three-year contract, which he accepted, essentially sealing Wheat's fate.

"It was necessary," York tried to explain to a raging McKeever. "We've got to do things, and we couldn't wait for you to get well."

"Three years weren't necessary," roared McKeever. "You could have given him one year, and I'd have got him next fall."[38]

Robinson had no intentions of stepping down and instead worked to release Wheat, battling McKeever, who continued to back the longtime outfielder. All of this was done via long-distance correspondence, as Robinson had retreated to his winter refuge in Georgia immediately following the season. With a managerial position unlikely, Wheat focused on a business venture with Cot Tierney. They planned a New Year's Day opening of a billiards and bowling business on Thirty-eighth and Main in Kansas City. The emporium was named "Tierney & Wheat Recreation." Wheat grew ill towards the end of December, before finally having his tonsils removed on January 18, 1927, at Trinity Lutheran Hospital.

On January 1, during Wheat's illness, Dodgers assistant secretary Fred Hanlon broadcast an announcement from Ebbets Field that Wheat had been released. Waivers from the other 15 clubs had been secured weeks before. Hanlon read a letter from Robinson:

> The board of directors at a recent meeting discussed the Wheat proposition. Inasmuch as it was deemed advisable to endeavor to build up a young team for 1927, with a view toward finishing higher up in the pennant race than in 1925 and 1926 with older players, some of whom have possible played too long in Brooklyn, and on account of the long and excellent service rendered the Brooklyn Club by Mr. Wheat, it was decided to give him his unconditional release, rather than offer him a contract at a salary less than his recent contracts called for. The board of directors join me in wishing Mr. Wheat the best of luck wherever he goes and trust he will remain a baseball star for many years to come.[39]

Robinson was much less sentimental when discussing the matter with members of the Brooklyn media. "We have to make room for kids," he said matter-of-factly.[40]

The longest-tenured National League player, Wheat put to rest any questions of whether or not he would continue playing. "I intend to play baseball somewhere next season, as I am feeling fine again and should have some more good baseball left in me. Under the circumstances I am sorry to leave Brooklyn, but if such is the fact I welcome my release," he said in a statement from his farm in Polo.

Wheat then turned his attention to his support for nearly two decades. "The Brooklyn fans have always treated me fine and I extend to them my kindest regards for a happy and prosperous New Year."[41]

Over three decades later, upon induction into the Hall of Fame, Wheat admitted to *Kansas City Star* sportswriter, Joe McGuff, how the treatment from the Dodgers had affected him. "I've never quite got over that," Wheat said. "It kind of soured me a little on baseball."[42]

Holmes eulogized Wheat in a lengthy article the day after the announcement was made public. "He was the most popular player Brooklyn ever claimed for its own. He was a great hitter, a valuable all-around athlete. He always gave his best. He was a gentleman. He was a landmark at Ebbets Field, something inseparable with the fans' idea of a Brooklyn ball club."[43]

For the next few decades, Holmes would be a huge proponent of Wheat's place in the Brooklyn franchise's history, especially during the glory years of the 1940s and into the '50s. Holmes frequently referred to Wheat as the greatest Dodger ever. When Wheat was up for election to the Hall of Fame, Holmes made it his mission to convince voters Wheat belonged. Wheat's impact on Brooklyn fans was indelible. They, too, continued to remember him in letters to the *Daily Eagle* for years to come.

Several teams were interested in Wheat's services, including: the Cubs, Senators, Yankees, and Giants. Only John McGraw, who was in the market for an outfielder to replace the vacancy left by the departure of Irish Meusel and the illness of Ross Youngs, indicated that Wheat would be an everyday player. Though Wheat had expressed interest in signing with a western team to be closer to the family farm, the Giants were said to be offering at least the $15,000 he made in 1926.

As rumors of Wheat's next team proliferated, the *Daily Eagle* was flooded with letters from Dodgers fans writing about Wheat, especially the poor treatment deemed unfair by the ball club. Much like the persistence of Holmes, longtime fans would write in to the *Daily Eagle* for decades to follow, comparing the modern Dodgers to Wheat and his place as one of the greatest players in franchise history.

A week after the National League owners' meeting, the Giants pulled off a blockbuster deal, but Wheat wasn't a part of it. McGraw sent Frisch and inning-eater Jimmy Ring to the St. Louis Cardinals for player-manager, Rogers Hornsby. Just a few months removed from helping the Cardinals to their first World Series title, the combative second baseman had run out of chances in St. Louis. Frequent disagreements with Cardinals owner Sam Breadon led to the parting of ways. In New York, fan favorite and team

9. Calm Amidst the Storm, 1925–1927

captain, Frisch, had been called out by McGraw for not setting a good example during the season. McGraw wasn't done, obtaining Grimes a few days later in a three-team trade with the Phillies.

On the evening of January 12, Connie Mack, manager of the American League Philadelphia Athletics, announced that he had signed Wheat for a contract between $16,000 and $18,000. "We need a high-class outfielder," said Mack, also the team's owner, "and I could not find one who looked better than Wheat."[44]

After a decade of wallowing in the second division, the A's had shown promise over the previous two seasons, finishing second in 1925 (Senators) and third in 1926 (Yankees). Mack, in his 27th year of a 50-year career as owner and manager of the A's—often known as the Mackmen—was looking for some veterans to get his team to the World Series. A catcher and contemporary of Robinson during his playing days, Mack had been patiently plotting since 1922, after being given more control of the roster following the death of original majority owner and team president, Benjamin Shibe. Mack's first move was on October 15, 1926, when he purchased Joe Boley, a star shortstop, from the Baltimore Orioles of the International League. The Orioles owner, Jack Dunn, was an old friend of Mack's, and the two would make frequent deals. Over the years, several A's stars started in Baltimore, including: Boley, second baseman, Max Bishop, and pitchers, George Earnshaw and the great Lefty Grove.

In late December 1926, Mack brought back Eddie Collins, a former member of the A's $100,000 infield that had won three of four World Series appearances with Philadelphia in the early 1910s, before being sold to the White Sox in December 1914. In his dozen years in Chicago, Collins helped the club to two World Series appearances, beating the Giants in 1917 and losing to the Reds in the tainted '19 series. He was one of the few players who was exonerated from the Black Sox Scandal, and stuck with the team during the trying early '20s. For the two years prior to his return to Philadelphia, he was player-manager, earning a salary of $35,000, and leading them to two fifth-place finishes. He was further placated by having his good friend, Kid Gleason on the A's coaching staff.

Mack eyed two of the biggest names left on the market: Tris Speaker, who just finished his eighth season as player-manager of the Red Sox, and Detroit Tigers outfielder and manager, Ty Cobb, who was six years in with co-op duties. Both had been recently cleared by Commissioner Landis for charges of betting. Mack went after Speaker first, enlisting Collins, who had been named team captain, to woo him to Philadelphia. At a banquet at the Penn Athletic Club, Collins said, "I have told Tris here, not once, but many times, that if he wants to come to a town where business can be combined with pleasure, he would do well to come to Philadelphia."[45]

The words didn't convince Speaker, as Clark Griffith of the Washington Senators outbid Mack, Yankees, Tigers, and White Sox for the outfielder's services in 1927 (Speaker would sign with the A's in '28). Mack then turned his sights to Cobb, travelling to Augusta, Georgia, to offer the 21-year-veteran outfielder a contract of around $50,000 to make him the game's highest paid player again. Cobb accepted. "Because of certain incidents that received prominence during the offseason I call this 'vindication year' and I am out to play the kind of baseball that will make folks write letters to their cousins in the country."[46] Wheat didn't voice his intentions like Cobb, but he too would be seeking his own vindication.

It proved to be a free-spending offseason as Mack spent somewhere in the range of $250,000 on his roster. On paper, it was one of the deepest in the league, and many sportswriters were picking them to win the 1927 pennant. There were four other future Hall of Famers on the '27 Athletics, for a total of seven: Al Simmons, outfielder; Jimmie Foxx, first baseman;

Wheat looked back fondly on his lone season (1927) with the Philadelphia Athletics. Pictured from left to right: Kid Gleason, Eddie Collins, Ty Cobb, Zack Wheat, and Connie Mack (Kenny Dixon photo collection).

9. Calm Amidst the Storm, 1925–1927

Mickey Cochrane, catcher; and Grove, pitcher. The group would be unable to contend with the Yankees, who went on to sweep the Pirates in the World Series and be considered one of the greatest teams of all-time. The 1927 A's finished in second place, laying the groundwork for three consecutive American League pennants from 1929–'31, winning back-to-back World Series titles over the Cubs and Cardinals in '29 and '30, respectively, and losing in a rematch with St. Louis in '31.

Wheat looked rejuvenated early on in A's spring training in Fort Myers. Brian Bell of the *Brooklyn Daily Eagle* wrote that the former Dodger "seems to have taken a new lease on life and it seems certain that he will be the regular left fielder and a powerful factor in the offense of the club."[47] Shortly after the report, Wheat fell ill and neither his legs nor arm were in shape by the start of the regular season. Over the first six weeks, Wheat appeared in 26 games—starting just four. He was being referred to as the "highest paid pinch-hitter of all-time." When asked to assess the newcomers, Mack was honest without naming names. "Some of them don't look so good," he said. "However, we are only getting started."[48]

By early June, the A's had lost five of six games and were in third place, seven games behind the powerhouse Yankees. In an effort to jumpstart Philadelphia's anemic offense, Mack inserted Wheat and Foxx into the starting lineup. Described as a "third-string catcher," in just a few short years Foxx would become one of the game's premiere sluggers, perennial All-Stars, and MVP candidates. The move worked, as the A's won five in a row. Foxx wouldn't see regular time until the following season, but Wheat temporarily moved into a more active role, starting 17 June games, and batting .410 with five doubles.

Wheat enjoyed the experience of playing under a new manager, especially one as knowledgeable as Mack. Wheat recalled how against the White Sox, Mack perfectly placed him in the outfield. By now, Wheat was playing deep, no matter who was at bat. When Chicago's left-handed hitting first baseman, Bud Clancy, came to the plate, Wheat was surprised to see Mack waving him in towards the infield. "But still he kept wig-wagging with the scorecard, and soon I was standing not more than 20 feet behind Joe Boley and Sammy Hale. I was mad clear through. 'Old Connie is a fool,' I said to myself."

Clancy promptly hit a line drive right at Wheat, who caught it and tossed to Collins at second base for a double play.

"Zack, I knew what the pitcher was going to throw and figured that Clancy would hit it in exactly the spot he did," said Mack, when Wheat returned to the dugout. "That's why I kept signaling you to come in. Always watch me and do as you're told. And then you'll never get in any trouble."

Wheat's production dropped off in July, but he wasn't meant to carry the team. The A's had a potent lineup of young players. None was better than Simmons, who led the team in all major batting categories: batting, .392 (second in the league to Heilmann's .398); doubles, 36; triples, 11; home runs, 15; and 108 RBIs. The 25-year-old from Milwaukee, Wisconsin, would finish fourth in the American League MVP race, tied with his teammate, Cochrane. A 24-year-old catcher, he batted .338 with a dozen home runs in 1927 and would win the MVP outright in 1928. He was also excellent behind the plate, wresting away pitch-calling duties away from Mack.

As a team, Philadelphia batted .304, second in the American League. Other .300 hitters on the A's included first baseman, Jimmy Dykes, .324; third baseman, Sammy Hale, .313; Boley, .311; and outfielder, Walt French, .304. Wheat batted .324 in 88 games with 12 doubles, a triple, and a home run. Collins also was a solid contributor, but, like Wheat, was limited due to several nagging injuries that started in spring training and never fully healed. Of Mack's pricey off-season acquisitions, Cobb fared the best. A switch of teams hadn't changed Cobb's demeanor. He was as defiant as ever—and backed his actions up. At age 40, he batted .357, with 32 doubles and 93 RBIs. He led the team in runs (104), stolen bases (22), and, a surprise to many, games played (133). With the pennant out of reach, he left the team in late September, with over a week remaining, to travel to a hunting excursion in Wyoming. That didn't mean he didn't have a positive influence, as both Cochrane and Foxx spoke glowingly of Cobb's impact on their early career. Wheat, too, found a good friend in Cobb. The pair talked regularly throughout the rest of their lives, and Cobb would be a strong advocate of Wheat's entrance into the Hall of Fame.

Overshadowed by their potent batting was the A's consistent 1927 pitching staff, led by Grove, a 27-year-old left-hander in his third season with the A's after spending five years with the Orioles. Lefty—real name, Robert Moses—burst onto the major league scene in 1925, leading the league in strikeouts (116)—his first of seven straight times doing so (four of those would be the major league-lead). In 1926, the six-foot-three Grove led the majors in ERA (2.51) and in 1927 won his first of six consecutive 20-win seasons. He would be at his best during Philadelphia's three-year run in the World Series, capped off by his 1931 MVP campaign when he led the majors in wins (31), ERA (2.06), complete games (27), and strikeouts (175). Supporting Grove during the '27 season was fellow lefty Rube Walberg (16–12), ageless 43-year-old spitballer Jack Quinn (15–10), Howard Ehmke (12–10), and Eddie Rommel (11–3).

After his down July, Wheat rebounded with a solid August—always one of his strongest months. On August 12, he recorded the 30th and final four-hit game of his career in a 7–1 win over the Boston Red Sox. Cobb

9. Calm Amidst the Storm, 1925–1927

collected four hits in the game, too. The next day, Wheat threw out two would-be runs at home plate. Though the A's went 21–7 in August, there would be no catching Miller Huggins' 110-win "Murderers' Row" Yankees. They had an undeniable lineup, highlighted by MVP Lou Gehrig (.373, 47 home runs, and 173 RBIs) and Babe Ruth (.356, 60 home runs and 165 RBIs). Like Philadelphia, New York's lineup eclipsed a solid pitching staff with six reaching double digits in wins, and Waite Hoyt leading the way with a league-high of 22.

Philadelphia didn't give in, climbing from fourth to second-place by the end of the month, where they remained for the duration of the season. They finished 91–63, 19 games behind the eventual World Series champion Yankees. Mack thought his team could have performed better. He blamed an unlikely source—harassment by a fan, Harry Donnelly, who had been a nuisance for the past few seasons. In mid–September, Mack had finally heard enough from Donnelly, who heckled players and umpires from the sparsely populated left-field bleachers at Philadelphia's Shibe Park. He was arrested and had to appear in court. Among other accusations, the A's manager said that the constant provocation Bill Lamar being released, Hale to make errors, and Wheat to asked to be pulled from a game after Donnelly's verbal barrage following a crucial error.

"I'm a regular rooter for them," contended Donnelly, who was instructed by the judge to stay away from the park or he would receive a hefty fine. "I've only been rooting so that they might get out there and win."[49]

In late September, Philadelphia scheduled an inter-league exhibition game against the Dodgers at Ebbets Field. Deemed "Buck Wheat Day," it had the makings of a special homecoming for Wheat, who continued to be a frequent topic in the *Brooklyn Daily Eagle*. He was the last of the veteran Athletics to get a recognition day at their previous team, and it proved disappointing, as a small crowd of roughly 2,000 showed up for the Monday afternoon game. The *Eagle* barely covered the game, reporting that Wheat started in left, went hitless in three at-bats, and, "what the crowd lacked in numbers it made up in enthusiasm when Buck Wheat idolized in Flatbush through his long and faithful service here, did anything at all."[50]

On October 12, Wheat was given his unconditional release by Connie Mack. Wheat cherished his experience under the legendary A's manager for years. "Mr. Mack was a wonder and I have often wished I had gone to work for him when I was in my prime," Wheat told Harold W. Langan of the *Sporting News* over a decade later.[51] He had a special fondness for Mack and the A's for giving him a chance. He called a photo of himself, Ty Cobb, and Eddie Collins "the finest memento I brought back from baseball."[52]

10

A Baseball Man Through Thick and Thin

Wheat was not ready to end his playing days. He turned down offers to manage and play for the Memphis Chickasaws of the Southern League and the International League's Jersey City Skeeters. Instead, he signed a contract with the Minneapolis Millers of the American Association in March 1928, departing a few days later for training camp in San Antonio, Texas. Things didn't get off to a good start. He reported 10 pounds underweight due to a severe case of the flu, and despite showing signs of being healthy during early workouts, he suffered a stone bruise in his right heel chasing a fly ball during an exhibition game in Wichita Falls, Texas. He tried to play through it, but it became so problematic that he returned home to Missouri in early April to see if surgery would be needed.

It took several weeks to heal, leaving Wheat relegated to pinch-hitting duties when the regular season started. "Wheat's mere attitude, stance and his swing indicated that he'll have to be a regular somewhere when his bruised heel gets into shape," wrote Charles Johnson of the *Minneapolis Star*.[1]

Yet to start a game, Wheat was still able to thrill the hometown crowd at Nicollet Park. Much like at Ebbets Field, he took advantage of the short porch in right field—roughly 280 feet down the line (with a 25-foot wall). He hit pinch-hit two-run homers on back-to-back days on May 5 and 6. The first one was the game-winner. The second tied the game, which the Millers eventually won.

Millers manager Mike Kelley voiced his concern over how long Wheat's injury lingered, and whether it might force him to retire. Finally, on May 20, Wheat started a game. Playing in left field and batting cleanup, Wheat hit a three-run homer over Nicollett's right field screen to give the Millers a first-inning lead over the Milwaukee Brewers. He was understandably rusty in the field but made a pair of nice catches in a 6–4 win. Kelley announced he would keep Wheat in the lineup as long as the veteran's legs would hold out. George Barton of the *Star Tribune* wrote, "It is

10. A Baseball Man Through Thick and Thin

worth a dollar of any man's money to see Wheat crouching over the plate, digging his feet in the dirt and waving the fence post which he calls a bat."[2]

The following day, the Millers made their first visit of the season to Kansas City. Just 50 miles from Polo, a celebration of Wheat had been in the works for the day game at Muehlebach Field. Prior to the game, players from both teams were pulled together with Wheat in the middle, where he was presented with a diamond ring by fans, many of them representing Polo. He had a first-inning single in the Millers 5–1 win over the Blues.

It was apparent Wheat's lack of mobility made him a liability in the field and base paths. Therefore, Kelley was judicious about starting him. All along, Wheat had been mentoring his teammates. One of them was St. Louis Cardinals prospect Ernie Orsatti. Despite finding success in limited time in 1926, he was sent to Minneapolis to work on his defense. The outfielder/

On May 21, 1928, Zack Wheat Day was held at Muehlebach Field in Kansas City, Missouri. Wheat, pictured with his son, Zack, Jr., was a member of the Minneapolis Millers, there to play the Kansas City Blues. In the stands behind them are (from left to right) Wheat's wife, Daisy; daughter, Mary Helen; and mother-in-law, Mary Forsman. Wheat would retire a few months later (Missouri Valley Special Collections, Kansas City Public Library, Kansas City, Missouri).

first baseman, who would become a key component of the Cardinals' Gas House Gang, raved about the changes Wheat made to his struggling game both defensively and offensively. "In a couple of weeks, Buck coached me on more hitting faults than I ever knew existed," said Orsatti when he returned to the big leagues after hitting .381 with 15 home runs and 84 RBIs for the Millers. "He could see mistakes of which I wasn't conscious and that nobody else could spot. It wasn't long before I snapped out of my slump and started to hit."

Orsatti's limitations in the field were more pronounced, particularly at first base. As a left-hander, he found problems throwing the ball to second and third base. In stepped Wheat to mentor him. "Wheat isn't left-handed as I am and, as far as I know, he never played first base. But he's been around a long while and I guess he know about everything there is to know about baseball. He made a first baseman out of me," said Orsatti, who returned to the Cardinals in late August and helped them to the World Series.[3]

By mid-July, the Millers were in fourth place, and Wheat was slumping at the plate. In a bold attempt to shakeup the lineup, Kelley moved Wheat into the cleanup spot, hoping he could rekindle some of his August successes of years gone by. It didn't take, and Wheat pressed even more when he was asked to play more regularly after Orsatti was called to the Cardinals. In an important series against the Indianapolis Indians, Wheat went one-for-11. He went to Kelley, telling him he was done. "I was hitting .300, but I knew I wasn't going any too well," recalled Wheat, "so early in August I told Mike I was quitting."[4]

Wheat appreciated the opportunity to give it one last try and the way Kelley handled him. "He treated me swell, just as he does all his players," said Wheat.[5]

Less than a week later, Wheat was placed on the inactive list to make room for Charley Miller, an outfielder from Dallas, Texas, and then unconditionally released. Wheat appeared in 82 games for the Millers—many of them pinch-hit appearances. He batted .309, with seven doubles, a triple, and five home runs. The local papers were honest about his shortcomings during the season but paid him tribute. Barton of the *Star Tribune* wrote, "Wheat at the age of 40 can look back over his long baseball record with pride. He was a great ball player and always was a credit to his profession."[6]

Wheat was tabbed to lead a group of American Association All-Stars "until the snow falls," as was reported in an Associated Press article. He retreated to his Polo, Missouri, farm, saying the only way he would return to professional baseball was as a manager of the Brooklyn Dodgers. He kept on playing ball over the next several years, occasionally suiting up for the Kansas City General Cabs, a top semi-pro team in the Kansas City metro

10. A Baseball Man Through Thick and Thin

area, as well as the Kansas City police department aggregation when he joined the force several years later.

In the desperate times of the depression, the Wheats became a target for robberies. In early November 1928, Daisy Wheat was assaulted by burglars at their home on Tauromee Avenue in Kansas City. She was home alone when the assailants barged through the front door, strangled her until she was unconscious, and made off with a diamond pin valued at $100 and a pair of medals Wheat had been given for winning the 1916 and '20 National League pennant. Troubles followed when they moved into a house on Pennsylvania Avenue several years later. Once again, they were victims of a theft, and once again, Daisy was physically accosted by the thief, who made off with a 41-diamond broach valued at $300.

All the while, Dodgers owner Steve McKeever was trying to plan out Wheat's return to Brooklyn. As far back as his first full season away from the professional game, 1929—much to the dismay of Robinson—McKeever wanted to implement a former Dodger at the helm upon the longtime manager's impending retirement. He became fixated on hiring either Grimes—who was thriving as a pitcher in his second of three stints with the Pirates—or Wheat. William McCullough of the *Brooklyn Times Union* reported the move. "They are respected by the fans here and baseball, as popular as it is in the town, would reach greater heights with Grimes or Wheat in the role of manager," McKeever had said.

"As for Wheat," the Dodgers owner explained, "he too would prove successful. There was never a more loyal player in the majors than Wheat was to the Brooklyn Club. His record here is unblemished and it is needless for me to say how the fans would take to him. Zack knows his baseball, too, and with the splendid material we have on hand, I think that he would give Brooklyn a first division team."[7]

Nothing ever materialized from those talks, but a comeback to baseball seemed on the horizon when it was reported that Wheat sold his interest in Tierney & Wheat Recreation to Guy Waite, one of the leading bowlers in the country, in April 1930. Later that year, McKeever dispatched a spokesman to Wheat's farm, where they came to an agreement that he would take over the managerial duties when Robinson was set to retire in October 1931. Wheat would retain the coaching staff—his old teammates Otto Miller and Ivy Olson—and be paid $10,000 a year. In the meantime, word spread that Wheat was going to be added to Robinson's coaching staff as first base coach. Despite his admiration for Wheat, McKeever ended the hearsay. "The manager of the team unconditionally released Wheat a few years ago and perhaps this would result in ill feeling if he were to return as coach. We do not want it said that we are handicapping the Brooklyn manager in any way."[8] Ultimately, Max Carey succeeded Robinson as manager in 1932. A rumor spread of Wheat joining Carey's coaching staff, but that was all it was, a rumor. The job went to Casey Stengel instead.

It was obvious that even after his departure, Robinson didn't want to leave baseball behind. For the next two seasons he was the president and manager of the Southern Association's Atlanta Crackers. At a league meeting in August 1934, he fell in his hotel bathroom, hitting his head on the tub and breaking his arm. While being attended to he joked, "Don't worry about it fellas. I'm an old Oriole. I'm too tough to die." Sadly, he was wrong. He suffered a brain hemorrhage, lapsed into a coma, and died days later with his wife by his side. He was buried in Baltimore's Cathedral Cemetery, not far from his old teammate, John McGraw, who had died less than six months earlier. In 1945, the Old-Timers committee voted Robinson into the Baseball Hall of Fame.

Wheat remained a full-time farmer until the summer of 1932, when the financial strain from the Great Depression and a devastating drought in 1930 were too much to bear. Without a pension from baseball, he was forced to sell his 12-room country home that sat on 160 acres to W.A. Rookstool, an oil contractor from Norman, Oklahoma, for $23,000. (For years an unsubstantiated rumor circulated that Wheat lost his homestead gambling.) Rookstool planned to convert three small valleys into lakes stocked with trout. Wheat had lived on the homestead for a dozen years, spending the majority of his time there since retiring. He wintered with his brother, Mack and his family in California and then returned to his residence in Kansas City to embark on another recreation business venture with Tierney. His official title was vice-president of Tierney-Wheat-Shepard, Inc.

Over the next several years Wheat sporadically played in old-timers' games and for local town ball teams, helped out at baseball camps, and occasionally was rumored to be managing one of those clubs. His absence from professional ball was curious to say the least, especially with the reverence with which he was held as a player. When he showed up at an American Association meeting in Kansas City, former players were telling stories about Wheat to the press. "Just about the toughest boy in the whole league to pitch to," said former Cardinals catcher, Vern Clemons. "That is, when there was something at stake. What was his weakness? I don't know. None of us did. He hit anything."[9]

In 1933, Wheat vied to manage the Reds. The biggest talk came when he was on a list of successors to Max Carey as manager of the Dodgers. Wheat's reported demands of $16,500 took him out of the running. He wrote an open letter to Brooklyn management questioning when these demands

10. A Baseball Man Through Thick and Thin

took place. "I guess I made the proposition sometime when I was asleep and now that I am awake I want to open up negotiations again."[10] Wheat's letter did nothing, and in February 1934, his old friend Stengel was named the Dodgers' new manager. It seems that the Brooklyn faithful still held Wheat in high regard, as the *Brooklyn Daily Eagle* was flooded with letters to get him on the coaching staff—citing the recent return of Honus Wagner as a coach of the Pirates. Nothing ever materialized, and it began a fruitless three-year reign for Stengel, who never finished in the first division.

After failing to get back into professional baseball, Wheat joined the Kansas City police squad in August 1935. In early April 1936, Wheat was given a silver lifetime pass to American and National League games. A few days later, on April 12, 1936, Easter Sunday, Wheat was in a near fatal car accident. "Another cop and I out in Kansas City were moving around in a radio car one night when a gang of gunmen shot out of a side street tore past us, going the other way," recalled Wheat. "We turned around and started after them, were closing in when it happened. Another car tearing across from a side street hit us squarely and I was thrown right through the door of the car and across the road."[11]

Wheat was lucky to be alive. He broke his wrist, nearly bit his tongue off, fractured his skull, broke two neck vertebrae, fractured multiple ribs (two of which punctured his left lung), and suffered a shoulder injury that required doctors to graft ligaments from his leg onto his arm. As word of the accident spread, and with his prognosis unknown, tributes and well-wishes flooded his way. Longtime friend and former teammate Casey Stengel called Wheat "one of the greatest outfielders, both defensively and offensively in baseball," and, "an athlete of the highest standing and a fine gentleman."[12]

Wheat was confined to Menorah Hospital for a few months, but by the summer he was back to being involved around the state—coaching a police team and throwing out a ceremonial first pitch as part of a semi-pro tournament. In August, the Dodgers sent out over 130 invitations to old-time players. On September 10, a celebration was set to take place at Ebbets Field, commemorating the 60th anniversary of the National League. Wheat emerged from the hospital just in time to make the trip to Brooklyn. It had been years since he had been there, and the ball park looked much different than during his glory days. Major renovations took place in 1931, with seating expansion being the main priority. In a few years, night baseball would come to Ebbets Field. At the festivities, Wheat was among a group of former major leaguers, including Babe Ruth and Honus Wagner, but it was Wheat who was the main attraction. He was the only one with an individual moment of recognition, much to the delight of the crowd, and reporters surrounded him with their cameras when he emerged on the field. "And sometime later, 'ol Buck bounced out of the dugout and was introduced at the home plate," reported Tommy Holmes. "They handed him a bat and he caressed it lovingly and flashed that old grin as he assumed his characteristic stance."[13]

A month later, Wheat was named a finalist to succeed Stengel as manager of the Dodgers. Of the 90 men who applied, it came down to Wheat; Grimes, now manager of the Louisville Colonels; Charlie Dressen, manager of the Reds; and former Yankees, Ruth and Tony Lazzeri. Wheat had no contact with the team. "If I'm being considered as manager of the Brooklyn club, its news to me," Wheat told the *New York Daily News*.[14] Grimes, who was supposedly considered for the job as early as July, was officially introduced as manager on November 5. Shortly thereafter, the "Wheat as a bench coach" campaign reignited, flooding Ed Hughes' column in the *Brooklyn Daily Eagle* for several years. It was in Wheat's best interest that he didn't get the job. Grimes did and suffered through two difficult seasons as manager before being replaced by Leo Durocher following the 1938 season. The Detroit Tigers also showed interest in Wheat, but as side effects of his accident lingered, doctors advised him not to pursue the offer.

In 1937, Wheat's name appeared on the Baseball Writers' Association of America Hall of Fame ballot. In his first year he received just five votes (2.5 percent). Interest would bottom out in 1945 (two votes/.8 percent) and peak two years later in 1947 (37/23 percent). It would still be over a decade until he was enshrined. Along the way were disappointments. His time on the regular ballot expired in 1953, and he was passed along to the Veterans Committee. However, his name was kept alive by Tommy Holmes of the *Brooklyn Daily Eagle* and former teammates like Stengel and Cobb, the latter of whom had made it his mission to get players he thought should be in the Hall of Fame elected.

Surprisingly, Wheat was unable to find work in the game, but his on-field accomplishments weren't forgotten. In 1937, James Hendry, described as a "sports historian and record-keeper," polled players from 1900–'39 to name their All-Star team for each decade, collecting more than 100 lists. Wheat's contemporaries had him listed as an outfield alternate on the 1910–'20 squad, beaten out by Joe Jackson for "starter." The other two first-string outfielders were Ty Cobb and Tris Speaker, with Sam Crawford joining Wheat as a bench player.[15]

In December 1937, Wheat lost a $50,000 damage suit when his evidence was insufficient that he collided with a car owned by a motor car company. Upon doctor's advice, the Wheats looked for a change of scenery following the accident. One of the first places Zack thought of was a resort on the shore

10. A Baseball Man Through Thick and Thin

of Lake of the Ozarks in Sunrise Beach, Missouri, a favorite spot that he frequented for hunting and fishing. One day, he and Daisy drove over to take a look. As luck would have it, the owner was looking to sell, and shortly thereafter, the Wheats were in possession of the property. They soon opened a 46-acre hunting and fishing resort with a dozen cabins, a boat landing, rowboats, motor launch, and duck blinds. Located in an area known as "Hurricane Deck," the resort became a popular destination for former players.

Daisy had taken to domestic life over the years. When the Wheats were still living in Polo, she would occasionally take the train to Chicago for some big-city entertainment. In the coming years she grew content living on the lake. As during the days when Zack's teammates would come for dinner, Daisy loved to make food for people. She canned and pickled fruits and vegetables from her garden, baked pies, and served the fish and game caught at the resort. Zack was still restless, yearning to be a part of major league baseball.

Wheat continued to try to find his way back into professional baseball, applying for a job as a scout in December 1939. He went through the summer of 1940 without being hired, but in the fall, Brooklyn owner Larry MacPhail invited a number of former Dodgers back to Ebbets Field for an Old-Timers event. He put them up at Brooklyn's ritzy Hotel Bossert and paid all their expenses. On September 22, 1940, Wheat was among two-dozen former Dodgers—some of them former teammates he hadn't seen in 15 years—who played a three-inning exhibition game against the current squad. The Old-Timers lost 6–3, but Wheat showed he was still a fan-favorite as the crowd's loudest cheers came when he caught fly balls in left field and then rapped a single to center to drive in a run in the third inning.

After the game, Wheat and a handful of former players walked a few blocks over to the apartment of the man who signed him for the Dodgers—Larry Sutton—who was in failing health. Wheat knew first-hand what these types of visits meant, once confessing that without the occasional drop-in of former teammates and other baseball figures, he'd be lost. "I feel like an old retired fire horse when he hears that fire bell," he once said. "I feel like I would rather be any place where I could see or hear or talk baseball."[16]

A year later, in 1941, Holmes named Wheat to his All-Time, All-Star Brooklyn Dodgers team. Many of Wheat's teammates were on the first team, including Jake Daubert, first base, and Jimmy Johnston, third base. Though Wheat had been retired for over a dozen years, his impact was still being felt. "Buck Wheat's classic batting style still rates discussion among young players who never saw him but have heard of him, sometimes second or third hand," wrote Holmes.[17]

Zack Wheat

Later in 1941, Harold W. Lanigan of the *Sporting News* visited Wheat at his home at Lake of the Ozarks. Lanigan and his photographer, George Dorrill, were met by Wheat, Daisy, and their son, Zack, Jr., a six-foot-four former football player at Wentworth Military Academy in Lexington, Missouri. The pair were treated to a wonderful visit, including a huge meal made by Daisy. Zack was in great spirits, and the seemingly only residual effect of the car accident that nearly took his life was, of all things, the wrist injury. "Some nights it's plain murder the way it hurts," said Wheat. As Lanigan and Dorrill left, Wheat "waved a cheery goodbye and called: 'Tell all the boys to come down when they want some good hunting or fishing.'"[18]

With the litany of all-time teams that Wheat was being named to, it is only necessary that he had a few of his own. He gave one to Lanigan during his visit, who listed a few comments from Wheat:

Catchers—Mickey Cochrane ("distanced all catchers")
Pitchers: Christy Mathewson ("greatest of all pitchers"), Pete Alexander ("no pushover"), Rube Waddell ("a wizard"), and Nap Rucker ("just as good as Rube, but Nap always had a poor club behind him")
First Base—Hal Chase
Second Base—Rogers Hornsby ("tops of all right-hand hitters")
Third Base—Pie Trainer
Shortstop—Honus Wagner ("class by himself as infielder")
Outfielders: Ty Cobb, Tris Speaker, and Joe Jackson

Wheat gave a few more over the years, including these two squads:
All-Star Brooklyn Club from his years on the team:

1st base—Jake Daubert
2nd base—George Cutshaw
3rd base—Jimmy Johnston
Shortstop—Ivy Olson
Left field—"I was the only LF there"
Center field—Hy Myers
Right Field—Casey Stengel
Catcher—Otto Miller
Left-handed pitcher—Nap Rucker
Right-handed pitcher—Dazzy Vance

All-Star National League Team

1st base—Gil Hodges
2nd base—Rogers Hornsby
3rd base—Pie Traynor

10. A Baseball Man Through Thick and Thin

Shortstop—Honus Wagner
Left field—"I was the only LF there"
Center field—Edd Roush
Right Field—Stan Musial
Catcher—Roy Campanella
Left-handed pitcher—Eppa Rixey
Right-handed pitcher—Christy Mathewson[19]

During World War II, Zack, Jr., served in the Army, stationed in Hawaii. Zack, Sr., aided the war effort by taking up work as a safety engineer at the Sunflower Ordinance Works in De Soto, Kansas. "The way I figure this war, it's the series for the real world championship, and if I'm too old to play, I'd rather be bat boy than sit in the stands," he said. "It isn't much like Ebbets Field, but I figure everybody that's helping out in the war is in the big leagues now, from the messenger boys up."[20] The war-depleted Dodgers also called on Wheat to help, bringing him back for the Tri-Cornered War Bond Game on June 26, 1944. In the three-way game between New York teams, Wheat and other stars from each franchise were part of the pre-game festivities. The final score was Dodgers, five; Yankees, one; and Giants, 0.

In the summer of 1949, Frank Graham, who a few years earlier had published a book chronicling the history of the Brooklyn franchise, put together his own all-time Dodgers team that was published in the *New York Journal-American*, and subsequently printed in *Baseball Digest*. It was still heavy with players from Wheat's era. "Since the passing of Zack Wheat after the season of 1926, his like has not been seen in Brooklyn—nor anywhere else, for that matter," wrote Graham.[21]

A few months later, in October 1949, a reunion of the 1916 pennant-winning Brooklyn club took place during the Yankees and Dodgers World Series, with 15 of the 18 surviving members in attendance. The group—many of whom hadn't seen each other in years—took in all the games (the Yankees won in five games), reminiscing throughout. The Dodgers Old-Timers dinner party was held at the Hotel St. George, hosted by Branch Rickey. Among attendees was Yankees manager Casey Stengel, a member of the '16 team. He put aside the gravity of the series, sitting next to and visiting with Dodgers manager Burt Shotton, and delivering the keynote speech, which included calling Wheat "one of the greatest hitters I ever saw in my life."[22]

Wheat and Stengel had an indelible connection. In October 1952, Wheat travelled to Los Angeles to surprise his old friend for the television show *This Is Your Life*. Stengel, coming off his fourth-straight World Series title as manager of the Yankees, was there under the assumption he was

Zack Wheat

there to receive an award from the *Los Angeles Times* National Sports Award Board. When he got to the Capitan Theater, he was greeted by a people from his past, including Wheat, who spoke on Stengel's first major league game.

Wheat's absence from the Hall of Fame continued to perplex many, and longtime fans and sportswriters took it upon themselves to push for his enshrinement—still several years away. In 1952, Holmes wrote, "Each year I vote that he be elected to Cooperstown, but too few of the present-day voters remember him."[23]

When Wheat passed two decades later, Fred Lieb wrote to Wheat's daughter, Mary, telling her, "For some time, in the 1930s and 1940s: I was peeved at my fellow writers in the Baseball Writers Association for not naming Zack to the Hall of Fame."[24]

Personally, 1953 was a trying year for Wheat. His brother, Basil, died on June 18 at the Leeds (Missouri) Sanitarium after a brief illness.

Wheat (middle) traveled to Los Angeles, California, to surprise Casey Stengel (right) on the television show *This Is Your Life*, which aired on October 29, 1952. Wheat is shown talking with host Ralph Edwards about Stengel's first major league game (courtesy *Sporting News*. All rights reserved. Reprinted with permission).

10. A Baseball Man Through Thick and Thin

Following his baseball career, Basil worked as a maintenance man at the Jackson County courthouse. A few months later, on November 1, Wheat's mother, Julia, passed at the age of 89. That same difficult year—Wheat's last on the regular Hall of Fame ballot—he was given some further respect by Jim Crusinberry. A charter member of the Baseball Writers Association, he named Wheat to his all-time National League team, but that didn't help his cause. The following year, 1954, Holmes announced that Wheat had dropped off the ballot indefinitely due to the 25-year statute of limitations following retirement. His fate was now put in the hands of the Hall of Fame Veterans Committee, established the year before. The eleven members were to meet in odd number years (changed to even in 1956) to elect players over the 25-year threshold. After electing six players in their first year, the committee was limited to two per session.

Reminiscences of Wheat continued to find a way into newspapers. Murray Robinson of the *New York Journal-American* recalled the exact moment his idolatry of Wheat began. "Zack Wheat became our hero one summer day long, long ago as we sat soaking wet in the left field bleachers in a sudden rainstorm. He made a one-handed catch in the rain and almost slid into the bleachers on top of us. He apologized—and won us all over for all time."[25]

It was evident Wheat still missed being a part of professional baseball a quarter century after he retired. He once said that each spring he regarded himself "the loneliest man on the planet."[26] At home he often simultaneously had a game on the television and one on the radio. He and Daisy occasionally travelled to Kansas City, St. Louis, or beyond to watch games, gaining entrance with his lifetime pass to any ballpark. He yearned for another Old-Timers game, too, anxious to see former teammates and once again feel the adulation of the fans. "That one a couple of years ago was great, too bad we can't have them more often," he told the *Brooklyn Daily Eagle* while watching the Dodgers play in St. Louis in August 1953. "It's great to see those guys you played with and I think the fans get a kick out of it, too."[27]

Wheat never publicly showed ill-will towards the modern game. He was always complimentary of players and never begrudged the increasing salaries. He wasn't one to dole out advice either, but, when he did, he said with a wink, "Tell them to learn to chew tobacco."[28]

Wheat got his wish to return to Ebbets Field a few years later in mid–August 1955, when an all-time, all-star Brooklyn team was honored between games of a doubleheader against the Phillies. He was the senior member of a team that included Duke Snider and Dixie Walker, outfield; Gil Hodges, first base; Jackie Robinson, second base; Pee Wee Reese, shortstop; Cookie Lavagetto, third base; Roy Campanella, catcher; and Dazzy

Zack Wheat

Vance, pitcher. The group was awarded silver platters by Commissioner Ford Frick. The 67-year-old Wheat received one of the largest ovations when he hit three pitches off former teammate, Dazzy Vance.

The following summer, 1956, Wheat was so desperate to get back in the game that he took on duties as a "bird-dog" scout for the Kansas City A's, whom he closely followed. He received no pay and no expenses for his services. "I've got a job, but I find it impossible to stay away from baseball in some form or other."[29]

In fall 1957, the Veterans Committee voted Wheat into the Hall of Fame. It was short-lived, when the group realized that Wheat was ineligible for election because he had been retired for less than the requisite 30 years. With the Veteran's Committee's voting schedule of every other season, Wheat would have to wait until the '59 session. It was frustrating, but to those that followed Brooklyn baseball, he remained a legend. In January 1958, baseball writers threw a party for Babe Hamberger, who worked in a number of capacities for the Dodgers, starting as a 14-year-old batboy in 1921 and finishing as the superintendent of Ebbets Field when the club moved to Los Angeles. They asked him who the best Dodger was in his nearly four decades with the organization. "That's easy," he replied. "Zack Wheat." A follow-up question of the greatest fellow of that time, "Zack Wheat. No contest," he answered.[30]

Dan Comerford, who served as Dodgers equipment manager for decades starting in 1906, listed Wheat as the greatest Dodger during his time, followed by Jake Daubert and Nap Rucker.[31]

On August 15, 1958, Wheat was named the tenth member of the Missouri Sports Hall of Fame, joining Carl Hubbell, 1951; Stengel and Phog Allen, 1952; Bill Corum and Don Faurot, 1953; Cal Hubbard, 1954; Vernon Kennedy, 1955; Brutus Hamilton, 1956; and C.E. McBride, 1957. A ceremony was held at the Missouri State Fair in Sedalia on August 22.

Finally, in February 1959, came the emotional call that Wheat had finally been elected into the Hall of Fame. He was the 84th man voted in and 11th by the Veterans Committee. It took the committee all of a half hour to decide. Of the 11 votes he received, ten were first-place, and one second place. During his 16 years on the BBWAA ballots (1937–'55), Wheat received a total of 276 votes. With the BBWAA only voting during even numbered years (a practice that lasted until 1967), he would be the lone inductee that year.

Wheat took the opportunity to scrutinize the Major League Baseball pension system that was put in place in 1947 by then commissioner, Happy Chandler. It left out all players that retired before then, including Hall of Famers, such as Wheat. "Some of them have no place to live and are entirely dependent on their children," he declared. "After all, they were pioneers in

10. A Baseball Man Through Thick and Thin

the game and helped get it established. It seems to me they are deserving of help."[32]

Casey Stengel chastised the Baseball Writers and Veterans Committee for taking so long to vote Wheat in, before paying tribute to his friend: "As a great outfielder and hitter, as a teacher and a friend, as a veteran who tried to help the kids, Zach was matchless. If I know anything about batting, I got my groundwork from Wheat."[33]

July proved to be a busy month for Wheat. On July 16, friends in Lake of the Ozarks gathered to pay tribute to him before his departure for Cooperstown. Four days later, on July 20, Wheat was in upstate New York, accompanied by his daughter, Mary Gottshall. It was a bitter sweet moment for Wheat, as Daisy was too ill to make the trip. "I would have been here anyway," said Mary, "but it is doubly important because mother is not well enough to make the trip and she despaired of finding out everything that happened from Dad."[34]

His plaque read:

> Zachariah (Zack) Davis Wheat, Brooklyn N.L. 1909–'26. Philadelphia A.L. 1927. Brooklyn outfielder for 18 years, holds Brooklyn record for—games played 2,318 at bat, 8,859, hits 2,804, singles 2,038, doubles 464, triples 171, total bases 4,003, extra base hits 766. Batted .375 (1923) .375 (1924) .359 (1925) league batting leader .335 (1918) lifetime batting average .317 with 2,884 hits, played 2,406 games.

Wheat's speech was brief, but emotional: "This is one of the greatest moments of my life. I'm here on my first visit and I saw a lot of things at the Hall of Fame yesterday which brought back memories. It's a beautiful setting for this sort of thing. I want to take this occasion to thank everyone for everything." The moment overtook him, and he paused for a moment. "I don't know what I was going to say. I had something planned but I can't remember it now. Again I want to thank everyone, each member of the old-timers committee of the Baseball Writers association and all of those who have made this day possible."[35]

As he walked back to his seat alongside his daughter, Wheat was greeted by Ty Cobb. Holmes wrote that he met his former teammate with outstretched hands, his "voice choked with emotion and eyes burning."[36]

Afterwards, Wheat mingled with them and others at the Otesaga Hotel, signing the occasional autograph. One man approached Wheat, asking, "You one of the old-timers?"

"That's right," replied Wheat.

"What's your name?" the man demanded, unaware of who he was talking to.

"Jesse James," retorted Wheat with a slight smile.[37]

Zack Wheat

Wheat during his Hall of Fame induction speech, July 20, 1959. He was the lone inductee that year (Kenny Dixon photo collection).

Wheat fielded endless interviews and was humble throughout. When he was pressed to compare himself to modern players, he was gracious. "The game has changed since the days when I played," he told Joe McGuiff of the *Kansas City Star*, adding, "The lively ball has made the big difference. They play the game so differently that you just can't make comparisons."[38]

Less than a week later, on July 26, Wheat was honored at Municipal Stadium, during an A's and Red Sox game. He had been a fan of the A's since playing for them in 1927, but even more so after the club moved from Philadelphia to Kansas City in 1955. He and Daisy frequently made the 150 mile drive to watch games. In the stands were some the game's greats: Franklin "Home Run" Baker, Ty Cobb, Jimmie Foxx, Lefty Grove, Rogers Hornsby, Ray Schalk and Paul Waner. Also there was Warren Giles, National League president. With Daisy once again absent, Mary and Zack, Jr. were in attendance. Wheat entered the field in a white Nash Rambler sedan and made his way around the warning track with a police escort before being dropped off by home plate. There, A's owner, Arnold Johnson, acknowledged the legends in attendance before a flattering tribute of Wheat, who was gifted a

10. A Baseball Man Through Thick and Thin

traveling clock and transistor radio. Wheat thanked those in attendance and was on his way back to his seat when Johnson called him back and handed over the keys of the vehicle and urged him to attend more A's games. A beaming Wheat once again stepped to the microphone and spoke about the last months, calling them "the greatest thrills of my life."[39]

Yet another celebration awaited Wheat in New York City. Since the Dodgers were now in Los Angeles, the Yankees took it upon themselves to honor Wheat during their 17th annual Old-Timers' Day. They paid Wheat's travel expenses, putting him up in the Savoy-Hilton on Fifth Avenue. He was the guest of honor amongst the 61 all-time greats in attendance (including 11 Hall of Famers), which spotlighted past Yankees, National League, and World Series heroes since 1921. In October, Wheat was the guest of the Dodgers, throwing out the first pitch before a record-breaking crowd prior to Game Five of the World Series between the Dodgers and Chicago White Sox at the Los Angeles Memorial Coliseum. Sportswriter Dan Parker wrote that the next day Wheat went to the game with Bill Veeck, Babe Herman, Parker, and his two sons and was denied entry until he bought a ticket.

Sadly, several weeks later, on November 29, 1959, Daisy Wheat died at the age of 71, at a Kansas City hospital, after an 11-day illness. She had been in good health in recent years other than a back injury a few years prior when she fell at home. After four-and-a-half decades of marriage, the loss was difficult for Wheat to handle.

A respite for Wheat during his sorrows was continued accolades. On January 31, 1965, he became the fifth player to receive the Sid Mercer Memorial Award from the New York Chapter Baseball Writers Association at their annual dinner at the Americana Hotel. He joined Ty Cobb, 1960; Rogers Hornsby, 1962; Max Carey, 1963; and Rube Marquard, 1964 (there was no recipient in 1961). The award was seen as a retroactive MVP award. Wheat won for his 1918 campaign, when he won his lone batting title. In a rare moment of genuineness, Stengel, who was manager and vice-president of the New York Mets, showered his longtime friend with praise: "One of the grandest guys ever to wear a baseball uniform, one of the greatest batting teachers I have ever seen, one of the truest pals a man ever had and one of the kindliest men God ever created."[40] Wheat became a regular at events for the Mets.

Several week later, in March 1965, Wheat travelled to Florida for the first time since 1927, when he was training with the Philadelphia Athletics in Fort Myers. He was a guest of the Manatee County Chamber of Commerce's second annual Hall of Fame banquet. Overdressed in a wool suit (with a modest Hall of Fame lapel pin), wool shirt, and carrying a raincoat, he gave a long interview to the *Tampa Tribune*, as memories of past spring trainings flooded his mind.

In 1969, during major league baseball's centennial season, writers and broadcasters once again selected an all-time Dodgers team. Wheat was the only player of his era to earn enough votes to make the roster. As a testament to his legacy, he was second place to Sandy Koufax (32½ votes to four) as the "Greatest Dodger of All-Time." Dodger fans voted for their own all-time team that year, too. Wheat was recognized as the franchise's greatest left fielder by them as well.

Wheat's Hall of Fame status continued to make him a draw for interviews and appearances. Wearing his Hall of Fame lapel, he travelled the country to be honored. It was at one of these gatherings in March 1972, that he contacted a virus that left him, his daughter, Mary, and Frank Frisch extremely sick. When they returned north, Wheat was still ailing, but wanted to make it to his home to recuperate. Driven by his grandson, Zachary E. Wheat, the elder Wheat grew gravely ill on his way back to Sunrise Beach. Mary was called, and the group headed for Bothwell Hospital in Sedalia, Missouri, with Zack laying in the back seat in agony. They arrived at the hospital on March 11, and as his grandson carried him in, Zack passed away. He was buried at Forest Hill and Calvary Cemetery in Kansas City, Missouri, alongside his wife, Daisy.[41]

In 1976, the National League held a centennial anniversary celebration. Among other actions, it named All-Star teams from four different era. Wheat was named to the 1901–'25 squad, along with Roger Bresnahan, catcher; Jake Daubert, first base; Rogers Hornsby, second base; Heinie Groh, third base; Honus Wagner, shortstop; Edd Roush and Max Carey, outfield; and Christy Mathewson and Eppa Rixey, pitchers.

In the mid–1980s, a push for more recognition for Wheat began. On the occasion of Wheat's 100th birthday, his grandniece, Frances Aardal, started an ambitious campaign to fund a lighted Zack Wheat ball field on his former farm near Polo, Missouri, for the Caldwell County Dodgers, a 14- to 18-year-old team (he also had a Little League named after him). Aardal reached out to as many people as she could, including the Los Angeles Dodgers. Team president O'Malley responded with a check for $500 and souvenirs. The cost proved too much, and the proposal eventually failed.

Wheat was honored in several ways in Missouri over the years. A stretch of Highway 13 running through Caldwell County is named Zack Wheat Memorial Highway. Nearby is a stone Zack Wheat Memorial that was originally erected on his Polo farm and then moved down the road to Stagecoach Park, where Zach Wheat Memorial Sports Complex sits.

10. A Baseball Man Through Thick and Thin

American Legion Post 624 in Sunrise Beach, Missouri, was named after him as the primary program of the Legion was baseball (this was initiated a month before his death). In late September 1974, a dedication was held for the Zack Wheat Memorial Roadside Park at the intersection of Route 5 and Lake Road 33. The Sunrise Beach community raised $1,645.17 for the Zack Wheat monument, and the ceremony was heavily attended. The guest speaker was Green County Sheriff, Mickey Owen, a former Dodger catcher. In 2010, the monument was moved to its current location at Zack Wheat American Legion Post 624.

Today, nearly a century of seasons has come and gone since Wheat retired, and almost a half-century has passed since his death. During the franchise's Brooklyn years, he was considered not only the Dodgers' most popular player, but its greatest. In the decades since, as the success of the teams and players of the 1940s and '50 took attention away from him and the franchise moved across country to Los Angeles, Wheat has been forgotten by many. Furthermore, he played in an era when numbers weren't worn, thus the franchise hasn't held a formal number retirement ceremony to keep his name alive. However, his impact is undeniable, as his name is littered throughout the Dodgers record book. He still leads in several career batting categories, with no one on the horizon to overtake him any time soon:

Games—2,322
At-bats—8,559
Hits—2,804
Singles—2,038
Doubles—464
Triples—171
Total Bases—4,003

Appendix: Major League Statistics

Zachariah Davis Wheat
Born: May 23, 1888, Hamilton, Missouri
Died: March 11, 1972, Sedalia, Missouri
Height: 5'10"
Weight: 170 lbs.
Bats: Left
Throws: Right
First Game: September 11, 1909
Final Game: September 21, 1927

Appendix: Major League Statistics

Year-by-Year Regular Season
Major League Batting Statistics

Year	Team	LG	G	AB	R	H	2B	3B	HR	RBI	SB	BB	SO	BA
1909	BRO	NL	26	102	15	31	7	3	0	4	1	6	13	.304
1910	BRO	NL	156	606	78	172	36	15	2	55	16	47	80	.284
1911	BRO	NL	140	534	55	153	26	13	5	76	21	29	58	.287
1912	BRO	NL	123	453	70	138	28	7	8	65	16	39	40	.305
1913	BRO	NL	138	535	64	161	28	10	7	58	19	25	45	.301
1914	BRO	NL	145	533	66	170	26	9	9	89	20	47	50	.319
1915	BRO	NL	146	528	64	136	15	12	5	66	21	52	42	.258
1916	BRO	NL	149	568	76	177	32	13	9	73	19	43	49	.312
1917	BRO	NL	109	362	38	113	15	11	1	41	5	20	18	.312
1918	BRO	NL	105	409	39	137	15	3	0	51	9	16	17	.335
1919	BRO	NL	137	536	70	159	23	11	5	62	15	33	27	.297
1920	BRO	NL	148	583	89	191	26	13	9	73	8	48	21	.328
1921	BRO	NL	148	568	91	182	31	10	14	85	11	44	19	.320
1922	BRO	NL	152	600	92	201	29	12	16	112	9	45	22	.335
1923	BRO	NL	98	349	63	131	13	5	8	65	3	23	12	.375
1924	BRO	NL	141	566	92	212	41	8	14	97	3	49	18	.375
1925	BRO	NL	150	616	125	221	42	14	14	103	3	45	22	.359
1926	BRO	NL	111	411	68	119	31	2	5	35	4	21	14	.290

Appendix: Major League Statistics

Year	Team	LG														BA
1927	PHI	AL	88	247	34	80	12	1	1	38	2	18	5			.324
Total			2,410	9,106	1,289	2,884	476	172	132	1,248	205	650	572			.317

World Series Batting Statistics

Year	Team	LG	Series	Opp	G	AB	R	H	2B	3B	HR	RBI	SB	BB	SO	BA
1916	BRO	NL	WS	BOS (L)	5	19	2	4	0	1	0	1	1	2	2	.211
1920	BRO	NL	WS	CLE (L)	7	27	2	9	2	0	0	2	0	1	2	.333
Total					**12**	**46**	**4**	**13**	**2**	**1**	**0**	**3**	**1**	**3**	**4**	**.283**

Source: Baseball-Reference.com

Chapter Notes

Preface

1. *Baseball Digest* (Gurnee, IL), March, 1965, p. 89
2. Donald Honig and Lawrence Ritter, *The 100 Greatest Baseball Players of All Time* (New York: Crown Publishers, Inc., 1981), p. 219.

Prologue

1. *Sporting News* (St. Louis, MO), February, 11, 1959, p. 3.
2. *Ibid.*
3. *Sporting News* (St. Louis, MO), February, 11, 1959, p. 2.
4. *New York Journal-American* (New York, NY), February 3, 1959, p. unknown. Zack Wheat Clippings File, National Baseball Hall of Fame and Museum (Cooperstown, NY).

Chapter 1

1. *San Bernardino Sun* (San Bernardino, CA), July 21, 1959, p. 13
2. *Baseball Magazine* (Boston, MA), January, 1917, p. 51.
3. *Harper Sentinel* (Harper, KS), July 6, 1916, p. 3.
4. *Brooklyn Citizen* (Brooklyn, NY), March 6, 1913, p. 4.
5. Lake of the Ozarks Association, *50th Anniversary, Bagnell Dam, 1931–1981* (Lake Ozark, MO: Lake of the Ozarks Association, 1989), p. 292.
6. Alfred H. Spink, *The National Game* (St. Louis: National Game Publishing Co., 1910), p. 256.
7. *Sporting News* (St. Louis, MO), November 20, 1941, p. 5.
8. *Gazette Globe* (Kansas City, KS), February 22, 1911, p. 3.
9. *Brooklyn Daily Eagle* (Brooklyn, NY), June 3, 1910, p. 23.
10. *Kansas City Kansan* (Kansas City, Kansas), October 8, 1920, p. 1.
11. *Sporting News* (St. Louis, MO), February, 11, 1959, p. 6.
12. *Kansas City Star* (Kansas City, MO), April 11, 1965, p. 109.
13. *Sporting News* (St. Louis, MO), November 20, 1941, p. 5.
14. *Kansas City Star* (Kansas City, MO), April 11, 1965, p. 109.
15. *Brooklyn Daily Eagle* (Brooklyn, NY), May 27, 1913, p. 22.
16. *Sporting News* (St. Louis, MO), November 20, 1941, p. 5.
17. *Brooklyn Daily Eagle* (Brooklyn, NY), February 19, 1911, p. 49.
18. *Montgomery Advertiser* (Montgomery, Alabama), June 21, 1909, p. 7.
19. Solomon's tip led to Ebbets allowing the businessman to become the vice president of the Newark Sailors (later Indians) of the Eastern League.
20. P.J. Dragseth, ed., *Eye for Talent: Interviews with Veteran Baseball Scouts* (Jefferson, NC: McFarland, 2014), p. 6.
21. *Baseball Magazine* (Boston, MA), July, 1915, p. 50.
22. *Kansas City Times* (Kansas City, MO), May 22, 1925, p.11.
23. Lee Allen, *The Giants and the Dodgers: The Fabulous Story of Baseball's Fiercest Feud* (New York: G.P. Putnam's Sons, 1964), p. 79.
24. Tommy Holmes, *The Dodgers* (New York: Macmillan, 1975), p. 146.
25. *Kansas City Star* (Kansas City, MO), February 8, 1959, p.5B

26. *Halstead Independent* (Halstead, KS), May 20, 1920, p. 2.
27. Allen, *The Giants and the Dodgers*, p. 79.

Chapter 2

1. Tom Simon, ed., *Deadball Stars of the National League* (Dulles, VA: Potomac Books, 2004), p. 271.
2. Edward E. Steele, *Ebbets: The History and Genealogy of a New York Family* (St. Louis: E.E. Steele, 2005), p. 104.
3. Frank Graham, *The Brooklyn Dodgers: An Informal History* (New York: G.P. Putnam's Sons, 1947), pp. 31–32.
4. *Sporting News* (St. Louis, MO), February, 11, 1959, p. 6.
5. *Brooklyn Daily Eagle* (Brooklyn, NY), October 3, 1909, p. 19.
6. *Sporting News* (St. Louis, MO), November 20, 1941, p. 5.
7. *St. Louis Globe-Democrat* (St. Louis, MO), June 12, 1910, p. 48.
8. *Kansas City Star* (Kansas City, MO) July 16, 1959, p. 1B.
9. *Kansas City Kansan* (Kansas City, Kansas), date and page unknown. Zack Wheat Clippings File, National Baseball Hall of Fame and Museum (Cooperstown, NY).
10. Allen, *The Giants and the Dodgers*, p. 81.
11. *Brooklyn Daily Eagle* (Brooklyn, NY), October 21, 1909, p. 26.
12. *Logansport Reporter* (Logansport, IN), November 24, 1909, p. 6.
13. *St. Louis Star and Times* (St. Louis, MO), February 13, 1910, p. 9.
14. Allen, *The Giants and the Dodgers*, p. 74.
15. *Kansas City Star* (Kansas City, MO), June 8, 1924, p. 13.
16. *Brooklyn Daily Eagle* (Brooklyn, NY), March 5, 1928, p. 24.
17. *Montana Standard* (Butte, MT), July 1, 1924, p. 8.
18. *Ibid.*
19. *Ibid.*
20. Holmes, *The Dodgers*, p. 147.
21. Lane, *Hitters* (Cleveland: Society for American Baseball Research, 2001), p. 24.
22. *Brooklyn Daily Eagle* (Brooklyn, NY), June 3, 1910, p. 23.
23. *Logansport Pharos Tribune* (Logansport, IN), June 24, 1910, p. 4.
24. Lane, *Hitters*, p. 46.
25. Lane, *Hitters*, p. 137.
26. *Brooklyn Daily Eagle* (Brooklyn, NY), September 21, 1940, p. 11.
27. *Orlando Evening Star* (Orlando, FL), January 22, 1958, p. 5.
28. *Baseball Magazine* (Boston, MA), July, 1915, p. 52.
29. Lane, *Hitters*, p. 29.
30. *Brooklyn Daily Eagle* (Brooklyn, NY), January 24, 1911, p. 23.
31. *Brooklyn Daily Eagle* (Brooklyn, NY), March 8, 1911, p. 25.
32. *Brooklyn Daily Eagle* (Brooklyn, NY), July 8, 1911, p. 13.
33. *Brooklyn Daily Eagle* (Brooklyn, NY), September 21, 1940, p. 11.
34. *Ibid.*
35. *Sporting News* (St. Louis, MO), January 25, 1969, p. 44.
36. *Brooklyn Daily Eagle* (Brooklyn, NY), September 10, 1936, p. 20.
37. *Brooklyn Daily Eagle* (Brooklyn, NY), January 3, 1912, p. 22.
38. *Brooklyn Daily Eagle* (Brooklyn, NY), October 3, 1920, p. 2.
39. John G. Zinn. *Charles Ebbets: The Man Behind the Dodgers and Brooklyn' Beloved Ballpark* (Jefferson, NC: McFarland, 2019), p. 124.
40. *Brooklyn Daily Eagle* (Brooklyn, NY), May 20, 1912, p. 6.
41. *Brooklyn Daily Eagle* (Brooklyn, NY), September 18, 1912, p. 22.
42. *Brooklyn Daily Eagle* (Brooklyn, NY), September 27, 1912, p. 20.
43. *Baseball Magazine* (Boston, MA), July, 1915, p. 52.

Chapter 3

1. *Brooklyn Daily Eagle* (Brooklyn, NY), March 14, 1913, p. 20.
2. *Brooklyn Daily Eagle* (Brooklyn, NY), March 27, 1913, p. 22.
3. *Brooklyn Daily Eagle* (Brooklyn, NY), June 25, 1913, p. 20.
4. *Brooklyn Daily Eagle* (Brooklyn, NY), June 1, 1913, p. 75.
5. *Baseball Magazine* (Boston, MA), July, 1915, p. 47.

Notes—Chapter 4

6. *Ibid.*
7. *Brooklyn Daily Eagle* (Brooklyn, NY), June 14, 1953, p. 17.
8. *Brooklyn Daily Eagle* (Brooklyn, NY), February 1, 1949, p. 11.
9. *Ibid.*
10. *Sporting News* (St. Louis, MO), February 11, 1959. P. 6.
11. Lane, *Hitters*, p. 69.
12. Carrie Polk Johnston and W.H. S. McGlumphy, *History of Clinton and Caldwell Counties, Missouri* (Topeka: Historical Publishing Company, 1923), p. 193.
13. *Kansas City Star* (Kansas City, MO), August 22, 1930, p, 14.
14. John Snyder, *Dodgers Journal: Year by Year and Day by Day with the Brooklyn and Los Angeles Dodgers since 1884* (Cincinnati: Clerisy Press, 2009), p. 127.
15. *Brooklyn Daily Eagle* (Brooklyn, NY), June 14, 1925, p. 39.
16. *Ibid.*
17. Simon, ed., *Deadball Stars of the National League*, p. 302.
18. *Brooklyn Daily Eagle* (Brooklyn, NY), June 14, 1925, p. 39.
19. Allen, *The Giants and the Dodgers*, p. 94.
20. Jack Kavanagh and Norman L. Macht, *Uncle Robbie* (Cleveland: Society for American Baseball Research, 1999), p. 56.
21. *Ibid.*, p. 95.
22. Lane, *Hitters*, p. 94.
23. *Kansas City Star* (Kansas City, MO), July 30, 1958, p. 28.
24. Graham, *The Brooklyn Dodgers*, p. 45.
25. Graham, *The Brooklyn Dodgers*, p. 29.
26. Graham, *The Brooklyn Dodgers*, p. 66.
27. Source unknown, September 21, 1953, page unknown. Zack Wheat Clippings File, National Baseball Hall of Fame and Museum (Cooperstown, NY).
28. Lane, *Hitters*, p. 21.
29. *Tampa Bay Times* (St. Petersburg, FL), May 22, 1915, p. 6.
30. *Baseball Magazine* (Boston, MA), July, 1917, p. 358.
31. *Brooklyn Daily Eagle* (Brooklyn, NY), April 29, 1915, p. 20.
32. *Ibid.*
33. *Brooklyn Daily Eagle* (Brooklyn, NY), May 2, 1915, p. 37.
34. Graham, *The Brooklyn Dodgers*, p. 50.
35. Harry Grayson, *They Played the Game* (New York: A.S. Barnes & Company, 1945), p. 143.
36. *Brooklyn Daily Eagle* (Brooklyn, NY), March 29, 1941, p. 9.
37. *Brooklyn Daily Eagle* (Brooklyn, NY), September 21, 1940, p. 11.
38. *Brooklyn Daily Eagle* (Brooklyn, NY), April 1, 1947, p. 11.
39. *Baseball Magazine* (Boston, MA), March, 1919, p. 279.
40. *Brooklyn Daily Eagle* (Brooklyn, NY), July 30, 1919, p. 18.
41. *Brooklyn Daily Eagle* (Brooklyn, NY), July 14, 1922, p. 8.
42. *Ibid.*
43. Lane, *Hitters*, p. 136–137.
44. *Baseball Magazine* (Boston, MA), July, 1915, p. 47.
45. *Baseball Magazine* (Boston, MA), January, 1917, p. 49–51.
46. *Brooklyn Daily Eagle* (Brooklyn, NY), May 20, 1920, p. 24.
47. Steve Gelman, *The Greatest Dodgers of the Them All* (New York: G.P. Putnam's Sons, 1968), p. 139–140).
48. Simon, ed., *Deadball Stars of the National League*, p. 304.

Chapter 4

1. Allen, *The Giants and the Dodgers*, p. 99.
2. Lawrence Ritter, *The Glory of Their Times* (New York: Perennial-Enlarged Edition, 2002), p. 179.
3. Graham, *The Brooklyn Dodgers*, p. 53.
4. Zinn, *Charles Ebbets*, p. 155.
5. *Brooklyn Daily Eagle* (Brooklyn, NY), July 14, 1922, p. 8.
6. *Brooklyn Daily Eagle* (Brooklyn, NY), February 1, 1949, p. 11.
7. *Brooklyn Daily Eagle* (Brooklyn, NY), July 9, 1916, p. 33.
8. *Brooklyn Daily Eagle* (Brooklyn, NY), September 20, 1915, p. 20.
9. Lane, *Hitters*, p. 35.
10. *Baseball Magazine* (Boston, MA), January, 1917, p. 51.
11. *Sporting News* (St. Louis, MO), November 20, 1941, p. 5.
12. Glenn Stout, *The Dodgers: 120 Years*

of Dodgers Baseball (New York: Houghton Mifflin, 2004), p. 68.
13. Allen, *The Giants and the Dodgers*, p. 100.
14. *Ibid.*
15. Ritter, *The Glory of Their Times*, p. 179–180.
16. *Baseball Magazine* (Boston, MA), November, 1916, p. 30.
17. *Brooklyn Daily Eagle* (Brooklyn, NY), October 8, 1916, p. 1.
18. The same two teams went 18 innings in the 2018 World Series, won 3–2 by the now Los Angeles Dodgers.
19. Zack Wheat Clippings File, National Baseball Hall of Fame and Museum (Cooperstown, NY), September 21, 1953, page unknown.
20. *Baseball Magazine* (Boston, MA), December, 1916, p. 79.
21. *Baseball Magazine* (Boston, MA), December, 1916, p. 22.
22. *Baseball Magazine* (Boston, MA), December, 1916, p. 80.
23. *Baseball Magazine* (Boston, MA), January, 1917, p. 51, 104.
24. Graham, *The Brooklyn Dodgers*, p. 61.
25. *Baseball Magazine* (Boston, MA), December, 1916, p. 55.
26. *Baseball Magazine* (Boston, MA), January, 1917, p. 104.
27. *Ibid.*
28. *National Farm Journal* (Philadelphia, PA), September, 1930, p. 14.
29. Gelman, *The Greatest Dodgers of the Them All*, p. 138.

Chapter 5

1. *Sporting News* (St. Louis, MO), February, 11, 1959, p. 6.
2. Graham, *The Brooklyn Dodgers*, p. 64–66.
3. *Brooklyn Daily Eagle* (Brooklyn, NY), February 28, 1929, p. 29.
4. Graham, *The Brooklyn Dodgers*, p. 64–65.
5. Zinn, *Charles Ebbets*, p. 171.
6. *Brooklyn Daily Eagle* (Brooklyn, NY), November 7, 1917, p. 25.
7. *Brooklyn Daily Eagle* (Brooklyn, NY), July 8, 1917, p. 31.
8. *Baseball Magazine* (Boston, MA), December, 1917, p. 217.

9. Holmes, *The Dodgers*, p. 21.
10. *Kansas City Star* (Kansas City, MO), February 8, 1959, p. 5B.
11. Donald Honig, *The Man in the Dugout: Fifteen Big League Managers Speak Their Minds* (Chicago: Follett, 1972), p. 36.
12. *Sporting News* (St. Louis, MO), February, 11, 1959, p. 6.
13. *Brooklyn Daily Eagle* (Brooklyn, NY), March 22, 1918, p. 1.
14. *Baseball Magazine* (Boston, MA), March, 1919, p. 312.
15. *Ibid.*
16. *Brooklyn Daily Eagle* (Brooklyn, NY), July 29, 1919, p. 20.
17. *Brooklyn Daily Eagle* (Brooklyn, NY), April 7, 1919, p. 18.
18. Jake Daubert (SABR BioProject). Accessed June 15, 2019. https://sabr.org/bioproj/person/3fca088a.
19. Ed Konetchy (SABR BioProject). Accessed September 27, 2019. https://sabr.org/bioproj/person/c6889260.
20. *Brooklyn Daily Eagle* (Brooklyn, NY), April 16, 1919, p. 20.
21. *Brooklyn Daily Eagle* (Brooklyn, NY), May 27, 1919, p. 18.
22. *Sporting News* (St. Louis, MO), November 20, 1941, p. 5.
23. *Ibid.*
24. *Ibid.*
25. *Central New Jersey Home News* (East Brunswick, NJ), January 29, 1950, p. 11.

Chapter 6

1. *Baseball Digest* (Gurnee, IL), November, 1969, p. 20.
2. *New York Times* (New York, NY), February 9, 1920, p. 17.
3. *Wisconsin Rapids Daily Tribune* (Wisconsin Rapids, WI), April 16, 1948, p. 3.
4. *Kansas City Star* (Kansas City, Missouri) June 2, 1964, p. 14.
5. *New York World Telegram* (New York, NY), July 17, 1959, p. unknown. Zack Wheat Clippings File, National Baseball Hall of Fame and Museum (Cooperstown, NY).
6. *Kansas City Star* (Kansas City, Missouri) June 2, 1964, p. 14.
7. *Brooklyn Daily Eagle* (Brooklyn, NY), July 1, 1920, p. 20.
8. Zack Wheat Clippings File, National

Notes—Chapter 7

Baseball Hall of Fame and Museum, Cooperstown, NY.
 9. Lane. *Hitters*, p. 136–37.
 10. *Daily Times* (Davenport, IA), September 3, 1920, p. 3.
 11. *Brooklyn Daily Eagle* (Brooklyn, NY), September 29, 1920, p. 10.
 12. *Lewiston Daily Sun* (Lewiston, ME), September 29, 1920, p. 8.
 13. *Ibid.*
 14. *Hutchinson Gazette* (Hutchinson, KS), October 1, 1920, p. 1.
 15. *Baseball Magazine* (Boston, MA), June, 1920, p. 322.
 16. *Washington Herald* (Washington D.C), October 5, 1920, p. 8.
 17. *Cleveland Plain Dealer* (Cleveland, OH), October 6, 1920, p. 17.
 18. *Hutchinson Gazette* (Hutchinson, KS), October 8, 1920, p. 1.
 19. *Abilene Weekly Reflector* (Abilene, KS), October 21, 1920, p. 8.
 20. *Cleveland Plain Dealer* (Cleveland, OH), October 8, 1920, p. 18.
 21. *Brooklyn Daily Eagle* (Brooklyn, NY), June 9, 1920, p. 14.
 22. *Star Tribune* (Minneapolis, MN), October 11, 1920, p. 15.
 23. *Gazette* (Cedar Rapids, IA), October 12, 1920, p. 1.
 24. *Gazette Times* (Pittsburgh, PA), October 13, 1920, p. 20.

Chapter 7

 1. *Kansas City Kansan* (Kansas City, Kansas), February 25, 1921, p. 16.
 2. *Brooklyn Daily Eagle* (Brooklyn, NY), March, 11, 1921, p. 24.
 3. *Lincoln Star* (Lincoln, NE), May 27, 1921, p. 14.
 4. Lane, *Hitters*, p. 81.
 5. *Ibid.*
 6. *New York Times* (New York, NY), February 5, 1959, p. unknown. Zack Wheat Clippings File, National Baseball Hall of Fame and Museum (Cooperstown, NY).
 7. *Pittsburgh Post-Gazette* (Pittsburgh, PA), September 24, 1940, p. 16.
 8. *Brooklyn Daily Eagle* (Brooklyn, NY), June 17, 1921, p. 24.
 9. *Brooklyn Daily Eagle* (Brooklyn, NY), May 10, 1922, p. 27.
 10. Lane, *Hitters*, p. 218.
 11. *Buffalo Courier* (Buffalo, NY), January 17, 1926, p. 106.
 12. *Brooklyn Times Union* (Brooklyn, NY), March 4, 1922, p. 10.
 13. John C. Skipper, *Dazzy Vance: A Biography of the Brooklyn Dodger Hall of Famer* (Jefferson, NC: McFarland, 2003), p. 32.
 14. *Kansas City Star* (Kansas City, Missouri) June 8, 1938, p. 15.
 15. *Sporting News* (St. Louis, MO), November 20, 1941, p. 5.
 16. *Brooklyn Daily Eagle* (Brooklyn, NY), May 10, 1922, p. 27.
 17. *Ibid.*
 18. *Brooklyn Daily Eagle* (Brooklyn, NY), August 9, 1922, p. 22.
 19. *Harrisburg Telegraph* (Harrisburg, PA), June 15, 1922, p. 14.
 20. *Brooklyn Daily Eagle* (Brooklyn, NY), March 11, 1923, p. 42.
 21. *New York World Telegram* (New York, NY), July 17, 1959, p. unknown. Zack Wheat Clippings File, National Baseball Hall of Fame and Museum (Cooperstown, NY).
 22. *Ibid.*
 23. *Brooklyn Daily Eagle* (Brooklyn, NY), September 24, 1935, p. 18.
 24. *Brooklyn Daily Eagle* (Brooklyn, NY), September 27, 1922, p. 1.
 25. *Brooklyn Daily Eagle* (Brooklyn, NY), December 10, 1922, p. 49.
 26. *Brooklyn Daily Eagle* (Brooklyn, NY), December 20, 1922, p. 26.
 27. *Kansas City Star* (Kansas City, Missouri) February 8, 1923, p. 12.
 28. *Ibid.*
 29. Graham, *The Brooklyn Dodgers*, p. 89.
 30. *Brooklyn Standard Union* (Brooklyn, NY), March 30, 1923, p. 18.
 31. Graham, *The Brooklyn Dodgers*, p. 90.
 32. Lane, *Hitters*, p. 29.
 33. Lane, *Hitters*, p. 27.
 34. *New York Morning Telegram* (New York, NY), July 23, 1923, p. 7.
 35. *Brooklyn Daily Eagle* (Brooklyn, NY), August 3, 1923, p. 16.
 36. *Baseball Digest* (Gurnee, IL), March, 1962, p. 48.
 37. *Brooklyn Standard Union* (Brooklyn, NY), August 31, 1923, p. 10.
 38. *Kansas City Star* (Kansas City, MO), June 8, 1924, p. 13.

39. *Ibid.*
40. *New York Morning Telegram* (New York, NY), September 23, 1923, p. 12.
41. *Brooklyn Daily Eagle* (Brooklyn, NY), January 27, 1924, p. 42.
42. Allen, *The Giants and the Dodgers*, p. 115.
43. *Brooklyn Daily Eagle* (Brooklyn, NY), November 2, 1923, p. 26.

Chapter 8

1. Lane, *Hitters*, p. 170.
2. *Brooklyn Daily Eagle* (Brooklyn, NY), April 4, 1924, p. 26.
3. *Brooklyn Daily Eagle* (Brooklyn, NY), May 25, 1924, p. 7.
4. Graham, *The Brooklyn Dodgers*, p. 102.
5. *Kansas City Star* (Kansas City, MO), February 8, 1959, p. 5B.
6. Lane, *Hitters*, p. 218.
7. Lane, *Hitters*, p. 215.
8. *Kansas City Star* (Kansas City, MO), February 8, 1959, p. 5B.
9. *Ibid.*
10. *Brooklyn Daily Eagle* (Brooklyn, NY), September 26, 1924, p. 26.
11. Letter from Fred Lieb to Mary Gottschall, March 18, 1972, Kenny Dixon's Zack Wheat memorabilia collection.

Chapter 9

1. *Brooklyn Standard Union* (Brooklyn, NY), March 28, 1925, p. 11.
2. *Brooklyn Standard Union* (Brooklyn, NY), March 28, 1925, p. 11.
3. Lane, *Hitters*, p. 35.
4. *Brooklyn Daily Eagle* (Brooklyn, NY), April 18, 1925, p. 1.
5. *Kansas City Star* (Kansas City, MO), February 8, 1959, p. 5B.
6. *Kansas City Star* (Kansas City, MO), February 8, 1959, p.1B.
7. Allen, *The Giants and the Dodgers*, p. 127.
8. Stout, *The Dodgers*, p. 90.
9. *Brooklyn Daily Eagle* (Brooklyn, NY), February 24, 1929, p. 38.
10. *Brooklyn Daily Eagle* (Brooklyn, NY), October 15, 1928, p. 26.
11. *Baseball Digest* (Gurnee, IL), May, 1959, p. 77.
12. Graham, *The Brooklyn Dodgers*, p. 97.
13. *Kansas City Star* (Kansas City, MO), February 8, 1959, p. 5B
14. *Brooklyn Daily Eagle* (Brooklyn, NY), June 27, 1925, p. 10.
15. *New York Times* (New York, NY), July 16, 1925, p. 15.
16. Lane, *Hitters*, p. 21.
17. Lane, *Hitters*, p. 129.
18. *Orlando Evening Star* (Orlando, FL), January 22, 1958, p. 5.
19. *Brooklyn Daily Eagle* (Brooklyn, NY), August 9, 1925, p. 32.
20. Lane. *Hitters*, p. 29.
21. Allen. *The Giants and the Dodgers*, p. 129.
22. *Brooklyn Daily Eagle* (Brooklyn, NY), October 15, 1928, p. 26.
23. Skipper, *Dazzy Vance*, p. 71.
24. Lane, *Hitters*, p. 186–87.
25. *Brooklyn Daily Eagle* (Brooklyn, NY), February 27, 1926, p. 14.
26. Walter "Rabbit" Maranville, *Run, Rabbit, Run: The Hilarious and Mostly True Tales of Rabbit Maranville* (Phoenix: Society for American Baseball Research, Inc., 2012), p. 56.
27. Maranville, *Run, Rabbit, Run*, p. 59.
28. Graham, *The Brooklyn Dodgers*, p. 103.
29. Holmes, *The Dodgers*, p. 28.
30. Graham, *The Brooklyn Dodgers*, p. 104–105.
31. Graham, *The Brooklyn Dodgers*, p. 105.
32. Unknown source, September 11, 1936, p. unknown. Zack Wheat Clippings File, National Baseball Hall of Fame and Museum (Cooperstown, NY).
33. *Brooklyn Daily Eagle* (Brooklyn, NY), July 19, 1926, p. 2A.
34. *Kansas City Star* (Kansas City, MO), February 8, 1959, p. 5B.
35. *Brooklyn Daily Eagle* (Brooklyn, NY), September 21, 1940, p. 11.
36. *Esquire* (New York, NY), October, 1955, p. 148.
37. Bill James, *The New Bill James Historical Baseball Abstract* (New York: Free Press, 2003), p. 129
38. Tommy Holmes, *Dodger Daze and Knights: Enough of a Ball Club's History to Explain its Reputation* (New York: D. McKay Co., 1953), p. 55.

Notes—Chapter 10

39. *Brooklyn Daily Eagle* (Brooklyn, NY), January 2, 1927, p. 35.
40. Allen, *The Giants and the Dodgers*, p. 136.
41. *Brooklyn Daily Eagle* (Brooklyn, NY), January 3, 1927, p. 24.
42. *Kansas City Star* (Kansas City, MO), February 8, 1959, p. 5B
43. *Brooklyn Daily Eagle* (Brooklyn, NY), January 3, 1927, p. 24.
44. *Brooklyn Daily Eagle* (Brooklyn, NY), January 13, 1927, p. 22.
45. *Philadelphia Inquirer* (Philadelphia, PA), January 30, 1927, p. unknown. Zack Wheat Clippings File, National Baseball Hall of Fame and Museum (Cooperstown, NY).
46. *Brooklyn Daily Eagle* (Brooklyn, NY), February 9, 1927, p. 22.
47. *Brooklyn Daily Eagle* (Brooklyn, NY), March 16, 1927, p. 24.
48. *Evening News* (Wilkes-Barre, PA), April 16, 1927, p. 9.
49. *Mount Caramel Item* (Mount Caramel, PA), September 16, 1927, p. 3.
50. *Brooklyn Daily Eagle* (Brooklyn, NY), September 27, 1927, p. 24.
51. *Sporting News* (St. Louis, MO), November 20, 1941, p. 5.
52. *Ibid.*

Chapter 10

1. *Minneapolis Star* (Minneapolis, MN), April 11, 1928, p. 12.
2. *Star Tribune* (Minneapolis, MN), May 22, 1928, p. 13.
3. *Brooklyn Daily Eagle* (Brooklyn, NY), August 29, 1928, p. 14.
4. *Sporting News* (St. Louis, MO), November 20, 1941, p. 5.
5. *Ibid.*
6. *Star Tribune* (Minneapolis, MN), August 28, 1928, p. 14.
7. *Brooklyn Times Union* (Brooklyn, NY), November 21, 1929, p. 15.
8. *Brooklyn Daily Eagle* (Brooklyn, NY), January 22, 1931, p. 22.
9. *Kansas City Times* (Kansas City, Kansas), November 13, 1933, p. 12.
10. *Kansas City Times* (Kansas City, Kansas), August 24, 1933, p. 10.
11. *Brooklyn Daily Eagle* (Brooklyn, NY), September 11, 1936, p. 22.
12. *Brooklyn Times Union* (Brooklyn, NY), April 13, 1936, p. 13.
13. *Brooklyn Daily Eagle* (Brooklyn, NY), September 11, 1936, p. 22.
14. *Kansas City Times* (Kansas City, Kansas), November 5, 1936, p. 15.
15. *St. Louis Globe-Democrat* (St. Louis, Missouri), October 11, 1939,
16. *Milwaukee Journal* (Milwaukee, WI), May 23, 1941, p. 66.
17. *Brooklyn Daily Eagle* (Brooklyn, NY), April 15, 1941, p. 14.
18. *Sporting News* (St. Louis, MO), November 20, 1941, p. 5.
19. Grayson, *They Played the Game*, p. 14.
20. *Milwaukee Journal* (Milwaukee, WI), July 19, 1943, p. 32.
21. *Baseball Digest* (Gurnee, IL), August, 1949, p. 18.
22. *Kansas City Star* (Kansas City, MO), October 8, 1949, p. 6.
23. *Brooklyn Daily Eagle* (Brooklyn, NY), April 10, 1952, p. 17.
24. Letter from Fred Lieb to Mary Gottschall, March 18, 1972, Kenny Dixon's Zack Wheat memorabilia collection.
25. *New York Journal-American* (New York, NY), September 4, 1954, p. unknown. Zack Wheat Clippings File, National Baseball Hall of Fame and Museum (Cooperstown, NY).
26. *New York Times* (New York, NY), February 2, 1959, p. C31.
27. *Brooklyn Daily Eagle* (Brooklyn, NY), August 3, 1953, p. 11.
28. *New York Journal-American* (New York, NY), February 3, 1959, p. unknown. Zack Wheat Clippings File, National Baseball Hall of Fame and Museum (Cooperstown, NY).
29. Zack Wheat Clippings File, National Baseball Hall of Fame and Museum (Cooperstown, NY).
30. *Orlando Evening Star* (Orlando, FL), January 22, 1958, p. 5.
31. *Kansas City Star* (Kansas City, MO), March 5, 1937, p. 28.
32. *Kansas City Star* (Kansas City, MO), February 8, 1959, p. 5B.
33. *New York World Telegram* (New York, NY), July 17, 1959, p. unknown. Zack Wheat Clippings File, National Baseball Hall of Fame and Museum (Cooperstown, NY).

Notes—Chapter 10

34. *San Bernardino Sun* (San Bernardino, CA), July 21, 1959, p. 13.
35. *Kansas City Star* (Kansas City, MO), July 20, 1959, p. 16.
36. *San Bernardino Sun* (San Bernardino, CA), July 21, 1959, p. 13.
37. *Kansas City Star* (Kansas City, MO), July 20, 1959, p. 17.
38. *Kansas City Star* (Kansas City, MO), July 22, 1959, p. 43.
39. *Kansas City Times* (Kansas City, MO), July 27, 1959, p. 4.
40. *Iola Register* (Iola, KS), July 16, 1956, p. 6.
41. Satchel Paige would be buried here a decade later, making it one of a handful of cemeteries to be the resting place for two or more Hall of Famers.

Bibliography

Books

Allen, Lee. *The Giants and the Dodgers: The Fabulous Story of Baseball's Fiercest Feud.* New York: G.P. Putnam's Sons, 1964.

Dragseth, P.J. *Eye for Talent: Interviews with Veteran Baseball Scouts.* Jefferson, NC: McFarland, 2014.

Gelman, Steve. *The Greatest Dodgers of Them All.* New York: Putnam, 1968.

Graham, Frank. *The Brooklyn Dodgers: An Informal History.* New York: G.P. Putnam's Sons, 1945. Reprinted with a new foreword by Jack Lang. Carbondale: Southern Illinois University Press, 2002.

Holmes, Tommy. *Dodger: Daze and Knights.* New York: David McKay, 1953.

_____. *The Dodgers.* New York: Macmillan, 1975.

Honig, Donald, and Lawrence Ritter. *The 100 Greatest Baseball Players of All Time.* New York: Crown, 1981.

Johnston, Carrie Polk, and W.H. S. McGlumphy. *History of Clinton and Caldwell Counties, Missouri.* Topeka, KS: Historical Publishing, 1923.

Kavanagh, Jack, and Norman L. Macht. *Uncle Robbie.* Cleveland, OH: Society for American Baseball Research, 1999.

Lake of the Ozarks Association. *50th Anniversary, Bagnell Dam, 1931–1981.* Lake Ozark, MO: Lake of the Ozarks Association, 1989.

Lane, F.C. *Hitters.* Cleveland, OH: Society for American Baseball Research, 2001.

Maranville, Walter "Rabbit." *Run, Rabbit, Run: The Hilarious and Mostly True Tales of Rabbit Maranville.* Phoenix, AZ: Society for American Baseball Research, 2012.

Ritter, Lawrence. *The Glory of Their Times.* Enlarged Edition. New York: Perennial, 2002.

Simon, Tom (editor). *Deadball Stars of the National League.* Washington, D.C.: Brassey's, 2004.

Skipper, John C. *Dazzy Vance: A Biography of the Brooklyn Dodger Hall of Famer.* Jefferson, NC: McFarland, 2007.

Snyder, John. *Dodgers Journal: Year by Year & Day by Day with the Brooklyn & Los Angeles Dodgers Since 1884.* Cincinnati, OH: Clerisy Press, 2009.

Spink, Alfred H. *The National Game.* St. Louis, MO: National Game Publishing, 1910.

Stout, Glenn. *The Dodgers: 120 Years of Dodgers Baseball.* New York: Houghton Mifflin, 2004.

Zinn, John G. *Charles Ebbets: The Man Behind the Dodgers and Brooklyn's Beloved Ballpark.* Jefferson, NC: McFarland, 2019

Newspapers

Abilene Weekly Reflector (Abilene, KS)
Brooklyn Daily Eagle (Brooklyn, NY)
Brooklyn Standard Union (Brooklyn, NY)
Brooklyn Times Union (Brooklyn, NY)
Buffalo Courier (Buffalo, NY)
Cleveland Plain Dealer (Cleveland, OH)
Daily Times (Davenport, IA)
Evening News (Wilkes-Barre, PA)
Gazette (Cedar Rapids, IA)
Gazette Globe (Kansas City, KS)
Gazette Times (Pittsburgh, PA)
Halstead Independent (Halstead, KS)
Harper Sentinel (Harper, KS)
Harrisburg Telegram (Harrisburg, PA)
Hutchinson Gazette (Hutchinson, KS)
Iola Register (Iola, KS)
Kansas City Kansan (Kansas City, KS)
Kansas City Star (Kansas City, MO)
Kansas City Times (Kansas City, MO)

Bibliography

Lewiston Daily Sun (Lewiston, ME)
Lincoln Star (Lincoln, NE)
Logansport Pharos Tribune (Logansport, IN)
Logansport Reporter (Logansport, IN)
Milwaukee Journal (Milwaukee, WI)
Minneapolis Star (Minneapolis, MN)
Montana Standard (Butte, MT)
Montgomery Advertiser (Montgomery, AL)
Mount Caramel Item (Mount Caramel, PA)
New York Journal-American (New York, NY)
New York Times (New York, NY)
New York World Telegram (New York, NY)
Orlando Evening Star (Orlando, FL)
Pittsburgh Post-Gazette (Pittsburgh, PA)
St. Louis Globe-Democrat (St. Louis, MO)
St. Louis Star and Times (St. Louis, MO)
San Bernardino Sun (San Bernardino, CA)
Star Tribune (Minneapolis, MN)
Tampa Bay Times (St. Petersburg, FL)
Washington Herald (Washington, D.C.)
Wisconsin Rapids Daily Tribune (Wisconsin Rapids, WI)

Magazines/Journals

Baseball Digest
Baseball Magazine
Esquire
National Farm Journal
Sporting News
The National Game

Websites

www.baseball-almanac.com
www.baseballhall.org
www.baseball-reference.com
www.retrosheet.com
www.sabr.org

Other

Clippings File, National Baseball Hall of Fame and Museum, Cooperstown, NY.

Index

Numbers in ***bold italics*** indicate pages with illustrations

Alexander, Grover Cleveland 50, 54, 60, 70, 132, 166; admiration of Wheat 50; Wheats admiration of 50
All Nations baseball team 6
Allen, Lee 12, 124, 138
American Association 14, 24, 30, 40, 134, 158, 160, 162
American Series (Cuba) 38, 111
Applegate, Joseph H. 127–128
Appleton, Ed 49
Atlanta Crackers 117, 162

Bagby, Jim 97, 99, 101
Baltimore Orioles 14, 40, 41–42, 120, 131, 153
Barnes, Jesse 93–94
Barnie, Billy 14
Baseball Digest 167
Baseball Magazine 84, 97
Baseball Players' Fraternity 36
Baseball Popularity Contest (1923) 121, 122, 124
Baseball Writers Association of America 88, 164, 168, 169, 170, 171, 173
Bell, Brian 155
Bell, George 24
Bender, Charles Albert "Chief" 6, 48
Bentley, Jack 133
Benton, Rube 78
Bergen, Bill 46
Bezdek, Hugo 79
Black Sox Scandal 9, 94, 153
Boley, Joe 153, 155, 156
Boston Beaneaters 10, 18, 19; *see also* Boston Beaneaters; Boston Doves
Boston Braves 26, 43, 44, 51, 54, 58, 62, 76, 77, 85, 86, 92, 95, 105, 115, 131, 132, 134, 144, 146, 148; *see also* Boston Beaneaters; Boston Doves
Boston Doves 17, 145; *see also* Boston Beaneaters; Boston Braves
Boston Red Sox 21, 28, 53, 63, 64, 65, 66, 67, 68, 69, 70, 72, 88, 102, 149, 153, 156, 172
Bottomley, Jim 118, 123, 141
Bowerman, Frank 117

Braves Field (Boston, Massachusetts) 64, 66
Bresnahan, Roger 39, 44, 174
Brooklyn Citizen (Brooklyn, New York) 29
Brooklyn Daily Eagle (Brooklyn, New York) 17, 22, 25, 28, 30, 31, 34, 36, 37, 39, 41, 49, 52, 59, 62, 73, 78, 85, 93, 105, 110, 112, 117, 128, 132, 145, 152, 155, 157, 163, 164, 169
Brooklyn Dodgers 1, 3, 6, 11, 12, 14–15, 17, 18, 19, 21, 22, 27, 29, 30, 31, 33, 35, 36, 38, 39, 40, 41, 43, 44, 46, 47, 48, 49, 53, 54, 55, 56, 57–58, 60, 61, 62, 72, 76, 78, 79, 81, 82, 84, 86, 87, 88, 93, 94, 95, 96, 105, 106, 107, 110, 112, 114–115, 116, 117, 118, 119, 121, 122, 123, 124, 127, 128–129, 131, 132–133, 134, 136, 139, 140, 143, 144, 145, 146, 147, 148, 149, 150, 151, 152, 157, 160, 161, 162–163, 164, 165, 167, 169, 170, 173, 174, 175; 1916 World Series 63–70; 1920 World Series 96–102; various nicknames 2, 25–26, 44; *see also* Los Angeles Dodgers
Brooklyn Standard-Union (Brooklyn, New York) 29, 119, 123
Brooklyn Times (Brooklyn, New York) 29, 111, 161
Brooklyn Tip Tops 42, 49, 54
Brown, Eddie 134, 144
Buck Wheat Day 157
bunting 23, 107–108
Burns, George 47, 55, 70, 78, 88
Byrne, Charles 14

Cable, Budge 9
Cadore, Leon 12, 76–77, 84, 87, 92, 95, 101, 110
Caldwell, Ray 97–98
Caldwell County (Missouri) 1, 5, 38, 91, 174
Campanella, Roy 167, 169
car accident 163
Carey, Max 70, 150, 162, 173, 174
Carrigan, Bill 63, 64, 66, 67, 68
Casey Stengel All-Stars 102, 124
Chadwick, Henry 138
Chalmers Award 38, 114
Chamber of Commerce building (Brooklyn, New York) 132
Chance, Frank 18, 42, 98

191

Index

Chandler, Happy 170
Chapman, Ray 96–97
Chase, Hal 24, 61, 70, 166
Cheney, Larry 27, 53, 60. 68, 84
Chicago Cubs 18, 27, 39, 42, 44, 45, 46, 51, 53, 55, 57, 58, 60, 70. 79, 81, 89, 94, 105, 109, 115, 131–132, 133, 136, 139, 143, 144, 146, 149, 152, 155
Chicago White Sox 9, 27, **35**, 42, 53, 57, 58, 63, 78, 82, 85, 96, 102–103, 110, 118, 153, 154, 155, 173
Cincinnati Reds 4, 21, 23, 28, 32, 42, 47, 50, 51, 53, 54, 60, 62, 77, 82, 84, 85, 87, 94, 96, 106, 111, 112, 118, 153, 162, 164
Clarke, Fred 18, 150
Clearwater, Florida 119, 126, 136, 146
Clement, Wally 16
Cleveland Indians 24, 64, 96–102, 112, 123
Cleveland Plain Dealer 99, 100
Cobb, Ty 18, 19, 25, 49, 60, 88, 141, 143, 153, **154**, 156, 157, 164, 166, 171, 172, 173
Cochrane, Mickey 154, 155, 166
Collins, Eddie 153, **154**, 155, 156, 157
Comerford, Dan 120, 170
Comiskey, Charles 118
contract negotiations 12, 18, 32, 33, 34, 42, 72–74, 79–80, 84, 92, 104, 105, 111, 117, 119 124–125, 136, 138, 140, 146, 153, 158
Coombs, Jack 48–49, 55, 60, 63, 67–68, 76
Cooney, Johnny 116
Cooper, Wilbur 51, 110
Cooperstown, New York 3, 168, 171
Coveleski, Stan 97, 98, 99, 100, 101, 102
Cox, Dick 128, 144
Crable, George 24
Cravath, Gavvy 62
Crawford, Sam 37, 164
Crusinberry, Jim 169
Curtis, Julian 142
Cutshaw, George 12, 27, 36, 37, 38, 61, 64, 65, 67–68, 69, 77, 78, 166
Cuyler, Kiki 141

Daffiness Boys 128, 148
Dalton, Jack 44, 45–46
Daly, Arthur 108
Daly, Tom 11
Daubert, Jake 12, 24, 26, 32, 33, 34, 36, 38, 39, 42, 44, **45**, 55, 61, 65, 66, 68, 70, 76, 84–85, 87, 120, 165, 166, 170, 174
Daytona Beach, Florida 47, 57
Dear, Joe 9
DeBerry, Hank 12, 76, 112, 133
Decatur, Art 134
Dell, William "Wheezer" 49, 55
Demaree, Frank 12
Detroit Tigers 21, 28, 37, 96, 141, 143, 149, 153, 154, 164

Dickerman, Leo 122–123, 127
Doak, Bill 100, 110, 122, 127, 132, 134, 136, 145
Donovan, Bill 55
Douglas, Phil 53, 114
Dover Hall (Brunswick, Georgia) 55, 139
Dressen, Charlie 164
Dreyfuss, Barney 89
Dunn, Jack 97, 153
Durocher, Leo 164
Dykes, Jimmy 156

Earnshaw, George 153
Ebbets, Charles 11, 12, 13, 14, **15**–16, 17, 18, 26, 28–29, 30, 32, 34, 35, 39, 42, 44, 45–46, 47, 48, 49, 50, 56, 57, 64, 67, 69, 70, 72–73, 74, 76–77, 78, 79, 80, 84, 85, 86, 89, 92, 94, 96, 97, 98, 104, 105, 107, 111, 112, 114–115, 117, 118–119, 124–125, 126, 127, 134, 138, 139, 140, 143, 145
Ebbets, Charles, Jr. 29, 125, 139
Ebbets, Genevieve 35
Ebbets, Maie 77–78
Ebbets Field (Brooklyn, New York) 29–30 34–35, 37, 43, 49, 54, 56–57, 59, 60, 63, 77, 86, 98, **99**, 109–110, 115, 119, 120, 121, 129, 130, 132, 133, **137**, 139, 140, 145, 147, 151, 152, 157, 158, 163, 165, 167, 169, 170
Ehmke, Howard 156
Election to Hall of Fame 3, 4, 138, 152, 156, 164, 168–169, 170–171, **172**, 174
Elias, Al 104
Evans Billy 10
Evers, Johnny 42

Fales, Harold 142
fan adoration of Wheat 37, 74, 86, 152, 169
Federal League 42, 44, 46, 48, 49, 50. 54, 57, 72, 73, 82, 85
Fenway Park (Boston, Massachusetts) 28, 64
Fewster, Wilson "Chick" 97, 98, 148, 150
fielding 7–8, 9–10, 19, 25, 52–53, 69, 85, 108–109, 116, 117, 131
Fisher, Tom 10
Flatbush 28, 34, 43, 157
Fogel Field (Hot Springs, Arkansas) 21
Forbes Field (Pittsburgh, Pennsylvania) 17, 126
Forsman, Daisy 30, 32; *see also* Daisy Wheat
Foster, Rube 63
Four-for-Zero Club 128, 146, 147
Fournier, Jack 118, 120, 121, 123, 126, 128, 133, 134, 136, 139, 141, 143, **144**, 146, 149
Foutz, Dave 44
Foxx, Jimmie 154, 155, 156, 172
Frazee, Harry 70
French, Walt 156
Frick, Ford 170
Frisch, Frankie 87, 107, 121, 124, 133, 153, 174

192

Index

Gainer, Del 64, 67
Gandil, Chick 9
Gardner, Larry 64, 66, 67, 68, 69, 97
Garvin, Lee 10
Gautreau, Doc 148
Gear, Dale 9–10
Gehrig, Lou 157
Gelman, Steve 71
Gibson, George 16–17
Giles, Warren 4, 172
Gottschall, Mary 3, 171; *see also* Wheat, Mary Helen
Graham, Frank 1, 16, 29, 46, 53, 70, 72, 74, 119, 149, 167
Granger, Bill 29
Grayson, Harry 23, 129
Griffins, Mike 14
Griffith, Bert 76, 116
Griffith, Clark 3, 89, 154
Griffith, Tommy 84, 110, 116
Grimes, Burleigh 2, 57, 78, 79, **80**, 84, 85, 87, 89, 90, 95, 98, 99, 101, 102, 104, 109, 110, 111, 112, 117, **122**, 123, 127, 128, 131–132, 133, 134, 136, 145, 147, 153, 161, 164
Groh, Heinie 174
Grove, Robert Moses "Lefty" 153, 154, 155, 172

Haines, Jesse 149
Hale, Sammy 156, 157
Hamberger, Babe 170
Hamilton, Missouri 1, 5, 177
Hanlon, Fred 151
Hanlon, Ned 14, 15, 40, 42, 44
Heitman, Harry 84
Hendry, James 164
Henriksen, Olaf 68
Henry, Dutch 136
Herman, Floyd "Babe" 140, 148–149, 150, 173
Heydler, John 80, 89, 96, 102, 115, 128, 142
High, Andy 76, 111–112, 116, 133–134
hitting streaks 36, 47, 55, 60–61, 81–82, 93, 94, 110, 121, 130–131, 134
Hoblitzell, Dick 67, 68
Hodges, Gil 166, 169
Hoefer, W.R. 59
Hoffman, Ralph W. 8, 100
Holmes, Tommy 22, 52, 78, 93, 139, 141, 142, 145, 147, 149, 152, 164, 165, 168, 169, 171
Honig, Donald 1, 79
Hooper, Harry 64–65, 66, 68, 69
Hornsby, Rogers 77, 82, 107, 114, 120, 123, 124, 125, **130**, 131, 133, 136, 141, 152, 166, 172, 173, 174
Hot Spring, Arkansas 19–20, 21, 25, 30, 72, 73, 79, 104
Hotel St. George (Brooklyn, NY) 148, 167
Hubbell, Carl 3, 170
Huggins, Miller 55, 87, 157

Hughes, Ed 28, 164
Hughes, Jim 15
Huston, Til "Cap" 55

injuries 10, 21, 27, 30, 31, 36, 48, 54, 62, 74, 77, 78, 93, 115, 121–122, 123, 149–150, 158; car accident 163, 166
International League 46, 79, 153, 158

Jackson, Joe 21, 166
Jackson, Travis 124
Jacksonville, Florida 19, 84, 92, 111
Jamieson, Charlie 97, 101, 102
Janvrin, Hal 64, 65, 67, 68, 69, 107
Jennings, Hughie 15, 40, 124
Johnson, Arnold 172–173
Johnson, Ban 40, 89
Johnson, Clarence 158
Johnson, Walter 10, 50, 70, 133
Johnston, Jimmy 57, **58**, 60, 66, 68, 84, 86, 93–94, 97, 99, 107, 110, 111–112, 114–115, 116, 121, **122**, 133, 134, 144, 165, 166
Johnston, Wheeler "Doc" 97, 99
Jordan, Tim 21, 24, 109, 133

Kansas City, Kansas 7, 8, 18, 34, 38, 104, 161, 162, 169
Kansas City, Missouri 7, 26, 54, 70, 81, 124, 151, 159, 160–161, 163, 173, 174
Kansas City Athletics 170; honoring Wheat 172; Wheat scouting for 170; *see also* Philadelphia Athletics
Kansas City Blues 159
Kansas City Kansan (Kansas City, Kansas) 9, 104
Kansas City Star (Kansas City, Missouri) 123, 152, 172
Kauff, Benny 49–50
Keefe, Tim 53
Keeler, Willie 15, 40, 60, 110
Kelley, Joe 15, 40
Kelley, Mike 158, 159, 160
Kilduff, Pete 95, 101, 107
Kingston, Missouri 5
Klem, Bill 31, 37, 89
Konetchy, Ed 85, 87, 95, 98, 99, 101, 107
Koufax, Sandy 174

Lajoie, Napoleon 70, 79, 131
Lake of the Ozarks (Missouri) 3, 165, 166, 171
Lamar, Bill 141, 157
Landis, Kenesaw Mountain 50, 102, 118, 143, 153
Lane, F.C. 22, 23, 37, 44, 63, 70, 78, 81, 82, 94, 110, 120, 126, 131, 138, 142–143, 145–146
Langan, Harold 157
Lannin, Joseph 70
Lardner, Ring 49

193

Index

Lavagetto, Cookie 169
Law, Ruth 48
Leonard, Hubert "Dutch" 63, 68
Lewis, Duffy 64, 67, 68, 69
Lieb, Fred 133, 168
Lindstrom, Fred 124
Los Angeles Dodgers 134, 170, 173, 174, 175; *see also* Brooklyn Dodgers
Louisville, Kentucky 30, 32, 33, 36
Lumley, Harry 12, 13, 18, 21, 26
Luque, Adolfo 51

Mack, Connie 48, 89, 153, *154*, 155, 156, 157
MacPhail, Larry 165
Magee, Sherry 47
Mails, John 98, 102
Majestic Park (Hot Springs, Arkansas) 21
Mamaux, Al 78, 79, 81, 87, 95, 96, 100, 101
managerial stint 87, 139–140, 143, 145, 146, 150, 161–162
Maranville, Rabbit 54, 116, 146–147, 149
Marquard, Richard "Rube" 41, 51, 53–54, 60, 64, 65, 68, 76, 84, 87, 93–94, 98, 100–101, 105, 173
Mathewson, Christy 16, 41, 43, 45, 50, 56, 62, 82, 88–89, 133, 166, 167, 174
Mays, Carl 63, 66, 67, 68, 96–97
McGeehan, Bill 55
McGowen, Roscoe 140
McGraw, John 1, 18, 44, 58, 62, 88–89, 107, 124, 133,153 ; interest in acquiring Wheat 152; pitching to Wheat 23, 93–94; relationship with Wilbert Robinson 40, 41, 42, 43, 55, 63, 82, *127*, 162
McJames, Doc 15
McKechnie, Bill 42, 150
McKeever, Edward 29, 32, 138, 139
McKeever, Jennie 35
McKeever, Stephen 29, 126, 138, 139, 145, 146, 147–148, 151, 161, 162
McNally, Mike 67
Meadows, Lee 86
Mendez, Jose 124
Menke, Frank 56
Merkle, Fred 62, 65, 68
Meusel, Bob 124
Meusel, Irish 124, 152
Meyers, John Tortes, "Chief" 6, 56, 63, 65, 76
Miller, Otto 12, 27, 46, 67, 93–94, 101, 111, 112, 117, 147, 161, 166
Minneapolis Millers (Minneapolis, Minnesota) 158, 159, 160
Missouri Sports Hall of Fame 170
Mitchell, Clarence 89, 101, 107, 110, 140
Mitchell, Fred 115
Mitchell, Johnny 131, 134
Mitchell, Mike 23
Mobile Sea Gulls (Mobile, Alabama) 10–13, 18

Monahan, Joe 57, 94
Montgomery Advertiser (Montgomery, Alabama) 11
Mowrey, Mike 56, 65, 66, 67, 68
Muehlebach Field (Kansas City, Missouri) 159
Murphy, James J. 117
Murray, Jack 49
Myers, Hy 12, 46, 52, 55, 57, *58*, 59, 60, 61, 65, 66, 67,68, 72, *75*, 76, 87, 93–94, 99, 105, 108, 116, 117, 118, 166

National Baseball Hall of Fame 164
Native American heritage 5–6
Neis, Bernie 102, 134, 146
New York Giants 1, 16, 28, 30, 31, 33, 35, 36, 38, 41, 42, 43, 44, 45, 47, 49, 53, 55, 56, 58, 62, 63, 64, 68, 70, 74, 78, 82, 87, 88, 93, 94, 95, 107, 110, 111, 114, 115, 121, 124, 129, 131, 132–133, 134, 143, 144, 145, 152, 153, 167
New York Sun (New York, New York) 147
New York Yankees 1, 24, 34–35, 55, 70, 87, 88, 92, 96, 97, 105, 111, 112, 115, 118, 124, 152, 153, 154, 155, 157, 164, 167–168, 173
Newark Peppers 48, 57
nickname 6, 22
Northern, Hub *25*

O'Day, Hank 58, 89, 116
Oeschger, Joe 92
offseason training 18, 70–71, 128, 145–146
Olson, Ivy 54, 65, 66, 68, 69, 76, 87, 93–94, 96, 100, 102, 107, 112, 115, 161, 166
O'Neill, Steve 97, 98, 99, 102
Orsatti, Ernie 159–160
Osborne, Tiny 136
Otesaga Hotel (Cooperstown, New York) 171
O'Toole, Marty 32
Owen, Mickey 62, 175

Penny, James Cash, 1
Perritt, Pol 49, 78
Petty, Jesse 128, 147
Pfeffer, Ed "Jeff" 12, 47, 49, 55, 60, *61*, 64, 65, 67, 68, 69, 76, 84, 95, 97, 98, 101, 107; fight with Wheat 87
Philadelphia Athletics 21, *35*, 41–42, 44, 48, 131, 141, 153, 155, 156, 157, 171, 172, 173; acquisition of Wheat 153; *see also* Kansas City Athletics
Philadelphia Phillies 26, 35, 36, 44, 47, 50, 53, 54, 55, 62, 64, 78, 79, 85, 86, *90*, 92, 93, 94, 95, 105, 107, 113, 120, 124, 126, 127, 131, 132, 140, 144, 145, 153, 169
Pig Town 28
Pipp, Wally 96, 118
Pittsburgh Pirates 4, 16, 18, 23, 32, 44, 51, 77, 78, 79, 82, 85, 87, 89, 107, 110, 111, 112, 114–115, 117, 126, 141, 145, 150, 154, 161, 163

194

Index

Polo, Missouri 38, 54, 59, 70, 72, 77, 81, 84, 92, 102, 105, 119, 122, 123, 125, 126, 134, 151, 159, 160, 165, 174
Polo Grounds (New York, New York) 13, 28, 36, 88, 93, 96, 111, 114, 142
Polo News-Herald (Polo, Missouri) 121

Quinn, Jack 156

Rafter, Bill 29
Raymond, Bugs 16
Reed, George 10, 12–13
Reese, John Bonesetter 36
Reese, Pee Wee 169
Reulbach, Ed 46, 48
Rice, Thomas 33, 49, 51, 52, 62, 76, 82, 85, 86, 93, 100, 108, 115, 121, 122, 132
Rickey, Branch 4, 92, 116, 167
Ritter, Lawrence 1, 56, 63
Rixey Eppa 50, 51, 92, 167, 174
Robertson, Dave 49, 78, 89
Robinson, Hannah 43
Robinson, Harry 43, 87
Robinson, Jackie 169
Robinson, Mary (daughter) 43
Robinson, Mary "Ma" 43
Robinson, Murray 4
Robinson, Stanley 18
Robinson, Wilbert 39–40, 44, 46 48, 50, 53, 54, 56, 57, 58, 60, 61, 64, 65, 66, 67, 68, 69–70, 76, 81, 84, 87, 95–96, 98, 100, 101, 102, 104,105, 107, 108, 112, 117, 119, **122**, 123, 126, 131, 132, 135, 142, 144, 148, 153; relationship with John McGraw 40, **41**, 42, 43, 55, 63, 82, **127**, 162; relationship with Zack Wheat 49, 135, 138, 139–140, 143, 145, 146, 147, 149–150, 151, 161–162
Robinson, Wilbert, Jr. 43, 81
Rogan, Bullet 124
Rommel, Eddie 156
Roush, Edd 77, 82, **83**, 167, 174
Rucker, Nap 19, 24–25, 26, **31**, 32–33, 36, 45, 46, 49, 63, 69, 76, 145, 166
Ruether, Walter "Dutch" 105, 110, 117, 120, 123, 124
Rumill, Ed 88
Ruppert, Jacob 55
Ruth, George Herman "Babe" 1, 63, 64, 66, 67, 70, 88, 92, 102, 107, 111, 115, 121, 124, 142, 157, 163, 164

Saccoman, John 14
St. Louis Cardinals 18, 19, 32, 40, 45, 55, 77, 85, 86, 92, 105, 107, 110, 111, 113, 116, 117, 118, 120, 121–122, 123, 127, 129, 130, 134, 136, 141, 149, 150, 152, 155, 159–160
Sallee, Slim 78
Schalk, Ray 172
Schmandt, Ray 110, 118
Schmidt, Walter 114
Schupp, Ferdie 62, 78, 107
Scott, Everett 66
Scott, Jack 143
Scott, Julia Davis 5, 7, 8, 18, 34, 76, 104, 169
Sewell, Joe 97, 99, 123
Sheckard, Jimmy 50
Shibe, Benjamin 153
Shibe Park (Philadelphia, Pennsylvania) **35**, 157
Shore, Ernie 63, 64, 65, 66, 69
Shorten, Chick 68, 69
Shreveport Pirates (Shreveport, Louisiana) 6, 9, 10
Simmons, Al 141, 154, 155–156
Sisler, George 114
Skelly, Roy 37, 59
Smith, Elmer 97, 101
Smith, Red **20**, 33, 35, 38, 44
Smith, Sherrod "Sherry" 12, 49, 55, 60, 66, 67, 76, 87, 93–94, 102, 105
Snyder, John 39
Society for American Baseball Research 2, 85
Solomon, George 11
Southern Association 9, 10, 12, 24, 30, 32, 111, 112, 117, 162
Southern League 10, 19, 158
Southworth, Billy 42, 124
Speaker, Tris 25, 64, 96, 97, 98, 99, 100, 101, 102, 123, 131, 153, 154, 164, 166
Spink, Alfred H. 7
Spink, C.C. Johnson 3, 4
Spink, J.G. Taylor 3
spitball 27, 44–45, 53, 79, 97, 98, 99, 100, 101, 102, 110, 117, 122, 127, 136, 156; legalization 89–91, 104–105; slippery elm 79, 89
Sporting News 3, 22, 157
Sportsman's Park (St. Louis, Missouri) 10, 125
Stengel, Casey 12, 26–27, 32, 35, 36, 37, 39, 42, 44–45, 46, 47, 54, 56, **58**, 61, 64, 65, 70, 72, 73, 74, 76, 77, 78–79, 102, 104, 105, 124, 162, 163, 164, 166, 167–**168**, 170, 171, 173
Stock, Milt 134, 144, 146, 166
Stoneham, Charles 88
Stout, Glenn 63, 129
Street, Gabby 48
Sutton, Larry 11, 12, 24, 27, 47, 112, 165

Taylor, Eddie 148
Taylor, Zack 96, 112, 122–123, 136, 144
Tener, John K. 40, 43
Terry, Bill 124, 145
Tesreau, Jeff 41
Texas League 6, 9
Thebo, Tony 10
This Is Your Life 167–**168**
Thomas, Pinch 66

195

Index

Thorpe, Jim 6
Tierney, Cotton 128, 151, 162
Tierney & Wheat Recreation 151, 161
Tierney-Wheat-Shepard, Inc. 162
Tinker, Joe 42
Toney, Fred 60
trade rumors 26, 32, 36, 49–50, 92, 73, 79, 91–92, 105, 111, 114–115, 117, 119, 124–125
Tyler, George 51

Van Bushkirk, Clarence 28, 34
Vance, Charles Arthur "Dazzy" 3, 12, 76, 112, *113*, 116, 117, 123, 124, 127, 128, 132, 133, 136, 145, 147, 148, 166, 170
Vaughn, James "Hippo" 51, 81
Veeck, William 89, 173
Veterans Committee 3, 4, 164, 169, 170, 171
Vila, Joe 147
Von der Horst, Harry 14, 29

Waddell, George Edward "Rube" 10, 166
Wagner, Honus 114, 163, 166, 167, 174
Walberg, Rube 156
Walker, Dixie 169
Walker, Tillie 64, 65, 66, 67
Walker Act 86
Walsh, Ed 27, 53
Walsh, Jimmy 67
Wambsganss, Bill 98, 101
Waner, Paul 144–145, 172
Ward, Chuck 78
Ward, John Montgomery 44
Washington Park (Brooklyn, New York) 17, 26, 28, 30–31, 32, 33, 34, 35, 42, 138
Washington Senators 10, 48, 133, 154
Wheat, Basil 5, 7, 9
Wheat, Basil, Jr. 5, 34, *91*, 92, 168–169
Wheat, Daisy 4, 6, 36, 54, 58, 72, 78–79, 81, *106*, 111, 112, *159*, 161, 164, 166, 169, 171, 172, 173; *see also* Daisy Forsman
Wheat, Mack 5, 6, 34, 48, 54, 81, *90*, 92, 104, 162
Wheat, Mary Helen 6, 36, 54, 58, *106*, 133, *159*, 168, 172; *see also* Gottschall, Mary
Wheat, Zack, Jr. 36, 81, *106*, *159*, 166, 172
Wheat resort (Sunrise Beach, Missouri) 2, 3, 164–165
Whittington Park (Hot Springs, Arkansas) 21
Williams, Ken 114
Willis, Vic 16–17
Wilson, Hack 124, 144
Wood, Joe 53, 63
Wooster 29, 111
World Series 16, 41–42, 44, 48, 57, 62, 76, 78, 82, 85, 87, 89, 94, 106, 107, 115, 124, 133, 139, 148, 152, 153, 155, 156, 157, 160, 167, 173; 1916 World Series 63–70; 1920 World Series 96–102
World War I 72, 81, 150
World War II 167
Wrigley Field (Chicago, Illinois) 140

Yager, Abe 29, 39, 62, 73, 74, 84, 85–86, 105, 139
York, Bernard 29
Youngs, Ross 88–89, 124, 152

Zack Wheat American Legion Post 2, 175
Zack Wheat Day 159
Zack Wheat Memorial 2, 174
Zack Wheat Memorial Highway 2, 174
Zack Wheat Memorial Roadside Park 175
Zach Wheat Memorial Sports Complex 2, 174
Zimmerman, Heinie 78
Zinn, John G. 30, 57, 74